Will and Political Legitimacy

Will and Political Legitimacy

A Critical Exposition
of Social Contract Theory
in Hobbes, Locke, Rousseau,
Kant, and Hegel

Patrick Riley

Harvard University Press
Cambridge, Massachusetts
and London, England 1982

Library of Congress Cataloging in Publication Data

Riley, Patrick, 1941-
    Will and political legitimacy.

    Includes bibliographical references and index.
    1. Social contract—History.   I. Title.
JC336.R53   320.1'1   82-3105
ISBN 0-674-95316-9   AACR2

In Memoriam
David L. Rinne
1941–1976

Preface

T HIS BOOK is meant to be a critical exposition of and commentary on the work of the four most eminent members of the social contract tradition in the seventeenth and eighteenth centuries—Hobbes, Locke, Rousseau, and Kant. To this has been added a study of Hegel's attempted "canceling and preserving" of the philosophical foundations of this tradition. The purpose of this book is thus both historical and philosophical: it is historical insofar as an effort has been made to render the unfolding of the contractarian tradition accurately; but it is primarily philosophical inasmuch as the main stress is placed on the analysis and evaluation of concepts—will, voluntariness, consent, contract—that all social contract theorists, in any historical period, seem to use. If the greatest stress has fallen on will and voluntariness, that is because those concepts are the best guides through the unfolding of the tradition. Hobbes, after all, urges that "wills... make the essence of all covenants" and that there is "no obligation on any man which ariseth not from some act of his own"; Locke, that "voluntary agreement gives... political power to governors for the benefit of their subjects"; Rousseau, that "the general will is always right"; Kant, that a mature, rational people could never will the continued existence of such an institution as unmerited hereditary rank; even Hegel, that "in modern times" we "make claims" for private judgment and private willing. So it certainly seems reasonable to view social contract theory as a form of political voluntarism, as a political expression of a general human capacity for free agency.

At the same time, it is the ambiguities and contradictions in the concept of will—the fact that will is viewed sometimes as a moral cause of imputable moral effects and sometimes as a mere appetite or desire—that lead to some of the main difficulties in contractarianism. At least Hobbes, Locke, Rousseau, Kant, and Hegel deal straightforwardly and fully with the relation of will to legitimacy and obligation; despite the renaissance of contractarianism in the last twenty years, the more recent contract theorists do not do as well with will and voluntariness. There is, however, a continuing use of an implicit voluntarism even in those contractarian theories that say very little about will in its relation to political legitimacy.

Now, one might think it rash, in understanding contract theory as a form of political voluntarism, to try to explain contractarianism through the notion of voluntary action of one's own; this seems to risk explaining the opaque by the still more opaque. After all, the notion of voluntary action of one's own is sufficiently problematical without deploying it as a means of shedding light on a formidable political tradition comprising figures as different as Hobbes and Kant. Indeed, the notion of voluntariness alone provides enough material for a substantial volume, as is seen clearly in J. L. Austin's subtle piece "A Plea for Excuses," with its infinite gradation of finely shaded distinctions—between *unwillingly* and *involuntarily*, for example. One might reasonably think that he would do better to confine himself to the notion of voluntariness, or at least to theories of human action, and not risk treating the subject of what social contract theory appears to be: an intersection of a theory of free action with a theory of politics in which will is treated as "cause" and legitimate political order as "effect." However rash it may be to go beyond the judicious cautiousness of an Austin (beyond only in range, certainly not in depth) it is inescapably the case that the central concept in social contract theory is will. At least, this is so when one brackets out of contractarianism some accompanying doctrines that are not themselves purely contractarian, such as natural law and natural rights in Locke's complete concept of political right. There is no doubting or denying the subtlety of recent work on notions such as will, intention, free action, reasons and causes, and the like, in attempts to link up voluntary action with rightful politics; that linkage was made and insisted on by the great contractarians, whose thought would be impoverished if one failed to examine the adequacy of this linkage. And, in the end, one can find consolation in the fact that contractarianism is a political outgrowth, a political expression, of a more general theory of human free action, one that gives contractarianism depth and wholeness. If its connection with voluntarism causes some of its problems, it is that same connection that helps to give it a satisfying completeness.

A word about the sense in which this book is a historical study may be warranted. Even if it is extravagant to think of all the members of the Great Tradition, from Plato to Rawls, as coexisting and conversing in a timeless *nunc stans*, it might still be that there are perennial, though not timeless, questions in philosophy that stretch over time. Since Plato's *Euthyphro*, for example, the question of whether there are any "eternal verities" that not even divine will can alter has recurred in every age of philosophy: in the seventeenth century, for instance, Descartes insisted that God would be neither creator nor omnipotent if A were necessarily equal to A, or if the good were necessarily good; but he was criticized by the neo-Platonists Leibniz and Malebranche, who argued that creation ought not to mean arbitrary willfulness, with Leibniz adding that *stat pro ratione voluntas* is "the motto of a tyrant." And a century later Kant resurrected the same problems near the end of the *Critique of Pure Reason,* siding, more or less, with Leibniz.

This is an example of a perennial speculative debate, and one that can and indeed must be carried on by abstracting a single thread—here the tension between always-having-been and coming-into-being—from the concrete wholeness of Platonism, Cartesianism, or Kantianism. To be sure, Descartes, as a Christian, worried about creation in a way that Plato did not: the *Timaeus* is less agitated than the *Response to the Six Objections* because salvation is not at stake. But in looking at a perennial question one (designedly) minimizes the historical particularities of Platonism and Cartesianism precisely in order to stretch a sufficiently abstract notion over time and space. One loses something, to be sure (though others will retrieve it); but one gains a clear view of the fact that there are permanent and recurring questions in philosophy, even if recurrence is never simple recapitulation. To bring this out one *heightens* what is general and perennial; one subordinates what is particular and time bound.

So too in political thought. Since Plato's *Crito* it has been a permanent question whether the legitimacy of government and the responsibilities of citizens depend on some free human action, for example the voluntary acceptance of benefits such as security and education, when one could have departed. To say that this question, very broadly conceived, appears in *Crito* and then twenty centuries later in Locke's *Second Treatise,* and then again in Michael Walzer's *Obligations,* is quite true. To be sure, it does not appear in exactly the same form: Locke had a highly developed notion of the moral significance of "voluntary agreement," while Plato had not. Furthermore, *Crito* is arguably anomalous in Plato's whole political corpus, since he usually stresses the rule of the wise rather than agreement. Locke, by contrast, must appeal to voluntary agreement, since for him all men are equal and there is no natural authority. These differences cannot be explained without some historical reference to Christianity's equality of all souls before God and its idea that, in St. Augustine's phrase, "consent" must be "voluntary." The notion of leaving history utterly out of account is absurd; but one can at least hope to find what Michael Oakeshott calls "the universal predicament" in the "local and transitory mischief."

Philosophy is not timeless, but within time there is sufficient continuity and recurrence to speak of perennial questions, and the social contract is one of those questions. Its central concern is to ask why political legitimacy and political obligation should be viewed as the voluntary creation of equal moral agents. That question, or at least the bare beginning of it, has been with us since *Crito;* but the most striking set of answers was provided by the great age of social contract theory, which flourished between publication of Hobbes's *Leviathan* (1651) and Kant's *Metaphysical Elements of Justice* (1797).

In order to appreciate contractarianism as a still serious doctrine and not as a mere accompaniment to the rise of the bourgeoisie, it seems right to treat precisely Hobbes and Kant, together with Locke and Rousseau. Of course, there is something in Quentin Skinner's insistence that it is hard to claim to have achieved "historical understanding" of a "period" if we continue "to focus our main attention on those who discussed the problems of political life at a level of abstraction and intelligence unmatched by any of their contemporaries." But even Skinner himself is forced to draw a distinction between "classic texts" and mere "ideologies," finally allowing that the main reason for "focusing" on the study of ideologies is that "this would enable us to return to the classic texts themselves with a clearer prospect of understanding them." Perhaps jewels do shine more brightly in a setting of paste, as some theologians have imagined that the blessedness of the elect is heightened by the misery of the damned; but Skinner himself never mistakes the gems for the settings. His own intelligence, so formidably displayed in *The Foundations of Modern Political Thought*, leads him, correctly, to "abstract" from an ideological "background" those feats of "abstraction and intelligence" that may indeed be qualitatively unrepresentative of a period but that do represent something higher: the possibility of remaining true enough over time to warrant being read. For surely the final reason to read Hobbes, Locke, Rousseau, Kant, and Hegel is that they may conceivably be right.

Intellectual debts are the only agreeable ones, and it is a pleasure to be able to acknowledge publicly the efforts of all those who had a hand in forming this book.

My attention might never have turned to political philosophy at all had I not encountered the late Martin Diamond in my first year of college; he was a remarkable teacher, and I wish that I had finished this book while he was still living. Those aspects of political philosophy that Diamond did not teach I first learned from James F. Doyle, who generously gave up his evenings to conduct small-group tutorials. In one of those sessions we read Michael Oakeshott's essays on Hobbes's *Leviathan,* and it was that which led, several years later, to Oakeshott's being my tutor at the London School of Economics. There is no adequate way of expressing everything I owe to Michael Oakeshott; his kindnesses to me now cover nearly twenty years. I owe to him especially the notion that much of modern political thought, and particularly contractarianism, rests on "will and artifice," rather than on the "reason and nature" of antiquity; indeed, that Oakeshottian distinction first led me to think of writing this book.

From the London School I went to Harvard University, where I worked with Judith Shklar. If I understand anything at all about Rousseau and Hegel, it is thanks to her efforts. Her seminar on the Enlightenment is what I still think about when I want to imagine the Platonic ideal of an academic course. I am grateful to her for her kindness over fifteen years' time, not least her reading and commenting on the manuscript of this book twice. She provokes, even without meaning to, immoderate feelings of esteem and affection.

My indebtedness to John Rawls is scarcely much smaller. One of the great pleasures of returning to Harvard as a visiting professor of government in 1980–1981 was the chance to hear him lecture once again. I will always be grateful for the helpful advice about Kant that he was good enough to give me. It was also at Harvard that I first knew George Armstrong Kelly; some years ago he gave me invaluble comments on an earlier draft of this book that greatly strengthened the final version. For that, and more particularly for years of friendship, I am thankful.

The invitation to spend a term back at Harvard I owe to Harvey Mansfield, Jr., whose fine lectures on Hume and Kant I had enjoyed as a graduate student. By 1981 Michael Walzer had left for Princeton, but I recall with pleasure a long conversation in Cambridge in the early 1970s about my early plans for this book. The familiar and welcome faces of Arthur Maass and Sam Beer made the Harvard government department a congenial place to put the finishing touches on the manuscript. Nearly at the last moment I received helpful advice from Michael Sandel and Stephen Holmes; meeting them was a splendid dividend.

I am grateful too to Harvard University Press and especially Aida Donald, editor for the social sciences, whose determined efforts led to this happy result. Her favorable comments on the manuscript gave me much-needed encouragement at just the right time. The Press also provided three anonymous readers of my manuscript, for whose helpful comments I am most grateful.

I also owe a great deal to the University of Wisconsin, which has given me a home and a wonderfully congenial work atmosphere for a decade. I have experienced nothing but kindness and encouragement from colleagues and students alike. A timely grant from the Wisconsin Graduate Research Committee permitted me to work with Locke manuscripts at the Bodleian Library and at the British Museum in 1976–77. The Wisconsin department of political science found the resources, thanks to Elizabeth Pringle, to type the manuscript; the actual typing was carried out not just well but cheerfully by Norma Lynch with the aid of Judith Lerdahl and Shari Graney. To all of these people I am most grateful; but I reserve special thanks for my colleague and friend Booth Fowler, whose support over ten years' time has been deeply appreciated.

I owe most of all, however, to my oldest and best friend, David L. Rinne, who died suddenly of a heart attack at the age of thirty-five in November 1976, soon after taking up his duties as conservator of antiquities at the Getty Museum in California. Had I not known David I probably would never have become devoted to philosophy and history, for surely it is people who first bring us to love what they love. His enormous interest in the philosophy of Aquinas and then in Aristotle finally touched me; thereafter, perhaps, we inspired each other. This makes him sound desperately earnest and sober, which is the reverse of the truth; he was wonderfully imaginative and irreverent. He was also the best friend that I and my wife and children could ever hope to have; this book is dedicated to his memory, which for us is a living one.

Several journals that published early versions of some of the chapters of this book have been good enough to permit me to reuse portions of my work. I am grateful to *Political Studies* (Oxford, 1973 and 1974) for permission to refashion articles on Hobbes and Locke into my present Hobbes and Locke chapters; to the *American Political Science Review* (1970), which published about half of what is now my Rousseau chapter; to *Political Theory* (Sage Publications, 1973), which published about two-fifths of what is now my Kant chapter; to *Journal of the History of Ideas* (1973), in which roughly half of chapter 1 appeared; and to the *Western Political Quarterly*, which published an earlier version of my Hegel chapter. For all of these generous permissions I am grateful.

Contents

Will and Political Legitimacy

How Coherent Is the Social Contract Tradition?

T_{HE} seventeenth and eighteenth centuries are commonly and accurately represented as the great age of social contract theory: the still popular doctrine that political legitimacy, political authority, and political obligations are derived from the consent of those who create a government (sometimes a society) and who operate it through some form of quasiconsent, such as representation, majoritarianism, or tacit consent.[1] On this view legitimacy and duty depend on consent, on a voluntary individual act, or rather on a concatenation of voluntary individual acts, and not on patriarchy, theocracy, divine right, the natural superiority of one's betters, the naturalness of political life, necessity, custom, convenience, psychological compulsion, or any other basis.[2] It is not necessary to lay too much stress on this point with American readers, who know that, according to the Declaration of Independence, governments derive their "just powers" from the consent of the governed; or with an English audience familiar with Locke's *Second Treatise*. It does not, indeed, take much effort to show that between the time of Hobbes in the middle of the seventeenth century and that of Hegel in the early nineteenth, consent emerged as the leading doctrine of political legitimacy. Even writers who rejected consent and willing as the basis of authority and obligation, such as Burke, thought it useful to say that society was based on a metaphorical contract of some sort.[3]

Political philosophy since the seventeenth century has been characterized, above all, by voluntarism, by an emphasis on the consent of individuals as the standard of political legitimacy. This theme is sounded by many of the most important thinkers between

Hobbes and Kant, though as significant a figure as Hume is an exception.[4] Even Hegel, though scarcely an "atomistic individualist" or a contractarian, explicitly argues that while "in the states of antiquity the subjective end simply coincided with the state's will," in modern times "we make claims for private judgment, private willing, and private conscience." When a social decision is to be made, Hegel continues, "an 'I will' must be pronounced by man himself." (This "I will" must have an "appropriate objective existence" in the person of a monarch; "in a well-organized monarchy, the objective aspect belongs to law alone, and the monarch's part is merely to set to the law the subjective 'I will.' ")[5] If even Hegel, who sometimes traces the origins of the French Revolution to Rousseauean notions of individual will and consent, allows this voluntarist turn in his own noncontractarian theory, it goes without saying that all of social contract theory can be seen a striking example of voluntaristic ideas. Its insistence on the artificial nature of society and government, on the derivation of their legitimacy, and sometimes their actual existence, from acts of will makes this clear.[6] Why voluntarism—political legitimacy through authorization by individual wills acting in concert—came to hold such an important place in Western thought requires a book to itself, a phenomenological study of political will.[7] What is probable, or at least what Hegel has made to seem probable, is that ancient quasiaesthetic theories of the good regime and the naturally social end of man gave way, with the introduction of Christianity, to thinking about politics after the model of "good acts." Just as good acts required both knowledge of the good and the will to do the good, politics now required moral assent, the implication of the individual in politics through his own volition. The freedom to conform voluntarily to absolute standards had always been important in Christian doctrine, particularly in its Pelagian and Arminian moods, emphasizing the significance and meritoriousness of individual good will.[8] The Reformation doubtless strengthened the element of individual choice and responsibility in moral thinking while subordinating the role of moral authority. And it was natural enough that the Protestant view of individual moral autonomy should spill over from theology and moral philosophy into politics, forming the intellectual basis of contract theory. To be sure, Luther was no contractarian in politics; but his views on the governance of the Lutheran church contained political implications that would have been difficult to control.

We all have the same authority in regard to the Word and sacraments, although no one has a right to administer them without the consent of the members of his church, or by the call of the majority (because, when something is common to all, no single person is empowered to arrogate it to himself, but we should await the call of the Church. . . . When a bishop consecrates, he simply acts on behalf of the entire congregation, all of whom have the same authority. They may select one of their number and command him to exercise this authority on behalf of the others.[9]

After the unfolding of the essential social ideas of the Reformation, the mere excellence of an institution would no longer be enough; it would now require authorization by individual men understood as "authors." However voluntarism and social contract theory arose—and here there is room for a great deal of plausible speculation—what is certain is that ideas of the good state increasingly gave way to ideas of the legitimate state; and after the seventeenth century this legitimacy was often taken to rest on the notion of willing.[10]

If what is suggested here is true, then it represents a substantial break with the ancient tradition, in which consent does not commonly function as a principle of legitimacy (perhaps because the concept of will rarely has major moral significance in ancient philosophy).[11] While the need for consent to fundamental principles of political society in order to create a political construct through will and artifice is a doctrine characteristic of what Michael Oakeshott has called the "idiom of individuality,"[12] the ancient conception of a highly unified and collective politics was dependent on a morality of the common good quite foreign to any insistence on individual will as the creator of society and as the basis of obligation. This conception turned on a view of political life as the highest, most all-embracing end of man, and was, moreover, considered both natural and prior to, ontologically if not chronologically, the independent existence of self-sufficient men. Given the ancient view of the morality of the common good and the supreme importance and naturalness of political life, ancient thought had no need of theories of political obligation, for these are necessary only when the duty to obey is in doubt. Politics being the highest end of man, obligation was not a real problem, and the task of the great legislator was not to show why men ought to obey but merely in what way—under what kind of regime—they should do so. Legislation was the task of giving the most perfect form to an intrinsically natural and valuable activity.[13]

It is true that in Aristotle's *Ethics,* for example, there is an extended treatment of legal responsibility in terms of whether a given action is voluntary or not. Indeed, as A. W. Adkins points out in his fine study of the development of Greek ethical theory, *Merit and Responsibility,* by looking only at certain passages in the *Ethics* one might imagine that the difference between Aristotle and modern voluntarists is not so great: "Since virtue is concerned with passions and actions, and since praise and blame are bestowed upon such as are voluntary, while to such as are involuntary pardon is granted, and sometimes pity, it is presumably necessary for those who are enquiring about virtue to distinguish the voluntary and the involuntary; and it is useful to those who have to make laws, with a view to determining rewards and punishments."[14] But Aristotle did not allow this voluntarism to extend into politics; he never suggested a theory of moral personality that required all legitimate actions to be voluntary, or chosen by private individuals. In fact, he went out of his way to repudiate contractarian views of society: any true *polis,* he urges in the *Politics,* must devote itself to the encouragement of goodness if the city is not to sink into a mere "alliance," a mere covenant that guarantees men's rights against one another.[15] And in Plato, with the exception of *Crito,* the will counts for even less: it is often simply assimilated to arbitrary caprice, as in the *Republic,* when Socrates attempts to refute Thrasymachus' view that justice is the will of the stronger,[16] or it is compared unfavorably with the eternally correct principles that even the gods themselves follow, as in the *Euthyphro,* where Plato makes it clear that the gods will holiness because it is holy, that holiness is not simply whatever they happen to will.[17]

The decisive turn in the voluntarization of Western social thought came with St. Augustine, who appropriated the *bona voluntas* of Cicero and Seneca and deepened it into a central moral concept.[18] In *De Libero Arbitrio* St. Augustine defines "good will" as "the will by which we seek to live honestly and uprightly and to arrive at wisdom"; but he is equally concerned with the "bad" will that accounts for responsibility and sin, saying that "I have a will...[and]...if I use it to do evil, to whom is the evil to be attributed, if not to me?"[19] (It must of course be bad will, and not just the body, that leads to sin: the cause of sin is "produced from the soul, not the flesh," as St. Augustine says in *The City of God.*)[20]

Here, good will and bad will have a far greater range than in Aristotle: they are not confined to mere legal accountability but color the whole of the moral life, even giving a new meaning to justice. St. Augustine insists that "unless something is done by the will, it can be neither a sin nor a good deed," so that "punishments and rewards would be unjust if man did not possess free will." That is why St. Augustine can say, in his late *De Trinitate,* that "one is nearly blessed when one is right in willing whatever one wills."[21]

This is not to say that St. Augustine is a voluntarist or contractarian in his explicitly political writings, above all *The City of God*; but it is certainly true that Augustine made important voluntaristic moral claims that later grew into political doctrines. In *De Spiritu et Littera,* for example, he insists that "consent is necessarily an act of will."[22] Without the strong link that Augustine forged between consent and will, social contract theory would be unthinkable, since it defines consent in terms of will. And St. Augustine's claim, in *De Libero Arbitrio,* that "the will, by adhering to the common and unchangeable good, attains the principal and great human goods," that such a will "sins whenever it turns from the unchangeable and common good and turns to its own private good,"[23] later made possible Pascal's insistence in the *Pensées* that "one must incline to what is general: and leaning toward oneself is the beginning of all disorder, in war, in policy, in economy, in the particular human body. Thus the will is depraved."[24] And that Pascalian Augustinianism is one of the ancestors of Rousseau's insistence that "general" will is good, "particular" will bad.[25] The leap from Augustine to Rousseau is, confessedly, great; but Rousseau is not conceivable without Augustine and various seventeenth-century transformations of Augustinianism.

Aristotle's limited doctrine of voluntary action, enlarged and deepened by St. Augustine, was taken over by the greatest medieval Aristotelian, St. Thomas Aquinas, who applied the idea of the voluntary not only to law but also, like Augustine, to sin and to good acts.

> The proper act of a free will is choice: for we say that we have a free will because we can take one thing while refusing another; and this is to choose...Now two things concur in choice: one on the part of the cognitive power, the other on the part of the appetitive power. On the part of the cognitive power, counsel is required, by which we judge one thing to

be preferred to another: and on the part of the appetitive power, it is required that the appetite should accept the judgment of counsel.[26]

Two things are necessary to a free moral action in St. Thomas: a rational standard provided by cognition and a conforming of one's will to the counsel of the cognitive power. A doctrine of this kind is necessary if every man is to be responsible for his salvation at least partly because of acts of his own; though how one reconciles such individual responsibility with divine prescience, divine grace, and causality has been a subject of endless dispute in Christian philosophy.[27] For the most part St. Thomas confines this voluntarist element of his thought to morality and does not ordinarily allow it to become a standard of political right. If, however, a political authority were to command the doing of an action contrary to divine or natural law, then of course the question of sinning by obeying the law would arise; and since sin, including political sin, involves willing, Thomistic politics can be indirectly and occasionally affected by voluntarism. A man might have a moral obligation to disobey, a possibility St. Thomas tends to minimize.[28]

This voluntarism becomes less indirect, more explicitly political, in some of the Christian political philosophers who succeeded Aquinas—most particularly William of Ockham and Nicholas Cusanus. Ockham urges in his *Quodlibeta* that "no act is virtuous or vicious unless it is voluntary and in the power of the will,"[29] and in his *Tractatus de Praedestinatione* that if God determined a "created" (human) will to act "just as fire does," then "no act of a created will would be imputable to [that will] itself," so that "merit and demerit would be done away with."[30] This general doctrine finds a political expression in his insistence that "no one should be set over a *universitas* of mortal men unless by their election and consent . . . what touches all ought to be discussed and approved by all."[31] For Ockham, then, Christian liberty is both the ground of virtue and the limiting condition of rightful politics.[32] A political voluntarism is even clearer in the greatest of the "Conciliar" theorists, Nicholas Cusanus, who argues in an almost contractarian vein that "since all men are by nature free," legitimate rulership can come only "from the agreement and consent of the subjects." Such subjects, Cusanus insists, must not be "unwilling," and whoever is "set up in authority" by the "common consent of the subjects" must be viewed "as if he bore within himself the will of all."[33] This will of all, to be sure, is not the will of all that Rousseau contrasts with a true general will. As Paul Sigmund has properly observed, "Cusanus' theory is not a theory of individualism like that of John Locke...consent is given by corporate groups rather than by individuals in a state of nature."[34] This distinction must be kept in mind in tracing the provenance of full-blown modern contractarianism, which has a broader purpose than the Conciliarist aim of limiting and constitutionalizing papal sovereignty.

The most advanced and subtle form of political voluntarism before the social contract school itself is contained in Francesco Suarez's magistral *On Laws and God the Law-Giver*. In this work Suarez draws an important distinction between intellect and will, treating the latter as a kind of "moral causality": "the intellect is able merely to point out a necessity existing in the object itself [e.g., $A = A$], and if such a necessity does not exist therein, the intellect cannot impart it," while the will "*endows* [something] with a necessity which did not formerly characterize it; and, in the matter of justice, for example, it *causes* a thing to be of a given importance."[35] This moral necessity with which will endows a political "thing" through its causality is made quite clear by a remarkable analogy: "just as freedom [of will] has been given to every man by the Author of nature, yet not without the intervention of a proximate cause—that is to say, the parent by whom [each man] is procreated—even so the power of which we are treating [political power] is given to the community of mankind by the Author of nature, but not without the intervention of will and consent on the part of human beings who have assembled into this perfect community."[36] For Suarez free will and political consent are analogous or even parallel; will is the "proximate cause" of the state. Suarez summarizes his doctrine with the observation that "human will is necessary in order that men may united in a single perfect community," and that "by the nature of things, men as individuals possess to a partial extent (so to speak) the faculty for establishing, or creating, a perfect community." Plainly, for Suarez that faculty is will: men can be "gathered together" into "one political body" only by "special volition, or common consent"; the people cannot "manifest" consent "unless the acts are voluntary." To be sure, "special volition," viewed as a kind of moral causality, does not simply create the *whole* of political right; "it is consonant with natural reason that a human commonwealth should [exist and] be subjected to some one," but since natural reason does not itself set up particular governments or appoint rulers, "natural law has not in and of itself, and without the intervention of human will, created political subjection."[37] This, as it happens, is almost the same as Locke's doctrine in section 81 of the *First Treatise*: government may well be ordained by God and required by natural law, but neither God nor natural law establishes governments; for Locke, as for Suarez, the "consent and contrivance" of men "translates" this ought into existence.[38]

All of this leads to the general reflection that will could not, or at least did not, become important in political philosophy until and because of Christian practical doctrines—doctrines that, after Augustine, turned precisely on will and choice.[39] The modern contractarian position involves an effort to view politics as legitimized through consent, through special volition, so that obligation and authority are products of everyone's original freedom and responsibility, effects of everyone's will as a moral cause. It is perfectly possible, of course, to treat contractarianism in terms of more modest notions: as an extension of certain medieval ideas about contracts between rulers and peoples,[40] as Conciliarism writ (very) large, as a theory of rational decision making,[41] and the like. The disadvantage of more modest treatments, however, is that they take inadequate account of the revolution introduced into political and moral philosophy by Christian ideas and thereby underemphasize the ethical components of contractarianism, such as autonomy, responsibility, duty, authorization, and willing.[42] By contrast, a large-scale view of modern consent theory—one that traces Christian antecedents—can at least explain what is most characteristic of political voluntarism since Hobbes: that the voluntary goes beyond the confines of legal responsibility, sin, and good acts to become the very foundation of all social legitimacy. In Rousseau, to take a good post-Hobbesian example, not only morality but also political authority and political obligation are derived quite explicitly from acts of consent, from willing.[43] And Thoreau carries consent even further, insisting on the right of a citizen to consent to or dissent from any act of government whatsoever.[44]

It would be tedious to point out at length what appears to be commonly recognized: that consent or agreement based on will, understood as a moral faculty, came to occupy a place in political philosophy in the seventeenth, and eighteenth, and early nineteenth centuries that it had never occupied so completely before—not, at least, in the political, as distinguished from the moral and legal, realms.[45] A few examples, however, may be of some use. Hobbes, for instance, urges in chapter 42 of *Leviathan* that "the right of all sovereigns is derived originally from consent of every one of those that are to be governed," and he insists in chapter 40 that human wills "make the essence of all covenants."[46] In his earlier *De Cive* he had even stated, in what some take to be a rather un-Hobbesian passage, "I say that... a man is obliged by his contracts, that is, that he ought to perform for his promise sake; but that the law ties him being obliged, that is to say, it compels him to make good his promise, for fear of the punishment appointed by law."[47] Here, Hobbes clearly states that obligations are derived from promises, from contracts of which will is the essence, and not from fear of punishment, which simply reinforces the intention that results from a promise.[48] Passing over Locke, who nonetheless argues that "voluntary agreement gives... political power to governors for the benefit of their subjects," and turning to Rousseau, one finds an insistence that "I owe nothing to those whom I have promised nothing... Civil association is the most voluntary act in the world; since every individual is born free and his own master, no one is able, on any pretext whatsoever, to subject him without his consent."[49] (One of the advantages of this passage is that it shows how clearly the ideas of consent, promise, and voluntary action are tied together.) As for Kant, in the *Metaphysical Elements of Justice* he urges that it is just for the nobility to be allowed to die out gradually, since the people could never have willed the establishment of a hereditary class that does not merit its rank, and that all legitimate laws must be such that rational men could consent to them.[50] Even Hegel, though clearly nervous about the possible dangers of allowing will or consent to be important, grants that in modern times "we make claims" for private willing and private judgment.[51]

If all of this seems so clear, what difficulties or problems are there that have kept generations of political theorists occupied? Why have contemporary consent theorists still so much to say? In the first place, none of this *is* so clear. What is clear is that certain claims for consent and for willing are made; but what begins to cloud this apparent clarity is the fact that, of the five main theorists who have a great deal to say about consent during the seventeenth, eighteenth, and early nineteenth centuries—Hobbes, Locke, Rousseau, Kant, and Hegel—at least four are ambiguous or inconsistent in setting up a philosophical framework that is adequate to explain the concept of consent as a source of authority and obligation. Much, if not all, of this ambiguity and inadequacy is due to the fact that consent theories must rest on a concept of will or voluntary action but that the will is one of the least clear of ideas, not only in the writers in question but in philosophy generally. What makes an understanding of will rather difficult in moral and political philosophy is that the term has at least two fairly distinct meanings, a "moral" meaning and a "psychological" meaning. At least since the time of the Scholastics the will has been treated as a moral faculty or an elective faculty or a rational appetite that is sharply set off from knowledge on the one hand and action, considered simply as motion, on the other. In a writer such as St. Thomas or Suarez, rectitude is the product of reason and volition combined.[52] The will is, on this view, defined as a choosing faculty, which examines various objects of knowledge and selects one or several on the basis of some reason or principle such as the idea of the good or divine law. Full knowledge and a striving to effect a chosen object of knowledge are thus essential to a completely moral act.[53] Such a position stresses the importance of the autonomy of the moral agent, the distinction between reasons, which persuade, and causes, which determine, and the like.[54] And this position implies a politics: one's "elective" will is what operates in consenting to (electing) a rightful political order.

Yet, at least since the time of Hobbes will has sometimes been defined in the language of physiological psychology as the "last appetite in deliberation."[55] Here too a distinction is drawn between knowledge and action, but on this view the will is only the efficient cause of an action, not a faculty that can legitimize or confer dignity on what is elected. A purely physiologico-psychological conception of will does not need to make autonomy important: such a conception of will is perfectly consistent with most notions of necessity, causality, and determinism.[56] According to a seventeenth-century exponent of such a view, such as Hobbes, or a twentieth-century one, such as Moritz Schlick,[57] one is free to act, not free to will; the antecedent causes determining will can always be found. In this doctrine men are responsible for what they do, in the sense that their will causes actions that are punishable; they could have acted otherwise, but only if the antecedent causes of volition had been different.

Stopping for the moment with this bare sketch—which is intended only to remind the reader of a certain range of problems disputed for hundreds of years, not to settle or indeed even fully state anything—one can at least say that consent appears to have some sort of relation to will. These writers do not ordinarily urge that consent is a function of mere knowledge, since men know a great many things, some of which they reject for reasons; nor is consent seen as purposeless motion. Consent is held, even by Hobbes, to be a voluntary act.[58] *Will* is, or once was, commonly taken to be a term that intervenes between knowledge and action, explaining the transition from merely knowing a great many things to attempting to do some particular thing. Here the notions of resolving and striving are often brought to bear, and Wittgenstein adds "trying, attempting, making an effort."[59] (There is less agreement as to whether the will is a faculty that adopts for itself what the intellect finds to be best or whether the will is an appetite determined by causes.) *Will*, then, is often used in a great variety of senses: as preference, as wish, as command, as "rational appetite," as the capacity to shape personal conduct, as "moral causality." It is beyond doubt that the extreme indeterminacy of the word *will*, the fact that it is used in both psychological explanations (based on causes) and moral explanations (based on reasons), is at the root of a great many of the unclarities in the doctrines of Hobbes, Rousseau, and Hegel; that Kant escaped confusion on this point, but only at the considerable cost of radically separating psychology and morality; and that Locke seems to avoid these difficulties only because he was fortunate or politic enough to treat consent and will in two different books, one of them published anonymously. Locke, actually, was quite right when he said, "If the ideas of liberty and volition were well fixed in our understandings, and carried along with us in our minds, as they ought, through all the questions that are raised about them, I suppose a great part of the difficulties that perplex men's thoughts and entangle their under-standings would be much easier resolved."[60] The only question is how far he succeeded in this himself; and that question, applied to him and to Hobbes, Rousseau, Kant, and Hegel, is the whole subject of this inquiry.

It has not been determined whether the will actually exists. Moreover, there seems to be no prospect of arriving at such a determination, at least if empirical proofs are required. Even Kant, who made the concept of the will the foundation of his moral theory, saying at one point that a good will is the only un-qualifiedly good thing on earth, never dared to call the will any-thing more than a "necessary hypothesis," a kind of hypothetical moral causality without which such concepts as responsibility, choice, praise, blame, and the like would be inconceivable.[61] In recent times as distinguished a philosopher as Gilbert Ryle has dismissed the idea of will altogether, calling it simply an aspect of a fundamentally mistaken view of man as a mind-body whose mental "acts" need to be connected with physical acts by a concept of volitional "thrusts"; the will, on this view, is simply part of the "ghost in the machine," originating in mistakes made by Descartes and some others.[62] It would be impossible to summarize even the kinds of arguments about the will made in the last few hundred years without going into an unendurable amount of detail.

Perhaps, however, without pretending in any way to adequacy on this point, one can say that if consent, or promise, is to have a meaning in the sense that consenting or promising so binds us to moral and political duties that violation of consent or promise would be wrong and not simply inconvenient or vexatious or illogical or illegal, the will becomes that faculty that binds us when we freely choose something—a certain kind of relation to other persons—that is not caused. One must assume the possibility of a free action that is binding for the reason that morality depends in part on undetermined choice: not undetermined in the sense that there is no reason for such willing but in the sense that we are free to accept or reject the reason, thereby earning justifiable praise or blame, and that the will is not determined, in the strictly causal sense in which a stone is necessitated to fall, by anything whatsoever. Being influenced or persuaded by reasons would not count as being determined by causes, precisely because making up one's mind is an "act of one's own," whereas falling or being pushed is not.[63] If a promise is obligatory, if consent imposes duties, if one owes political allegiance because one has agreed to have this "debt," it is because there is in the actor a possibility of willing or not willing a given action that is the source of his being a free agent who could have done something else that would not have produced a moral debt. This is not a complete or sufficient moral theory, except for those who derive morality solely from will (Sartre, for example, as will be seen); but it is a necessary element in a moral theory that gives the notion of voluntariness some weight.

This argument is quite conventional and familiar, if not exactly self-evident or universally accepted. It is also, at best, hypothetical, in the sense that the idea of undetermined choice as the foundation of moral freedom and as the origin of the obligatoriness of promising and consenting can be nothing more than a "necessary hypothesis," as Kant says.[64] But it can also be urged that it can be nothing less, and without necessary hypotheses, assuming that the possession of facts is out of the question, it is impossible to account for a great deal of what appears to be common moral experience.

What has just been suggested is, of course, an extremely abstract version of a general moral position that would be only more or less acceptable to some of the most eminent voluntarists of modern times. How far such a position is either required or accepted by Hobbes, Locke, Rousseau, Kant, and Hegel will have to be taken up in detail. Among more recent voluntarists the degree of divergence from this position varies, but they never depart from it altogether. T. H. Green, for example, who was eager to develop a theory of will that would avoid opening up a gulf between psychology and morality, adhered to the distinction between reasons and causes and between causality and autonomous self-determination, but in a way that reunited psychology and morality via the notion of "motive."

> The world of practice—the world composed of moral or distinctively human actions, with their results—is one in which the determining causes are *motives*; a *motive* again being an idea of an end, which a self-conscious subject presents to itself, and which it strives and tends to realize. An act of will...is thus always free, not in the sense of being undetermined by a motive, but in the sense that the motive lies in the man himself, that he makes it and is aware of doing so, and hence, however he may excuse himself, imputes to himself the act which is nothing else than the expression of the motive.[65]

Green's painstaking distinctions between desire and will, between both of these and intellect, and between all of these and action compose one of the most subtle efforts to say what will is and what its relations are to moral and political obligations.[66]

In *A Theory of Justice* a more recent contractarian and voluntarist, John Rawls, while not eliminating all consideration of the notion of will, concentrates mainly on the idea of rational choice, on the social institutions that rational men could agree to. The will is present, presupposed; but it lies in the background. Just principles for the "basic structure" of society, he says,

> are the principles that free and rational persons concerned to further their own interests would accept in an initial position of equality as defining the fundamental terms of their

association...This way of regarding the principles of justice I shall call justice as fairness.

No society can, of course, be a scheme of cooperation which men enter voluntarily in a literal sense...yet a society satisfying the principles of justice as fairness comes as close as a society can to being a voluntary scheme, for it meets the principles which free and equal persons would assent to under circumstances that are fair. In this sense its members are autonomous and the obligations they recognize self-imposed.[67]

Although it seems to be important that society be a "voluntary scheme," that men be autonomous and self-obligating, neither the term *will* nor the term *consent* appears often in Rawls's text. The ideas are there, and the whole construct seems to depend on them, but no long discussions are devoted to them.[68]

What this shows is that the modern voluntarist tradition is rather broad. A theorist can discuss more or fewer voluntarist ideas and still rely on will and consent, at least as distinguished from utility, the fiat of God, custom, prescriptive rights, or whatever. Most voluntarists, however much or little they talk about will and its relations to other mental faculties or processes, agree on the importance of consenting and promising. Most of them would agree that when someone says, "I shall probably be at the railway station, if I can find the time," he merely predicts a possible action, but that if he says, "I promise you that I shall be at the railway station, barring circumstances beyond my control," then he is bound to be there, though not as a result of what he merely knows, since knowledge is broader than what one wills and includes what one rejects, nor as a result of action in the sense of simple motion. On this view will can be seen as a kind of moral causality that, to use Hegel's phrase, consists in "setting in motion what was unmoved, and in bringing out what in the first instance lay shut up as a mere possibility."[69]

Doubtless there is a great deal that is unsatisfactory in all this. That the will is used as both a moral and a psychological concept to explain everything from the raising of one's arm to the undertaking of the sublimest duties creates infinite confusion; and ordinary language faithfully reflects this confusion. When one speaks of an action as willful, one ordinarily means capricious or arbitrary, while if one speaks of a meritorious act as voluntary, as distinguished from coerced or even interested, one usually means that merit can be imputed to an agent. If what has been indicated about willing and consenting is at all correct, then some serious difficulties appear for the consent theorists who are usually held to make up the social contract tradition. These difficulties arise from two main causes: either the theorist treats the will as a phy-siologico-psychological idea—perhaps as appetite or desire and not as a moral or elective faculty—at the same time that he treats voluntary consent as the main foundation of political legitimacy (as seems to be so in the cases of Hobbes and Locke); or the theorist finds the will alternately attractive and repellent, depending on whether he is considering it as a moral causality or as capricious and egoistic (which seems to be true of Rousseau and Hegel). Either or both of these difficulties can make a theory of voluntary consent incoherent, or at least deprive it of its philosophical foundations, even if its political persuasiveness, taken by itself, is unimpaired. A few examples should make an abstract point more concrete.

Beginning again with Hobbes, it is clear that despite what he says about consent and about obeying because one has voluntarily promised to do so, the will itself is formally defined as the "last appetite in deliberating" or the last impulse before action. As a result of this definition Hobbes suggests that animals, no less than persons, have wills. Here the will no longer seems to be something that can bind morally: *voluntary* can refer to anything from lifting one's arm to promising to obey, in that they both differ from, say, circulation of the blood, over which volition has no control.[70] One can understand how a moral or political obligation could arise out of a will defined in Kantian terms as the capacity to act according to the conception of a law,[71] since this would involve a conscious decision "of one's own," the understanding and application of a rule. But it is not clear how such an obligation can issue out of a will understood as an appetite, unless a notion such as obligation is considered to be either derivative from or reducible to a fact of psychology such as appetition. A further complication concerns the way in which Hobbes defines consent in chapter 5 of *De Cive*. Hobbes criticizes Aristotle for calling some animal societies (of bees or ants) political, on the grounds that such societies are not to be considered political because "their government is only a consent, or many wills concurring in one object, not (as is necessary in civil government) one [sovereign] will."[72] In short, the reason that these societies of ants or bees fail to be political is not that there is no consent but that there is no sovereign. But these animals do have wills that concur in one object. Clearly, the problem is that Hobbes's conception of consent is as broad as his conception of what is voluntary, and that breadth seems excessive in both cases, at least since Hobbes wants to use consent as the foundation of authority and obligation. Some of his seventeenth-century critics, particularly Bishop Bramhall, suggested that he draw a distinction between a moral will and a will that causes physical actions; but Hobbes explicitly rejected this solution, saying, "It is all one to say, my will commands the shutting of my eyes, or the doing of any other action."[73] What, then, is one to make of the traditional view that Hobbes based both authority and obligation on voluntary acts of consent?[74] Or are those interpreters right who say that terms such as *consent, promise,* and *obligation* should be understood in a purely metaphorical sense in his system? And if they are right, what should be made of Hobbes's claim that wills "make the essence of all covenants"?[75]

In Rousseau the problem is no less acute. Despite the fact that he sometimes treats moral notions as if they simply arise in a developmental process, in the course of socialization, he often, particularly when speaking of contract and obligation, falls back on a kind of moral a priorism in which the wills of free men are taken to be the causes of duties and of legitimate authorities. Thus, in an argument against obligations based on slavery in the *Social Contract,* Rousseau urges that "to deprive your will of all freedom is to deprive your actions of all morality"; the reason that one can derive no notion of right from mere force is that "to yield to force is an act of necessity, not of will."[76] In the *Discourse on Inequality,* in a passage that almost prefigures Kant, he insists on the importance of free agency, arguing that while physics might explain the "mechanism of the senses," it could never make intelligible "the power of willing or rather of choosing," a power in which, he says, "nothing is to be found but acts which are purely spiritual and wholly inexplicable by the laws of mechanism."[77] Despite this voluntarism in his moral and political theory, his fear of arbitrary willfulness, of what he calls "particularism" and "egoism," led him to suspect the notion of will as much as to praise it. As a result, as he claims, in his *Political Economy,* "The most absolute authority is that which penetrates into a man's inmost being, and concerns itself no less with his will than with his actions."[78] Only consent can create duties, but men do not know what they ought to consent to; as a result, great legislators must somehow guide the wills of men while leaving those wills free.[79] This requirement got

Rousseau into serious difficulties. Throughout his work he tried to retain will as a source of right while seeking to control or sometimes even obliterate it as a source of self-love and inequality through a process of socialization and education that lessens the autonomy of individuals.[80]

In Hegel, particularly in his later works, the concessions to voluntarism, always somewhat hesitant and tentative, were largely withdrawn as he considered the abyss of subjectivism and relativism to which theories of private willing can lead. What a person is, he says in the *Philosophy of Right,* is the series of his actions. But, he goes on, "if these are a series of worthless productions, then the subjectivity of his willing is just as worthless. But if the series of his deeds is of substantive nature, then the same is true also of the individual's inner will." That is, Hegel says, the will has a value when it wills what is objectively right. "What is right and obligatory is the absolutely rational element in the will's volitions," he continues. And what is rational is contained in, among other things, the state as the objectification of reason, since the state is an "ethical substance." When men are part of an objective ethical substance—a state—then the "self-will of the individual has vanished together with his private conscience which had claimed independence and opposed itself to the ethical substance." When a man no longer opposes what is "universal"—again the state—then "he knows that his own dignity and the whole stability of his particular ends are grounded in his same universal, and it is therein that he actually attains these." Since the will, though of some value, is subjective, and the state, as ethical substance, is objective, mere morality based on personal good will must give way to ethics.[81] But since the state constitutes ethics and can be judged only in the court of universal history, private will is more and more reduced by Hegel until one is sometimes inclined to wonder why he often claimed that modern Christian voluntarism represented an advance over ancient morality.[82] In the end Hegel reduces the consent element of his theory to the monarch's saying "I will" to legislation produced by a universal class of rational and disinterested civil servants, though he does argue that ordinary citizens will the state insofar as they recognize it as the concrete actualization of a rational freedom—insofar as they know it for what it is.[83] (It is worth pointing out that with Hegel the concept of real will as a kind of knowing begins.)

Only Kant avoids most of the difficulties to be found in these other political theorists. He erects a theory of will as the capacity to act according to the conception of a law, to shape one's own conduct in terms of reasons that one understands. Kantian theory is adequate to account for promising, consenting, and other practical notions, though Kant reserves those ideas for morality proper and suggests only that the political order must be one that men could rationally consent to obey. Since Kant confronted so many complex problems, it may be sufficient to say no more than this: that Kant believed that the only "unqualifiedly" good thing on earth is a good will; that he thought that moral activity consists of a good will willing a universal standard—respect for the dignity of men as ends in themselves.[84] He believed that politics is important because a state can set up a legal context in which morality is more nearly possible. Just as the principle of morality involves conforming the will to universal principles of practical reason, so political right consists in conforming external actions to a rule consistent with similar freedom for everyone.[85] Laws must be principles that men could reasonably consent to, while moral rules require actual willing and striving. In short, Kant makes contractarianism hypothetical: actual consent is not involved, but the state ought to evolve in the direction of "republicanism," such that one day a universe of republics will legislate only those things that are congruent with the demands of morality, though the grounds of moral and political obligation will remain distinct.[86] The most important thing is that Kant explains how a will can act as a kind of moral causality, which is distinguished from mere inclination or appetite (though this is only a "necessary hypothesis"), and how quasicontractarian politics can provide a context that will at least not contradict what morality requires. Kant has his problems, to be sure, among them his "pathological" treatment of psychology; but they do not undermine his fundamental achievement.

With the exception of Kant, then—assuming for the moment that his theory of will is unproblematical—what one finds is that the great age of social contract theory did not, on the whole, establish the philosophical underpinnings of consent on a sound enough footing. The main reason for this is that the concept of will has always been unclear in philosophy and has been used to explain many different kinds of experience. There is a further paradox: the age of Scholastic philosophy attained to an adequate, or at least helpful, philosophical explanation of will and consent but rarely applied it to such things as political rights and duties, unless the question of sinning by obeying the law arose. Of course, this is less true of Ockham or Cusanus than of St. Thomas and still less true of Suarez. However, though seventeenth- and eighteenth-century political theorists affirmed consent, indeed celebrated consent as the foundation of political legitimacy, they often moved farther and farther away from those theories of will that provided better explanations of consent, promise, and obligation than their own. As a consequence, anyone interested in consent theory should not hesitate to examine Scholastic philosophy quite seriously; though it is true that the Scholastics told us little when they said that clocks were operated by "horologic faculties" or that the drowsiness induced by sleeping potions was caused by a "soporific potency" or a "dormative virtue," it is also true that what they said about the will in relation to choosing, consenting, and promising is worthy of the closest attention. And this is particularly true of Suarez.

By the time one reaches Nietzsche, the idea of will as moral agency is no longer even respectable: the will, Nietzsche insists in the *Twilight of the Idols*, is the invention of priests who want to make men feel guilty and thus dependent on them for absolution.[87] (Nietzsche was, however, a partisan of will in quite another sense: the creative will of great artists). Strictly speaking, will in Nietzsche is double—good and bad. Christian and Kantian good will is really bad in that men are counted as free so that they can be found guilty ("responsible") and then punished. Will as the capacity to be guilty is nothing but "the metaphysics of the hangman." The "moral world order" that one ought to will, according to the "calamitous spider" Kant, is the "foulest of theologians' artifices," one that "infects" the "innocence of becoming."[88] But will as power, as creation, as mastery, as assertion—as in Goethe, Heine, and pre-*Parsifal* Wagner—is essential.[89] It is particularly important as a counter to Schopenhauer's "nihilistic" view that will is an unworthy "will-to-live," a grasping at a life that is a grotesque and doomed game "not worth the candle," that life as will and painful striving should undergo a "free denial" and "surrender."[90] The two kinds of will in Nietzsche—Christian and creative—illuminate the celebrated distinction between good and evil and good and bad. The "moral" pair (good and evil) is Augustinian and Kantian—and false; the aesthetic pair (good and bad) bears only on the "wealth of creative power,"[91] and this comes out not just in art but even in science, where "striving for power" should replace the inadequate notions of cause and dynamics: "every living thing does everything it can not to preserve itself but to become more."[92] After this Freudianism seems tame; but its significance for voluntarism is to shrink will as rational self-determination. In *Psychopathology of Everyday Life* and *Totem and Taboo* the notion of will as a faculty of the mind disappears altogether, and notions such as responsibility, duty, and guilt are traced only to a "dread of the community."[93]

It is true, of course, that there are some contemporary voluntarists who are more voluntaristic than anyone ever was; Sartre is a perfect example. Indeed, in his rejection of all "ideal" and a priori standards, in his insistence that since there is no "human nature," no human "essence" that precedes and shapes human "existence," man is "what he wills," Sartre puts himself in a position in which he is able to conclude that man is "as he conceives himself after already existing—as he wills to be after that leap toward existence."[94] But Sartre's voluntarism simply makes clearer what the contractarian tradition had been and to some extent still is: the combining of consenting and promising and willing with ideals such as legality, majoritarianism, sovereignty, that Sartre would reject as a prioristic. He insists that in willing for oneself one is willing for all men; that if one is honest, one must will universally. But this touch of Kantianism seems somewhat arbitrary, particularly if, as Sartre suggests, "there is this in common between art and morality, that in both we have to do with creation and invention...we cannot decide a priori what it is that should be done."[95] Sartre clearly has a relation to an older voluntarist tradition; but what he has excluded, except in the gratuitous insistence that willing be universal, is the shaping of will by definite social objectives, such as creating a legitimate authority. The contractarian tradition was never interested in will as creative of values that did not exist; it was interested in legitimizing principles and institutions whose value was not simply derivative from voluntarism as such.[96] Its proponents wanted men to consent but rarely urged that whatever is consented to is valid simply because will has come into play. The tradition held that some things deserve or merit consent, that political willing involves consenting to institutions that ought to reflect and support autonomy but that are not simply the effects of will.[97] Some philosophers—the older Hegel is the best example—would say that voluntarism in any form, contractarian or existentialist, leads to subjectivism, solipsism, and moral anarchism, to will's taking the place of reason. Yet even Hegel almost always tried to preserve will in some form—most often as "real" will, or reason itself—which shows how hard it is to bracket the notion of willing out of modern political philosophy.[98]

What one starts with in analyzing the social contract tradition, including its contemporary extensions, is an importance given to will that had never appeared before, at least not so fully, in the history of political philosophy.[99] Whoever doubts this can try to imagine how far he can make Hobbes, Locke, Rousseau, Kant, and even Hegel intelligible if the idea of will is left out. By comparison, Plato, Aristotle, and Cicero would be left almost wholly intact even if will were excised from their systems.[100] It is hard to avoid the conclusion that Christianity, which made individual choice and responsibility so important, was not the main force in effecting this change; certainly something like Suarez's analogy between free will and political consent makes this plausible. But to explore modern consent theorists by concentrating on will as a thread that holds the modern tradition together while setting it off from the classical tradition—and there is good reason to do this, since will illuminates political, moral, and psychological theory and their relations simultaneously—one must give up all efforts to say simply what a theorist is: a liberal, an authoritarian. Clearly, one can build authoritarian politics on liberal voluntarist foundations (as in the case of Hobbes) or hold that the people alone have the right to consent but lack suitable knowledge of what is worth consenting to (as in the case of Rousseau). What is important is not to characterize theorists with a small handful of labels but to trace the consistency of their designs by using an essential concept such as will as a guide. This process will yield conclusions that appear less firm; one will no longer say that Rousseau is either a liberal or a totalitarian, but one's judgments will be better grounded and less arbitrary.[101] Sometimes one will be able only to show how or why a particular line of argument is not quite coherent, or consistent with other major strains in a theorist's argument. But if this is all that can honestly be done, then it is not only enough but is a kind of limit that ought to be respected. Even within this limit, however, a great deal of light can be shown on difficulties in the contractarian position through a careful examination of the way in which contract theorists treat the will, which is, as Hobbes says, the "essence of all covenants."[102]

This kind of analysis has not yet been made in anything like an adequate way. But if, to take an example, interpreters of Hobbes who cannot agree whether there are real promises and obligations in the Hobbesian system were to compare the way in which Hobbes defines the will, in terms of appetite and aversion, with the way in which he uses the notion of willing in defining the essence of covenants, they might see that the reason that it is difficult to determine whether there are promises and obligations in Hobbes is that he uses the term *willing* in different and sometimes mutually exclusive senses, switching without notice from the physiologico-psychological notion of will as caused appetite to the moral notion of will as free cause of moral effects.[103] If one reads the *Essay concerning Human Understanding* as well as the *Second Treatise,* something comparable turns out to be true of Locke as well—at least in the first edition of the *Essay,* though Locke tried to remedy this defect in later editions.[104] In short, if the contractarian tradition can be approached from an angle not so much new as uncommon, perhaps both the strengths and the weaknesses of social contract theory can be thrown into higher relief. To judge from its own language, contract theory appears to require a notion of will as a moral causality that produces legitimacy, obligation, and the like, as effects. The question is: to what extent do Hobbes, Locke, Rousseau, and Kant provide a coherent account of that "causality"?

⸙ 2 ⸙

Will and Legitimacy
in the Philosophy of Hobbes

IN *Leviathan* Hobbes says that "wills...make the essence of all covenants" and that once a man has "transferred" his right to a "beneficiary" such as a sovereign, "then he is said to be OBLIGED, or BOUND, not to hinder those, to whom such right is granted...from the benefit of it: and that he *ought*, and it is his DUTY, not to make void that voluntary act of his own: and that such hindrance is INJUSTICE, and INJURY, as being *sine jure* [without right]."[1] Here the ideas of will and voluntary acts color and shape the notions of covenant, ought, duty, justice, and right. It is therefore not surprising that Hobbes should go on to base the authority or legitimacy of rulers, as well as the obligation of the ruled, on consent and voluntary agreement.

This voluntarism in turn leads one to expect a philosophical underpinning for the theory of consent that will show why legitimacy and duty are to be conceived as the consequences of agreeing and promising. That is, one expects a theory of moral personality, of moral agency, in which moral value is derivative, at least in part, from choice. Now, what is remarkable in Hobbes is that there seems to be a disjunction between the voluntarism that is at the heart of his notions of authority and obligation—most clearly in his doctrine that wills make the essence of all covenants but also in the notion that there is "no obligation on any man which ariseth not from some act of his own"[2]—and his account of the will and of the nature of voluntary actions in the rest of his system. If this apparent disjunction turns out to be a true disjunction, then many of the difficulties with which interpreters of Hobbes struggle may be due to the fact that, despite his voluntarism, there is a gulf between his ethical theory and his account of volition.[3]

One of the most interesting questions in the interpretation of Hobbes is whether there is a genuine doctrine of duties in his political philosophy, or whether terms such as *promise, duty,* and *obligation* must be understood in a metaphorical sense, as what is logically necessary to the creation and preservation of society but not morally necessary or dutiful. Clearly, murder can be forbidden on the rational ground that it will bring on a series of murders, including the murder of the first murderer. The logic of life—assuming that life is a good, or at least the precondition of all further goods—thus demands that men abstain from murder, perhaps as part of a more general endeavor of "seeking peace." It is quite possible to view Hobbes's "natural law" prohibiting murder in this way; but it is quite another thing to say that men should abstain from murder because it is wrong and not merely contradictory of a social logic.

For a long time it was commonly held that Hobbes viewed moral principles purely in terms of self-preservation and social logic. The reason that a man adheres to his promises, for example, is not that he is morally bound to fulfil his voluntary act but that it would be contradictory or "absurd" to make social arrangements only to violate them. In short, moral behavior is self-interested rational behavior.[4] There are plenty of passages in Hobbes that lend weight to such a view; for example, in chapter 2 of *De Cive* he urges that "the whole breach of the laws of nature consists in the false reasoning or rather folly of those men who see not those duties they are necessarily to perform in order to their own conservation."[5] It was held that a Hobbesian promise, for example, could not involve an action that was morally binding because one had promised (spoken words that were tokens of one's will, as a faculty or agency tht binds one), but that a promise could only mean a prediction of future behavior. For this interpretation of Hobbes there were again a number of reasons: he had insisted that the will is simply the last appetite preceding action, that will is causally determined and not free;[6] and he had denied that good and evil are objective concepts, urging instead that they are merely descriptive of the psychological state of the person using the terms.[7] These statements led to a general conclusion that all moral terms must be equally psychological in Hobbes and that none of his statements about rights and duties could be taken in a conventional sense.[8]

Yet, there were unresolved difficulties. Hobbes states quite clearly that, because of the equality of all men, there is no natural authority among them, that all authority has to be instituted by the consent of those who authorize a sovereign to make law and permit his will to stand for theirs instead of using their own unlimited but useless natural right to preserve themselves.[9] In short, there seems to be a doctrine of authority based on consent in Hobbes. But it is difficult to see how consent could be morally binding or how authority could be granted if the will is not a moral agency or faculty. Mere knowledge cannot give rise to duties, since one can know everything that is to be rejected as well as what is to be accepted; and mere motion, independent of any particular purpose, cannot be conceived as bringing about duties either. Hobbes himself seems sometimes to recognize this, particularly in his discussions of obedience to God and in his discussions of sin.[10] Obedience to God, Hobbes declares in chapter 18 of *De Cive*, is "not in the fact, but the will and desire wherewith we purpose and endeavor as much as we can to obey for the future."[11] The terms *will* and *purpose* and *endeavor* seem to be distinguished here from simply knowing something or simply moving; but a passage such as this is the exception in Hobbes. More commonly he speaks of will as an appetite—any appetite, so long as it is the last in a process of deliberation.[12]

In view of this, some seventeenth-century critics of Hobbes, and particularly Bishop Bramhall, revived the Scholastic distinction between will in a physical sense and will in a moral or elective sense, insisting that Hobbes ought to adhere to this distinction: that one kind of will permits us to open or shut our eyes while another kind ("elective" or rational) is the source of moral choices. But Hobbes, who did not want to perpetuate the Cartesian distinction between mind and body, explicitly denies that there is a difference between a will understood in terms of physiological psychology and a will understood in terms of moral choice. "It is all one to say, my will command the shutting of my eyes, or the doing of any other action."[13] Indeed, he goes on, "I do not fear it will be thought too hot for my fingers, to show the vanity of such words as these, *intellectual appetite...rational will, elective power of the rational will*." Partisans of "such words," like Bishop Bramhall— who also relish the absurd thought that "the will hath a dominion over its own acts" and that "the power to will is...determinable by ourselves"—are saying things "as wild as ever were any spoken within the walls of Bedlam."[14]

In denying any distinction between a physiological-psychological will and a moral or elective will, Hobbes was, as he was quite aware, rejecting a tradition that stretches at least from St. Augustine and St. Thomas,[15] and in some slight degree Aristotle,[16] to seventeenth-century churchmen like Bishop Bramhall. When he insists in chapter 6 of *Leviathan*, that the will is simply the "last appetite in deliberation" and not an "elective faculty," he is explicitly repudiating the Scholastic view of the relation of will to choice, duty, and promise that had long been a relatively fixed point in Christian doctrine. While it is true that Hobbes repudiates "the definition of the Schools" and even urges that will is causally determined by "extrinsic" forces and by "appetites" and "aversions,"[17] his definition of willing does not always seem to accord with some of his most important pronouncements about promises, duties, obligations, and the like arising from consent. Hobbes may, in fact, require a theory of will that he repudiates if his system is to be intelligible. Indeed, it is hard to imagine what consent could mean, beyond the bare fact of fortuitous concord, if the will is simply the last of any appetites. It could not be something within a moral personality that binds anyone to anything. The chief question in Hobbes, for present purposes, is: Does he provide an adequate philosophical foundation for the explanation of will and consent as the source of legitimacy and of duty, or do those terms in his system not mean what they are ordinarily taken to mean?

That consent, promise, and agreement as the foundation of covenants—contracts depending on trust—are fundamental in defining what Hobbes means by the political legitimacy of sovereigns and the political obligations of subjects is scarcely open to doubt.[18] First, and most important, he consistently defines the sovereign power of a commonwealth in terms of those ideas. "The right of all sovereigns," Hobbes urges in chapter 42 of *Leviathan*, "is derived originally from the consent of every one of those that are to be governed." The authority of any prince, he claims in chapter 40, "must be grounded on the consent of the people, and their promise to obey him." The advantage of looking at both formulations together is that the first defines the right to rule in terms of consent, while the second draws in authority and promise as well, showing the intimate relation of these ideas to each other. The fullest statement of this view is to be found in chapter 21 of *Leviathan*:

> In the act of our submission [to a sovereign] consisteth both our obligation, and our liberty. . . there being no obligation on any man, which ariseth not from some act of his own; for all men are equally and by nature free. And because such arguments, must either be drawn from the express words, *I authorize* all his actions, or from the intentions of him that submitteth himself to his power. . . the obligation and liberty of the subject is to be derived either from those words or others equivalent.[19]

To make it clear that covenants between men for the establishment of sovereignty are *voluntary*, Hobbes speaks, in chapter 40 of *Leviathan*, of "wills, which make the essence of all covenants."[20] Such covenants, or contracts depending on trust, are just as important in a "commonwealth by acquisition" (a polity gained by conquest) as in a "commonwealth by institution." The difference between them is that in the former men contract directly with the conquering sovereign to obey in exchange for life and security, while in the latter they contract with each other to make a sovereign the beneficiary of their agreement to give up the exercise of their natural rights, as long as they are protected. As a result even the conqueror of a subjected people derives his rights over them not from his power but from their consent: "It is not therefore the victory that giveth the right of dominion over the vanquished," Hobbes says in chapter 20 of *Leviathan*, "but his own covenant. Nor is he obliged because he is conquered. . . but because he cometh in, and submitteth to the victor."[21] As Hobbes puts it in a passage from *Liberty, Necessity and Chance*, which has the incidental merit of showing that death is not invariably his *summum malum*, some people believe that "conquerors who come in by the sword, make their laws also without our assent," that "if a conqueror can kill me if he please, I am presently obliged without more ado to obey all his laws." But, Hobbes asks, "may not I rather die, if I see fit?" He concludes, "The conqueror makes no law over the conquered by virtue of his power; but by virtue of their assent, that promised obedience for the saving of their lives."[22] In the end, the difference between commonwealths by institution and by acquisition is not fundamental, since both derive their legitimacy from voluntary acts of (potential) subjects.[23]. In both, wills "make the essence of all covenants."

It is not only sovereign power, however, that is authorized or legitimized by consent. In the English version of *De Cive* Hobbes redefines the Aristotelian concept of distributive justice not in terms of desert or merit but in terms of what has been agreed to: if I give "more of what is mine to him who deserves less, so long as I give the other [who deserves more] what I have agreed for, do I no wrong to either." This redefinition depends, of course, on Hobbes's view that all men are, or must be taken to be, equal, which rules out the possibility of preeminent natural merit.[24] He takes up the same position in chapter 11 of *Leviathan*, where he holds that "a man may be worthy of riches, office, and employment, that nevertheless can plead no right to have it before another; and therefore cannot be said to merit or deserve it," for merit "presupposeth a right, and that the thing deserved is due by promise."[25] Even merit and desert themselves, as distinguished from worth, are redefined in terms of voluntary acts, not of intrinsic excellence; any Platonic notion of natural justice is made impossible. Not surprisingly, in view of his version of merit, Hobbes goes on to claim in both *De Cive* and *Leviathan* that the distinction between masters and servants exists "by consent of men," and that it is "not only against reason, but also against experience," to hold that servants or slaves are intrinsically inferior to masters or that "masters and servant were not introduced by consent of men."[26]

The validity of law, moreover, is in some ways dependent on consent. While Hobbes often characterizes law as the command or the will of the sovereign—as distinguished from counsel, or mere advice—it remains true that law is not just "a command of any man to any man; but only of him, whose command is addressed to one formerly obliged to obey him."[27] Since this former obligation is itself defined in terms of consent, law is a valid command only when pronounced by an authorized person—a person whose authority has been willed, established by consent. Command alone has no more significance in Hobbes than power alone.

Passing beyond these immediately practical matters, Hobbes views the creation and use of language as the result of agreement; it exists, he says in chapter 3 of *De Cive*, "as it were by a certain contract necessary for human society." At one point, in chapter 18 of *De Cive*, Hobbes even goes so far as to insist that "to know truth, is the same thing as to remember that it was made by ourselves by the common use of words."[28] His theory of language as something wholly conventional is important not only as an instance of his general reliance on agreement or consent in the explanation and/or justification of social phenomena but also in relation to his theology, which does much to shape his concept of will. Since, in Hobbes's opinion, language is imposed on the world, and since we cannot truly know God, "words, and consequently the attributes of God, have their signification by agreement and constitution of men." That is, what we know of God is not really something we know; we ascribe attributes to him that we think "honorable."[29] Voluntarism has surely gone far in a philosopher if he defines not only language but God as well in terms of concepts simply agreed to.

In view of such radicalism it is not very astonishing that Hobbes goes on, in *Liberty, Necessity and Chance*, to redefine revelation in the light of this voluntarism, and in a way that deprives ecclesiastics, the prime causes of political chaos, of all right, except by delegation, to interpret Scripture. Hobbes's argument is so bold and sweeping that it must be fully cited:

> The Bible is a law. To whom? To all the world? He [Bishop Bramhall] knows it is not. How came it then to be a law to us? Did God speak it *viva voce* to us? Have we any other warrant for it than the word of the prophets? Have we seen the miracles? Have we any other assurance of their certainty than the authority of the Church? And is the authority of the Church any other than the authority of the Commonwealth, or that of the Commonwealth any other than that of the head of the Commonwealth, or hath the head of the Commonwealth any other authority than that which hath been given him by the members? . . . They that have the legislative power make nothing canon, which they make not law, nor law, which they make not canon. And because the legislative power is from the assent of the subjects, the Bible is made law by the assent of the subjects.[30]

What is of interest here, apart from the sheer audacity and formidable logic of this passage, is not simply the assertion that the Bible is law only if made canonical by the sovereign but the reassertion that the general right of that sovereign is derived from the assent of the subjects, that through the sovereign considered as their agent the people will the Bible to be what it is.

Hobbes does not stop at redefining legitimacy, obligation, distributive justice, language, the attributes of God, and the canonical character of Scripture in terms of consent and agreement; he also conceives the relation of God to his chosen people, the Jews, as a consequence of consent. "By the Kingdom of God," he says in chapter 35 of *Leviathan*, "is properly meant a Commonwealth, instituted, by the consent of those which were to be subject thereto, for their civil government, and the regulating of their behavior." Both the ancient Jews and modern Christians, in Hobbes's opinion, are linked to God by consent: both recognize his authority: the Jews in an actual earthly kingdom under a kind of regency of Moses and the Christians in a kingdom to come. One can even say that there are two levels of consent in God's relation to his chosen peoples: first, there is a covenant between those who subject themselves to God as a sovereign; but second, our knowledge of this covenant comes from Scripture, which is itself valid only because we have agreed to consider it as such, by allowing the civil sovereign to make the Bible canonical. We consent, then, to believe that God's relation to his chosen peoples is also based on consent. In any case God's kingdom, whether of the Old Testament or covenant or of the New, exists "by force of our covenant, not by the right of God's power."[31]

This last observation turns out to be quite important later on, inasmuch as for Hobbes all authority and right exist by covenant or agreement unless there is an "irresistible power" in some sovereign, whether God or man, a power that, according to Hobbes, gives rise to absolute rights of "dominion."[32] God was entitled to give laws to the Jews as their civil sovereign, because he was the beneficiary of an antecedent obligation created by covenant to obey; but he could have ruled them by natural "irresistible power."[33] It is essential to point this out because it shows one of the limits to consent in Hobbes's political theory. Indeed, of the several impediments that stand in the way of considering him a consent theorist pure and simple, one of the most problematical is the way in which he treats the relation of power to the right to rule. While it is undoubtedly true, as Michael Oakeshott maintains, that one of Hobbes's central doctrines was the belief that there is "no obligation on any man, which ariseth not from some act of his own,"[34] in both *De Cive* (chapter 14) and *Leviathan* (chapter 31) Hobbes says that irresistible power carries with it a right to rule. But if the right to rule can be derived from the possession of irresistible power, then a theory of obligation or legitimacy based on voluntary acts of one's own is made superfluous: "that obligation which rises from contract...can have no place...where the right of ruling...rises only from nature."[35] Or rather, such acts would be superfluous if there were any person on earth possessed of irresistible power; but the fact that only God actually has such power makes artificial right—right depending on covenant—necessary. If the natural right of a man to all things were conjoined with irresistible power, then that power would entitle him to rule, and all other men would be obliged to submit an account of their weakness. As Hobbes says in chapter 31 of *Leviathan*,

> Seeing all men by nature had right to all things, they had right every one to reign over all the rest. But because this right could not be obtained by force, it concerned the safety of every one, laying by that right, to set up men, with sovereign authority, by common consent, to rule and defend them: whereas if there had been any man of power irresistible, there had been no reason, why he should not by that power have ruled, and defended both himself, and them, according to his own discretion.[36]

Hobbes does not always, or even usually, reduce right simply to power as does, for example, Spinoza.[37] He supports the right to all things in the state of nature in the name of self-preservation, not in the name of arbitrary whim or lust for domination.[38] And since the natural right of man is not really comparable to the power of God—both because natural right is defended in terms of a self-preservation which no God requires, and because we cannot, according to Hobbes, really know God—he seems inconsistent in comparing the natural right to rule of an irresistible man with a similar right in God. Indeed, an irresistible man would, by definition, have no need of a right to self-preservation and hence no natural right to rule everyone in terms of that self-defense.

While dwelling on those aspects of Hobbes's theory that keep him from being simply a consent theorist it is important to note that Hobbes never allows the concept of natural rights—the liberty of self-preservation that leads at once to a right to all things and to universal warfare because that right is equal for all men—to be restricted even by a man's own consent. "The right men have by nature to protect themselves, when none else can protect them," he urges in chapter 21 of *Leviathan*, "can by no covenant be relinquished." It is for this reason that Hobbes says that a criminal on the way to his execution has a right to resist his executioners, notwithstanding the fact that by authorizing the sovereign to make any laws he has consented to all the laws: "a covenant not to defend myself from force, by force, is always void...no man can transfer, or lay down his right to save himself from death, wounds and imprisonment...and therefore the promise of not resisting force, in no covenant transferreth any right; nor is obliging."[39]

Natural rights, then, are ultimately inalienable, though the sovereign may have a concurrent absolute right, given by covenant, that will conflict with natural rights; for example, he may have a right to kill me even though I have a right to avoid being killed.[40] The case, however, is rather different with natural law. While Hobbes calls the laws of nature "dictates of reason," which are "immutable and eternal,"[41] in a passage in *Leviathan* that recalls Cicero's famous formulation in book 3 of *De Republica*,[42] he nonetheless holds in *Liberty, Necessity and Chance* that it is "absurd" to say that "the law of nature is a law without our assent," for the law of nature "is the assent itself that all men give to the means of their own preservation."[43] The natural laws may be only "conclusions, or theorems concerning what conduceth to the conservation and defense" of all men, and that dictate the seeking of peace as well as all the corollaries of such an endeavor—gratitude, equity, acknowledgment of equality; but Hobbes still speaks of assent in connection with them.[44]

Despite the fact that Hobbes views natural rights as unabridgeable—though the exercise of those rights may be channeled by a society, set up by agreement, that protects them—virtually every other political concept in Hobbes's philosophy is defined, in whole or in part, in terms of will and consent. The authority of sovereigns, the obligations of subjects, the nature of justice and merit, the validity of law, the origin of language, and even the attributes of God and the authority of Scripture are all made possible by voluntary acts: by promising, by consenting, by agreeing. To a certain degree this is even true of natural law as accepted by men, though its content is simply rational. Hobbes's position does not, of course, involve consent or agreement in the day-to-day operation of the state; one consents only in authorizing the representative person to stand for one's will.[45] Consent makes most of its appearances in Hobbes with respect to concepts of obedience and submission. This limitation, however, does not make consent unimportant for him; it simply restricts its scope. As a consequence it remains true that covenant is an essential concept in Hobbes, and that wills "make the essence of all covenants."

A theory that defines so many essential concepts—especially the authority or right of sovereigns and the obligations of subjects—in terms of consent, promise, and covenant and that suggests that wills make the essence of all covenants might be expected to develop a notion of will as a moral faculty whose free choice gives rise to authority and to obligation. The family of voluntarist notions on which Hobbes relies seems to need a certain kind of theory of will in order to be usable. Perhaps the traditional Christian view of moral choice would serve Hobbes's purpose. His moral and political philosophy often seem to depend on the idea of will as moral agency, of the choosing, self-obligating person as a moral person, as a possible subject of duties.[46] But when one turns to what he actually says about volition, it is hard to find much congruence between his definition of the will and the practical use he appears to make of it. Hobbes said something—though not very much—about the will in *Leviathan;* he said far more in *Liberty, Necessity and Chance,* to which one must turn after examining the relevant passages from *Leviathan.* Since, however, Hobbes's concept of will is almost always discussed with respect to "deliberation" and "deliberation" with respect to "appetite" and "fear" (or "aversion" in later works);[47] and since, moreover, the most concise statement of the relation of will to deliberation, appetite, and fear (or aversion) is to be found in chapter 12 of *The Elements of Law,* a brief look at that chapter will prove profitable.

Hobbes begins this chapter with his usual view that only "external objects cause conceptions," and that these conceptions cause "appetite and fear, which are the first unperceived beginnings of our actions." Appetite and fear succeed each other in the mind, Hobbes goes on, until an action is done, or until "some accident" makes action impossible. This alternating succession of appetites and fears, Hobbes continues, "during all the time the action is in our power to do, is that we call Deliberation." In this process of deliberation "the last appetite, as also the last fear, is called will (viz.) the last appetite will do; the last fear will not to do, or will to omit." After distinguishing true volition from mere inclination Hobbes urges that voluntary actions are "such as a man doth upon appetite and fear"—not upon reason or upon deliberation in a purely rational sense—and distinguishes these from involuntary actions such as falling or being pushed. He goes on to claim that the will itself is not voluntary since, if it were, a man could will to will, and will to will to will, ad infinitum, and this would be "absurd." In a crucial passage he insists that "as will to do is appetite, and will to omit, fear, the causes of appetite and of fear are the causes also of our will. But the propounding of benefits and harms, that is to say, of reward and punishment, is the cause of our appetite and our fears, and therefore also of our wills... and consequently our wills follow our opinions, as our actions follow our wills."[48]

To treat an opinion simply as an appetite is to run the risk of conflating causes with reasons, reactions with actions, and, most important, being determined with being persuaded. This passage shows that Hobbes does not always distinguish rational mental processes from physiological-psychological ones: being averse in general cannot explain the reasons for having an aversion to something. Having a reason for aversion, an averse opinion, is not the same as being determined by aversion as a general psychological cause.[49] There is a species of reductionism at work in Hobbes that, in its effort to trace all mental operations to perception ("conception"), appetite, and aversion, attempts to prove that the will is caused in rather too easy a way. This point is directly relevant to a consideration of Hobbes's consent theory, since he ends the passage on the will in the *Elements* by saying that "when the wills of many concur to some one and the same action, or effect, this concourse of their wills is called consent."[50] Obviously, a great deal depends on the possibility of distinguishing different kinds of will, deliberation, and consent. If will and deliberation can be defined simply in terms of appetite and aversion, with opinion reduced to one of the other of these, then consent means only an appetite that a certain number of men happen to have in common. This is a definition from which it would be difficult, to say the least, to derive ordinary views of obligation and authority, unless we assume that an appetite's being shared raises it to the level of an obligation. However, if there are different kinds of deliberation, some of them rational and involving the choice of beings who understand alternatives, then there is a possibility of understanding will and consent as the operations of a person, as distinguished from an animal.

A fundamental definition of the will appears in chapter 6 of *Leviathan* and is amplified in chapter 46.[51] Since the definition in chapter 6 is central to all further analysis, it is indispensable to quote it in full:

> In *deliberation*, the last appetite, or aversion, immediately adhering to the action, or to the omission thereof, is that we call the WILL; the act, not the faculty, of willing. And beasts that have *deliberation*, must necessarily also have *will*. The definition of the *will*, given commonly by the Schools, that it is a *rational appetite*, is not good. For if it were then could there be no voluntary act against reason. For a *voluntary act* is that, which proceedeth from the *will*, and no other. But if instead of rational appetite, we shall say an appetite resulting from a precedent deliberation, then the definition is the same that I have given here. *Will* therefore *is the last appetite in deliberation.*[52]

This concept of the will appears to be so broad, covering everything from the raising of a hand (or paw) to the understanding of the sublimest duties, that it is too undifferentiated for use in a moral theory based on will. For example, if fleeing from an enraged mob, on the one hand, and promising to obey a sovereign, on the other, are both voluntary acts, as compared with, say, the circulation of the blood, then this idea of the voluntary is too diffuse to be helpful in a consent theory. The equal ascription of deliberation and hence of will to men and beasts seems inadequate to serve as the philosophical foundation of promise, authority, and duty. Finally, the criticism of the Schools for calling a rational appetite does not hold up, since in the Scholastic view it is necessary only that a voluntary decision involve appetite's accepting the counsel of reason, not that all voluntary decisions be solely the product of reason.[53] Hobbes makes it quite clear, though, in the chapter 46 extension of his definition of will that it is precisely the Scholastic view of volition that he wants to overturn: "For cause of the will, to do any particular action, which is called *volitio*, they assign the faculty, that is to say, the capacity in general, that men have, to will sometimes one thing, sometimes another, which is called *voluntas*; making the *power* the cause of the *act*. As if one should assign for cause of the good or evil acts of men, their ability to do them."[54]

It would seem that a theory that grounds authority and

obligation on covenant, of which will is the essence, should seek to uphold the doctrine that men have a "capacity" to "will sometimes one thing, sometimes another," and that "the cause of the good or evil acts of men" is indeed "their ability to do them." What Hobbes assaults is in fact exactly what he ought to defend. But it soon becomes clear why he cannot accept the Scholastic view; it contradicts his theology. The Scholastic position, he urges, was "made to maintain the doctrine of free-will, that is, of a will of man not subject to the will of God," or, to put it another way, a will not subject to the efficient or second natural causes of the physical world that God, as first cause, has created.[55] It is clear why Hobbes wanted to deny that the will could be a free faculty, the cause of its own motion. Of course, a faculty of freely willing would have overthrown his theory of universal determinism; for Hobbes nothing is "self-moved."[56] But in addition to this, Hobbes had an excellent theological reason for adopting his view, despite its apparent consequences for his notion of will: the Christian philosophers had never succeeded in showing how God could be both the first cause of everything and yet not the cause of the choices, whether good or evil, of men. Hobbes was combatting the kind of doctrine found slightly later in Leibniz's *Theodicy:* "free will is the proximate cause of the evil of [guilt and] punishment; although it is true that the original imperfection of creatures, which is already presented in the eternal ideas [in the mind of God], is the first and most remote cause."[57] A view of this kind, which tries to distinguish between what God "wills" and what he "permits," between "moral" necessity and "metaphysical" necessity, was simply nonsense to Hobbes; it was "vain philosophy."[58] Thus his theology—which there is no conclusive reason for not taking seriously—demands a concept of determined volition, or caused volition, even if some might see this as a contradiction in terms.

These observations lead directly to the third and last passage in *Leviathan* in which Hobbes treats the will.

> *Liberty,* and *necessity* are consistent: as in the water, that hath not only *liberty,* but a *necessity* of descending by the channel; so likewise in the actions which men voluntarily do: which, because they proceed from their will, proceed from *liberty;* and yet, because every act of man's will, and every desire, and inclination proceedeth from some cause, and that from another cause, in a continual chain, whose first link is in the hand of God the first of all causes, proceed from necessity. So

that to him that could see the connection of those causes, the *necessity* of all men's voluntary actions, would appear manifest...For though men may do many things, which God does not command, nor is therefore author of them; yet they can have no passion, nor appetite to any thing, of which appetite God's will is not the cause.[59]

This passage, from chapter 21, simply confirms what has been said already, and is perhaps unavoidable if mind is treated as an epiphenomenon of matter.[60] It states with particular force Hobbes's view that will is caused by desire and inclination or appetite, which are themselves caused by perception of a world caused by God. All of this is quite appropriate to an "empirical" psychology but less appropriate to a theory that derives authority and obligation from voluntary acts. What one starts with, then, in turning to *Liberty, Necessity and Chance* for Hobbes's most extensive consideration of volition is the view that causality and theology, which all but coincide in this case, demand caused volition; that the will is the last appetite or aversion in deliberation; and that there is no difference between appetite and aversion simply and appetite and aversion that are brought about by opinion or reasoning.

In *Liberty, Necessity and Chance,* a long work containing Hobbes's and Bishop Bramhall's mutual refutations of each other's doctrines of will, Hobbes begins with a position that simply reinforces his familiar stance. Bramhall thinks, says Hobbes, that a man can "determine his own will." But no man can do this, he says, "for the will is appetite; nor can a man more determine his will than any other appetite, that is, more than he can determine when he shall be hungry and when not." True liberty, Hobbes goes on, "doth not consist in determining itself, but in doing what the will is determined unto"[61]—assuming, of course, that there is no "impediment to motion," which is Hobbes's most common definition of liberty.[62]

A little later in the treatise Hobbes declares that deliberation is common to men and animals, pointing out that horses, dogs, and other beasts "do demur often times upon the way they are to take: the horse, retiring from some strange figure he sees, and coming on again to avoid the spur." And "what else" than this does a deliberating man do, he asks, who proceeds at one time "toward action, another while retire[s] from it, as the fear of greater evil drives him back"? What Hobbes appears to do in this case, as in many others, is to reduce deliberation to reaction or even to stimulus and response. He is certainly able to find instances in which animal fear and human fear are comparable, but whether it is legitimate to define deliberation in terms of this lowest common denominator is doubtful. Bramhall objected that "deliberation implyeth the actual use of reason." Hobbes himself, in the very passage in which he likens human and animal deliberation, suggests that "voluntary presupposes some precedent deliberation, that is to say, some consideration and meditation of what is likely to follow" an action of ours, which seems in some degree to grant Bramhall's point, unless we suppose that animals meditate.[63]

About a third of the way into *Liberty, Necessity and Chance* Bramhall begins to develop the well-known argument that if the will is caused, men are not free moral agents and hence not responsible for their actions, the political consequence of which would be that they could neither authorize sovereigns to make laws nor be obligated by those laws. Hobbes claims, says the Bishop, now speaking of lawbreaking rather than lawmaking, that "not the necessity, but the will to break the law makes the action unjust." Bramhall goes on, "I ask what makes the will to break the law; is it not his necessity? What gets he by this? A perverse will causeth injustice, and necessity causeth a perverse will. He saith, 'the law regardeth the will, but the precedent causes of action.' To what proposition, to what term is this [an] answer?"[64] Hobbes had already provided an answer to this in an earlier part of the work, albeit an answer that could never please a Christian voluntarist who wants to use the will for purposes other than imputation of legal fault. We blame men for wrong voluntary acts, Hobbes urges, "because they please us not." Is blaming, he continues, "anything else but saying the thing blamed is ill or imperfect? May we not say a horse is lame, though his lameness came from necessity? or that a man is a fool or a knave, if he be so, though could not help it?"

It is sufficient to say that the examples are not very apt, since one does not blame animals in any ordinary sense, and folly is not comparable to knavery, as Hobbes himself suggests in an immediately preceding remark, in which he urges that we sometimes "represent reasons" to people in order to "make them have the will they have not." Reasons might be useful to a knave but not to a true fool. If, however, knavery and folly are equally caused, the place of reasons is hard to understand.[65]

The question is not just one of lame horses, knaves, and fools. In one of the most bold and striking passages of *Liberty, Necessity and Chance* Hobbes acknowledges that his notion of caused will might seem to be an impediment to divine justice, for someone might say that "if there be a necessity of all events" and no free will, "then praise and reprehension, reward and punishment, are all vain and unjust"; and "if God should openly forbid, and secretly necessitate the same action, punishing men for what they could not avoid, there would be no belief among them of heaven or hell."[66] Here Hobbes states the case against himself with a power that was not in Bramhall's power.

In Hobbes's view a bishop should not be so ignorant of Scripture as to forget St. Paul's letter to the Romans, chapter 9, in which St. Paul asks whether God's exercise of irresistible power might ever be unjust. "Is there unrighteousness with God?" St. Paul asks. And the answer is: "God forbid." Has not "the potter power over the clay, of the same lump to make one vessel unto honor and another unto dishonor?" And cannot God rightfully shape the actions of men in just the same way? The problem with Bishop Bramhall, Hobbes goes on, is that he fails to see what a reading of St. Paul could have shown him: that "the power of God alone, without other help, is sufficient justification for any action he doth." Whatever God does, even to agents with wills, "is made just by his doing." This is obvious to anyone who sees that "the name of justice," as used in human discourse, is "not that by which God Almighty's actions are to be measured." If St. Paul is not clear enough, there is the Book of Job:

> When God afflicted Job, he did object no sin to him, but justified that afflicting him by telling him of his power. *Hast thou* (says God) *an arm like mine? Where wast thou, when I laid the foundations of the earth?* and the like . . . Power irresistible justifieth all actions really and properly, in whomsoever it be found. Less power does not. And because such power is in God only, he must needs be just in all his actions. And we, that not comprehending his counsels, call him to the bar, commit injustice in it.[67]

Here irresistible divine power works against free will, just as in chapter 31 of *Leviathan* it works against the covenants of which will is the essence. It is passages such as these that make it impossible to agree with John Dunn that Hobbes "did not believe in permitting theological categories to deflect human terrestrial judgment."[68]

As the treatise unfolds, the advantage is sometimes on the side of Hobbes, sometimes on that of Bramhall. The Bishop, for example, makes a strong point when he suggests that Hobbes has confused the persuasiveness of reasons with the determination of causes (and Hobbes does sometimes speak of reasons as causes of the will). "Motives," by which Bramhall means reasons or principles, "determine not naturally, but morally; which kind of determination may consist with true liberty."[69] Being persuaded, that is, is consistent with true liberty because we determine ourselves by accepting reasons as valid. Hobbes, however, holds that "nothing is determined by itself," thus making a distinction between moral and natural determination impossible.[70] The Bishop found what he took to be a perfect example of Hobbes's mistake on this point: Hobbes says, urges Bramhall, " 'that we are not moved to prayer or any other action, but by outward objects, as pious company, godly preachers, or something equivalent.' " Hobbes's error here, the Bishop continues, "is to make godly preachers and pious company to be outward objects; which are [in fact] outward agents."[71] The error is to make a person who persuades into an object that causes. Bramhall suggests, not unreasonably, that if Hobbes's opinion were true that "the will were naturally determined by . . . extrinsical causes, not only motives were vain, but reason itself and deliberation were in vain." A little later in the treatise he complains that "now [Hobbes] tells us, that 'those actions which follow the last appetite, are voluntary, and where there is only one appetite, that is the last.' " But earlier, he goes on, Hobbes had said that " 'voluntary presupposeth some precedent deliberation and meditation of what is to follow, both upon the doing and abstaining from action.' " Hobbes, he says with some exasperation, "confounds all things," "human will with the sensitive appetite, rational hope or fear with irrational passions, inclinations with intentions," but particularly "imagination with deliberation."[72]

This last charge is particularly interesting, since it bears accurately on a rather odd passage in Hobbes's part of *Liberty, Neccesity and Chance*, one that puts reason on a footing with imagination and seems to weaken the use that he wanted to make of reason in science and in the rationality of natural law. "Consideration, understanding, reason, and all the *passions* of the mind," Hobbes declares, "are imaginations." Shortly after this, deliberation is added to the list of imaginings: "I do indeed conceive that deliberation [which is "nothing else but so many wills alternatively changed"] is an act of imagination or fancy; nay more, that reason and understanding are also acts of the imagination."[73] Here,

Hobbes goes so far in reducing deliberation, will, understanding, and reason to imagination that science and natural law are shaken, and this in the interest of showing that all mental operations are of one kind: traceable to sensory causes.

Hobbes, in his effort to overthrow the ordinary view of volition, even endangers his own notion of reason by likening it to fancy; but it is far from clear how one can reconcile this with the concept of natural laws as "immutable and eternal...dictates of reason."[74] Nevertheless, he often catches Bishop Bramhall in absurd arguments and even more often puts his finger on a standard point of Christian doctrine that is nearly impossible to make plausible. If the human will were not truly free, Bramhall had said, if men did not choose to be evil, then God would be a "tyrant" for creating "millions to burn eternally without their fault, to express his power." To this, a problem that troubled even so great a genius as Leibniz, Hobbes replied with a harsh but cogent remark.

The Bishop is nearer the calling him a tyrant, than I am; making that to be tyranny, which is but the exercise of an absolute power; for he holdeth, though he see it not; by consequence, in withdrawing the will of men from God's dominion, that every man is a king of himself. And if a man cannot praise God for his goodness, who creates millions to burn eternally without their fault, how can the Bishop praise God for his goodness, who thinks he hath created millions to burn eternally, when he could have kept them so easily from committing any fault?[75]

Hobbes is a master at tripping up those who want to attribute the same concepts of universal justice and good will to God and man alike, who want to make God the first cause of everything but not the creator of human wrongdoing. His simple doctrine of irresistible power, accompanied by the idea that we attribute goodness and justice to God as marks of honor—that is, of our opinion of his power—has at least the merit of consistency and shows why he cannot consider human will to be free.

Perhaps the most interesting of Hobbes's observations on will in *Liberty, Necessity and Chance* is one in which he most nearly approaches Spinoza's view that liberty is an illusion arising from our imperfect knowledge of causes. "Is there any doubt," Hobbes asks, "if a man could foreknow, as God foreknows, that which is hereafter to come to pass, but that he would also see and know the causes which shall bring it to pass, and how they work, and make the effect necessary?" It is because we do not see and know true causes, he suggests, that "we impute those events to liberty, and not to causes." At another point in the same work Hobbes contrasts not just liberty and causality but will and causality, saying that "a wooden top that is lashed by the boys, and runs about sometimes to one wall, sometimes to another, sometimes spinning, sometimes hitting men on the shins" would fancy, if it were "sensible of its own motion," that it "proceeded from its own will, unless it felt what lashed it." Is a man, Hobbes asks, any wiser than the top when he "runs to one place for a benefice, to another for a bargain, and troubles the world with writing errors and requiring answers" simply because "he thinks he doth it without other cause than his own will, and seeth not what are the lashings that cause his will?"[76]

Somewhat earlier, in a passage apparently designed to make the same point, Hobbes shows that Bramhall's distinction between moral determination, or persuasion, and natural determination, or causality, is something of which he takes inadequate account.

> When there is no compulsion, but the strength of temptation to do an evil action, being greater than the motives to abstain, necessarily determines him to the doing of it, yet he deliberates whilst sometimes the motives to do, sometimes the motives to forbear, are working on him, and consequently he electeth which he will. But commonly, when we see and know the strength that moves us, we acknowledge necessity; but when we see not, or mark not the force that moves us, we then think there is none, and that it is not causes, but liberty that produceth the action.[77]

It is not self-evident that it is useful to think of a motive as causal. To speak of motives as working on someone is a mechanistic metaphor not adequate to account for mental processes. In short, even in a passage designed to show that uncaused will and deliberation are illusory, Hobbes uses ideas that are hard to conceive in terms of causality. Bramhall, not being a Kant, could only suggest this in sometimes rather unclear language.[78]

The upshot of *Liberty, Necessity and Chance*, taken as a whole, is that while Hobbes is usually more forceful and cogent than Bramhall, the bishop makes a good point in distinguishing between reasons and causes, between being persuaded and being determined. Hobbes, while treating will as necessitated, does sometimes distinguish, in fact if not in principle, between deliberation and will both in a rational sense and in a sense of alternating appetite and aversion. Hobbes's theology requires him to insist that "if God had made either causes or effects free from necessity, he had made them free from his own prescience, which had been imperfection."[79] This work, then, tends to confirm what Hobbes says about the will in *The Elements of Law*, in *De Cive*, and in *Leviathan*. Little of it suggests a theory of volition on which could be built the obligation of promises or the legitimacy of authorized rulers.

What has unfolded thus far is a rather stark contrast between a moral and political theory that requires a family of voluntarist concepts as its foundation, and a theory of volition as appetite and aversion which is ill suited to account for the moral importance of consenting, promising, and agreeing. There appears to be a radical disjunction between an important part of Hobbes's social theory and its philosophical underpinnings.

In Hobbes's case the question to ask is this: If all human activity consists of motion caused by appetite and aversion, themselves caused by "conception" of a caused world, how does one account for ordinary moral and political concepts? In a caused world there is no room for reasons, for judgment, for obligations. Where causality explains everything, there is no need of "determining oneself" in terms of principles that one understands. Yet, Hobbes says, there is "no obligation on any man, which ariseth not from some act of his own," which is the perfect expression of a voluntarist and contractarian point of view. But this act cannot be just any act: it cannot be, say, the mere feeling of an appetite such as lust, because in a world of appetites and aversions the notions of obligation and authority could not exist at all. (By world of appetite and aversion is meant just that: a world in which all motion is caused by caused appetites and aversions. It is hard to see how reasons could be present in such a world even as ex post facto rationalizations of caused behavior.) For the coherence of his practical doctrines Hobbes needs not just any act but a free act on the part of a free agent, but he cannot provide such an agent without overthrowing the foundations of other parts of his system.

He needs a being who can shape his own conduct in terms of reasons and principles, such as natural law, that he understands. All this he needs; but he provides a being whose sole liberty consists in "doing what his will" (the "last appetite" or "last aversion") is "determined unto." On such a view reasons do not serve as motives, since the notion of a motive is swallowed up by a determinism of appetite and aversion. Thus, when Michael Oakeshott complains—in his essay "Logos and Telos," nominally a review of Spragens's *The Politics of Motion: the World of Thomas Hobbes*—of those who reduce Hobbesian "emotion, memory, imagination, will, choice, speech, deliberation, agreement and disagreement, and even self-consciousness to 'appetite' and 'aversion,'" to that "inertial motion which is common to all bodies," and who will not allow "Hobbes' cosmology to contain intelligent movement" such as the choice of a political order, he is right in saying that Hobbesian politics becomes unintelligible on an extreme reductionist view.[80] But did not Hobbes himself set this reductionism in motion by treating will precisely as the last appetite in deliberation, so that his voluntarist and contractarian ethics and politics become intelligible only by assuming a gulf between his psychology and his practical philosophy?

There is a way of avoiding this kind of conclusion: one can say either that some statements in Hobbes are not really meant, or meant literally, or that Hobbes "changes the meaning of words," as Leibniz and other anti-Hobbesians suggest, to make the new versions of traditional concepts consistent.[81] Perhaps Hobbes changes the meaning of words insofar as definitions are concerned but then uses the terms for traditional purposes. The best way to find out how this disjunction, if it does exist, affects his political philosophy is to examine a few passages in which Hobbes seems to be saying one thing about the relation of right to will, then to examine passages in which he appears to say something different, and finally to examine passages that are ambiguous and could lend themselves to various interpretations.

Among certain relatively recent interpreters of Hobbes, particularly A. E. Taylor, there has arisen a conviction that he was concerned not simply with prudent action—action based on rational foresight—not simply with self-preserving action, not simply with non-self-contradictory action, but with duties conceived as the consequence of voluntary choices.[82] Many of these recent interpreters are most impressed by a passage in chapter 14 of *De Cive* that reads: "I say that...a man is obliged by his contracts, that is, that he ought to perform for his promise sake; but that the law ties him to being obliged, that is to say, it compels him to make good his promise, for fear of the punishment appointed by law."[83] In this passage Hobbes makes the justice of contracts derivative from the promise a man makes and the good intention that he ought to have, whereas legal compulsion is something merely external. This, of course, conflicts with Hobbes's repeated assertion that justice simply is the law[84]—though as we have seen he defines distributive justice, at least, in terms of consent. More significantly, this passage seems to make justice a combination of a rational principle—contract as the foundation of peace—coupled with a good will or a right intention; but surely this is what Hobbes was arguing against in the Scholastics. There is another passage, in *The Elements of Law*, that is not cited by Taylor but that in making a point roughly comparable to the one just discussed has the additional advantage of drawing in the concept of will in a moral sense and of showing that promise and covenant are to be understood as products of this will. "Promises therefore, upon consideration of reciprocal benefit," Hobbes declares, "are covenants and signs of the will, or last act of deliberation, whereby the liberty of performing or not performing is taken away, and consequently are obligatory."[85] Promise, covenant, and obligation are all quite clearly related to willing—and willing in a way that would not make sense as the last of any appetites. Moreover, taking away the liberty of nonperformance cannot be a physical impediment to liberty, since covenants without the sword are only words.[86] This must then refer to a moral restriction on liberty. Of course, in the very next sentence of the *Elements* Hobbes goes on to say that as long as covenants consist only in mutual trust but are not guaranteed by coercive power, the "first performer" of a bargain will only "betray himself thereby to the covetousness or other passion of him with whom he contracteth"; that in a state of nature, without a sovereign, such covenants are of "none effect." (The creation of a sovereign can, of course, make these covenants "effectual.")[87] To speak, however, of what makes something effectual is not to say what its whole nature is. What the sovereign provides in this case—safety for performers—is not something out of which promise, covenant, or obligation can be deduced, since safety is only the condition of effectual covenants. It is not implausible to say that promises define the nature of covenants but that such covenants will be effective only when it is safe for everyone to adhere to obligations. This is an odd theory, to be sure, in that obligations are measured in part by circumstances; but to say that promises must be looked at in the light of considerations of safety is not to say that promises are unimportant in Hobbes's theory. Nor can it be denied that in this passage from the *Elements* promise, covenant, obligation, and will are intimately bound together in a way that looks rather conventionally voluntaristic. Hobbes evidently thought this passage correct enough to repeat it, almost word for word, in chapter 2 of *De Cive*.[88]

These passages could be written off as slips of the pen, albeit rather long ones, were there not other passages in all three of Hobbes's major political works in English—*The Elements of Law, De Cive,* and *Leviathan*—in which he distinguishes clearly between justice based on good will or good intention and justice that simply involves external command. In *De Cive*, for example, he says:

> He who hath done some just thing, is not therefore said to be a just person, but guiltless; and he that hath done some unjust thing, we do not therefore say he is an unjust, but a guilty man. But when the words are applied to persons, to be just signifies as much as to be delighted in just dealing, to study how to do righteousness, or to endeavor in all things to do that which is just; and to be unjust is to neglect righteous dealing, or to think it is to be measured not according to my contract, but some present benefit. So as the injustice or injustice of the mind, the intention, or the man, is one thing, that of an action, or omission, another.

Hobbes seems to be saying that justice is not simply what the law commands but that a man's good will or right intention is superior to mere legal compulsion; what is more, contract takes precedence over benefit. (As he urges in chapter 14 of *De Cive*, "in contracts we say, I will do this...[and]...a contract obligeth of itself.")[89] In any case, much of what has just been pointed out treats will as something other than the last of any appetites and upholds the derivation of right from a voluntary "act of one's own."

There is, nevertheless, a considerable weight of text and interpretation that supports a contrary view: that duty is simply a rational, metaphorical obligation not to do those things that will contradict one's continued existence by bringing on death, the end of all felicity. Some passages to this effect are juxtaposed with some of the ones just cited that show that there is a doctrine of willed duties in Hobbes. In chapter 3 of *De Cive*, in a passage separated from that on justice as good intention by only a single paragraph, Hobbes argues that

> the breaking of a bargain . . . is called an injury. But that action or omission is called unjust, insomuch as an injury, and an unjust action or omission, signify the same thing, and both are the same with breach of contract and trust. . . And there is some likeness between that which in the common course of life we call injury, and that which in the Schools is usually called absurd. For even as he who by arguments is driven to deny the assertion which he first maintained, is said to be brought to absurdity; in like manner, he who through weakness of mind does or omits that which before he had by contract promised not to do or omit, commits an injury, and falls no less into contradiction than he who in the Schools is reduced to an absurdity . . . An injury, therefore is a kind of absurdity in conversation, as an absurdity is a kind of injury in disputation.[90]

While it is certainly true that justice is likened to consistency, to being logical, there are perhaps a few points to be made. First, this passage is intended as an analogy; to say what something is like in some respects is not to say what the whole of it is. Second, Hobbes still uses the words *promise* and *contract* in speaking of justice, neither of which can be derived from the notion of logical consistency alone. Nonetheless, the passage as a whole treats justice as a matter of non-self-contradiction.

Perhaps the greatest difficulty to be faced by anyone who wants to treat Hobbes as a consent theorist is the definition of consent given in chapter 5 of *De Cive*. The "consent of many," Hobbes begins, "consists only in this": that those who seek security by establishing a social order "direct all their actions to the same end, and the common good." He goes on to show not only that in order to produce such a society the rational dictates of natural law must be followed but that a sovereign power, a single will, must be set up. He then observes that "Aristotle reckons among those animals which he calls politic, not man only, but divers others; as the ant, the bee, etc." Aristotle, Hobbes insists, was wrong in doing this, but not because such political animals fail to consent to a single social order. Indeed, Hobbes says that they do consent: "though they be destitute of reason, by which they may contract and submit to government, notwithstanding by consenting (that is to say) ensuing or eschewing the same things, they so direct their actions to a common end, that their meetings are not obnoxious unto any seditions." But, he continues, the government of these animals is not political, "because their government is only a consent, or many wills concurring in one object, not (as is necessary in civil government) one will."[91] Here, a number of things need to be said. In the first place, consent is initially defined as "ensuing or eschewing the same things," which certainly involves no moral content at all; any number of political animals could simply happen to do this. In the second, Hobbesian animals actually do have wills that concur in one object; the reason that they fail to be political is not that they do not consent—Hobbes says that they do—but that there is no "representative person" who provides one will for the commonwealth. But how, one might ask, does any representative person get his authority? Is it not by consent, covenant, promise, all of which require willing? After all, the sovereign is not merely one will: he is an authorized, representative will whose right to make law is derived from a "previous obligation" of subjects to obey. The concept of consent may even become unintelligible as the source of duties if it is used as broadly as in this passage, though it could continue to be intelligible as a common appetite. In chapter 42 of *Leviathan* Hobbes had said that "the right of all sovereigns is derived originally from the consent of every one of those that are to be governed." But now consent is made too imprecise to allow for the notion of right to be derived from it.[92]

Thus far some of Hobbes's statements about duty and promising look almost conventional, while others seem to define those ideas in terms of non-self-contradiction and converging appetites. Between these extremes there are other intermediate cases, which can be interpreted in either way. In *The Elements of Law*, for example, Hobbes defines a promise as "the affirmation or negation of some action to be done in the future."[93] Whether "to be done" means "ought to be done" or "will be done by anyone who is self-consistent" is not clear. There are many such instances, though these intermediate cases must usually be assimilated to one general interpretive viewpoint or another. At any rate, we have seen how difficult it is to settle on one general interpretive view that takes account of everything that Hobbes says about consent, promise, duty, and will, and does so without asserting that a given passage is not important or not to be taken literally. It is hard to know, in determining what is essential and what peripheral, whether one is satisfying Hobbes or oneself.

An examination of chapter 16 of Spinoza's *Theologico-Political Treatise* helps throw some light on the meaning of will, consent, promise, obligation, and covenant in Hobbes, because Spinoza actually does say much of what Hobbes is alleged to have said. While the differences between them are sometimes rather subtle, they are very instructive.

What is remarkable about chapter 16 of the *Treatise* is that it outlines a kind of contract theory that seems to rely little, if at all, on any idea of voluntary acts or on any idea of being morally bound by voluntary acts. Hobbes's view, of course, is relatively clear and very different on this point. He asserts in chapter 14 of *Leviathan* that once a man has voluntarily transferred the exercise of his natural right to a "representative person," he is "obliged, or bound, not to hinder those, to whom such right is granted, or abandoned, from the benefit of it: and that he *ought,* and it is his duty, not to make void that voluntary act of his own."[94] Spinoza almost never speaks of duties and obligations that arise out of voluntary actions. This is no accident, for in his contractarianism Spinoza diminishes volition almost to the vanishing point, since it is his view that will is an incoherent notion, a mere cover for our ignorance of determining causes. Hence, Spinoza cannot view the will as an autonomous moral causality capable of producing a morally binding covenant. The decisive passage is in *The Improvement of the Understanding*, where Spinoza says that "men are deceived because they think themselves free, and the sole reason for their thinking so is that they are conscious of their own actions, and ignorant of the causes by which those actions are determined." Ignorance, then, creates in men an illusion of liberty, for "as to saying that their actions depend upon their will, these are words to which no idea is attached." Indeed, those who pretend to know "what the will is," and who try to find "seats and dwelling-places of the soul," usually "excite our laughter or disgust." It is revealing that Spinoza treats will in a section called "Of Falsity," and when he gives examples of persons who fancy that they will freely, he invariably picks those with defective understandings: "the infant believes that it is by free will that it seeks the breast; the angry boy believes that by free will he wishes vengeance; the timid man thinks it is with free will that he seeks flight; the drunkard believes that by a free command of his mind he speaks the things which when sober he wishes he had left unsaid." Spinoza concludes that it is especially "the madman, the chatterer, the boy" who "believe themselves to be free."[95]

One would not expect Spinoza to speak of society as being maintained by covenant, or the perpetual will to preserve peace. Indeed, he confines himself to saying that natural right, which is the same as natural power ("the rights of an individual extend to the utmost limits of his power as it has been conditioned")[96] is to be "handed over" to governors who will keep people from injuring each other. The use of the phrase *handed over*, a purely mechanical phrase having no relation to willing or duty or obligation, is not accidental. Nor is Spinoza's claim that "a compact is only made valid by its utility"[97] and thus a man need not, for example, give a highway robber what he has promised to give him. Hobbes, by contrast, always says that if a man has promised and has thereby gained a benefit, he is obligated unless the civil law says otherwise.[98]

Now Hobbes is sometimes said to maintain very nearly this same doctrine: that promises in themselves do not give rise to any morally binding relations, but that fear and calculation of rational self-interest bring us to promise certain things and that only the sword, or power, can cause us to have a lively enough sense of fear—this time of the sovereign—to honor our commitments.[99] Spinoza does indeed say something quite like this:

> Everyone has by nature a right to act deceitfully, and to break his compacts, unless he be restrained, by the hope of some greater good, or the fear of some greater evil. . . The sovereign right over all men belongs to him who has sovereign power, wherewith he can compel men by force, or restrain them by threats of the universally feared punishment of death. . .
>
> If each individual hands over the whole of his power to the body politic, the latter will then possess sovereign natural right over all things.[100]

Compacts have no intrinsic validity; the right of the sovereign belongs to him because of his power; and individuals do not convey rights to the commonwealth but simply hand over a quantum of power. Hobbes, though he is sometimes represented as saying no more than this, and though he occasionally does say something like this, quite often says something more, and something different—something perhaps less consistent but more suggestive as well.

In chapter 14 of *Leviathan*, having defined natural right in terms of the liberty of self-preservation, and liberty as the absence of external impediment to motion, Hobbes goes on to consider the idea of a right as if it were a mere power in a way that looks Spinozistic.

> To *lay down* a man's *right* to anything, is to divest himself of the *liberty*, of hindering another of the benefit of his own right to the same. For he that renounceth, or passeth away his right, giveth not to any other man a right which he had not before; because there is nothing to which every man had not right by nature: but only standeth out of his way, that he may enjoy his own original natural right, without hindrance from him; not without hindrance from another. So that the effect which redoundeth to one man, by another man's defect of right, is but so much diminution of impediments to the use of his own right original.[101]

Giving rights to a sovereign, then, is rather like tearing down everyone's walls except the ruler's; in a transfer we allow the sovereign his full natural right while curbing our own. This is as far as Hobbes goes in agreeing with Spinoza's idea that right simply is power—except in the case of irresistibly powerful beings, though Hobbes never makes clear why their power involves rights. As was indicated earlier, a right to rule cannot be compared with a right to self-preservation; if the sovereign's right to rule were derived from his natural right, then it would be excusable if he killed all his subjects because he honestly thought that they constituted a potential threat to him, which only he could judge. Hobbes's occasional effort to derive the right of rulers from general natural right does not work, and he does not ordinarily rely on it; indeed, he uses it mainly when consent arguments seem implausible—for example, when he treats the right of the sovereign to punish criminals as a consequence of his natural right, it not being plausible that a criminal would consent to be executed.

Actually, to be more precise, Hobbes explains the right of the sovereign to punish on two quite different grounds, one involving the consent of the criminal, the other the natural right of the sovereign. A comparison of these two ground shows a great deal about his (occasional) efforts to derive political right from natural right. In chapter 21 of *Leviathan* he urges that "nothing the sovereign power can do to a subject...can properly be called injustice, or injury; because every subject is author of every act the sovereign doth...And therefore it may, and doth often happen in commonwealths, that a subject may be put to death, and yet neither do the other wrong." Execution is clearly justified by consent, by the subjects' having willed or authorized any act of the sovereign. This is also the case in chapter 15 of *Leviathan*. But in chapter 28 Hobbes, perhaps forgetting this argument, or wanting to use a different one that others might prefer, insists that "the right which the commonwealth, that is, he, or they that represent it, hath to punish, is not grounded on any concession, or gift of the subjects." Before commonwealths existed, he says, every man had a right to everything and had the liberty to do whatever he thought necessary for his self-preservation. "And this [natural right] is the foundation of that right of punishing which is exercised in every commonwealth." Subjects did not give such a right to the sovereign; but "in laying down theirs, strengthened him to use his own, as he should think fit, for the preservation of them all."[102] The phrase "for the preservation of them all" makes no sense as an extension of natural right, which is a right to self-preservation usually at the expense of others. These two versions of the right to punish show clearly that natural right cannot be used to explain the sovereign's right to rule and that in consenting to let him rule, subjects must convey a right that is something other than his own natural right. This shows again that right for Hobbes is often a consequence of consent, of a voluntary act, whereas in Spinoza this is not the case, largely because Spinoza does not ordinarily define natural right in terms of self-preservation or attach importance to willing.[103]

It was remarked, in comparing Hobbes with Spinoza, that there is a contract in the latter only in the sense that one hands over power to rulers and that one obeys only because of a rational fear of the consequences of not doing so. In chapter 15 of *Leviathan*, however, Hobbes says something quite unlike this. He grants that a covenant without the sword is only words and that terror is a necessary condition of political justice; but it seems clear that fear is neither a sufficient condition nor the only important one.

> Because covenants of mutual trust, where there is fear of not performance on either part...are invalid; though the original

of justice be the making of covenants; yet injustice actually there can be none, till the cause of such fear be taken away...Therefore before the names of just and unjust, can have place, there must be some coercive power, to compel men equally to the performance of their covenants, by the terror of some punishment...and such power there is none before the erection of a commonwealth...where there is no commonwealth, there nothing is unjust. So that the nature of justice, consisteth in keeping of valid covenants: but the validity of covenants begins not but with the constitution of a civil power, sufficient to compel men to keep them.[104]

In this passage Hobbes makes a distinction, not perfectly clear but certainly there, between the "original of justice" and its actuality, between its nature and its validity. This distinction seems to mean that the obligation produced by a covenant, of which will is the essence, is not derived from but only supported by the fear of power. This is confirmed by what Hobbes says about the relation of covenant to sentiments of fear and honor, at the end of chapter 14 of *Leviathan*.

The force of words, being...too weak to hold men to the performance of their covenants; there are in man's nature, but two imaginable helps to strengthen it. And those are either a fear of the consequences of breaking their word; or a glory, or pride, in appearing not to need to break it. This latter is a generosity too rarely found to be presumed on, especially in the pursuers of wealth, command, or sensual pleasure; which are the greatest part of mankind. The passion to be reckoned upon, is fear.[105]

In this case Hobbes speaks of performance of covenant (as distinguished from the nature of covenant, which involves consent), of "helps to strengthen it." By this he seems to mean that covenant itself is one thing—the source of duties—whereas fear, in most cases, or a sense of glory, in a few cases, is what reinforces obligations. A man is not obligated because he is afraid, though fear seems to be required to force men to fulfil their obligations. It would make sense to say that Hobbes distinguishes between a reason for obeying—promise or consent—and a cause—an external force—that will insure obedience. A man ought to obey because he has promised and has authorized the sovereign to will on his behalf; but his voluntary act must be shored up by psychological motives, above all fear, because he will not always adhere to his bargains.

This is not an inevitable or irresistible construction of Hobbes's meaning; there is in fact much to be said against it, some of it by Hobbes himself, particularly in chapter 14 of *Leviathan*.[106] It has the advantage, however, not only of significant textual support but also of clarifying one of the most serious problems in Hobbes: the question of how the social contract can be obligatory if no contracts are valid until they are backed by sovereign power.[107] As Leibniz insisted in a criticism of contract theory generally, and of Hobbes particularly, it is possible to refute "those who believe that there is no obligation at all in the state of nature, and outside of government; for, obligations by pacts having to form the right of government itself, according to the authors of these principles, it is manifest that the obligation is anterior to the government which it must form."[108] Viewing covenant, consent, promise, and agreement in themselves as the nature of justice and the source of duties, even in a state of nature, can help explain how the Hobbesian social contract would be, in a sense, legitimate before the erection of actual power, despite Hobbes's assertion that a covenant not guaranteed by sanctions lacks validity. If we consider as well that the first Hobbesian law of nature—to seek peace and follow it[109]—is, though rational, also assented to, and that a covenant of society, in pursuance of this natural law, forms the "original" of justice, one can at least say that there is a lot of evidence to suggest that fear of sanctions should be seen as a reinforcing element only, that consent and will are fundamental. This is actually suggested by Hobbes himself in chapter 14 of *Leviathan*, in which he says that "covenants entered into by fear, in the condition of mere nature, are obligatory"; but something cannot be at once obligatory and not valid. Hobbes did not make very clear the relation between duty based on contract and "helps" based on fear and threats. Sometimes he seems to say that agreements are always binding—unless they involve an agreement such as to kill oneself—sometimes that agreements are invalid unless they can be guaranteed by coercive power.[110] But he never says, with Spinoza, that compacts are made valid by their utility.

If one wanted to look for support for the idea that voluntary actions bind morally in Hobbes (as does A. E. Taylor), one might think that one had found it in chapter 15 of *Leviathan*, where Hobbes discusses once again the difference between a just action and a just man. Just as a righteous man does not lose that name because of a few unjust actions, so too the unrighteous man does not rid himself of that character because of a few just actions that he performs out of fear. This is so because the unrighteous man's will "is not framed by the justice, but by the apparent benefit of what he is to do."[111] Taylor goes so far as to liken this distinction to the Kantian one between "action done merely *in accord* with law, and action done *from* law,"[112] and there is some plausibility in this. But the next two sentences of Hobbes's text give the distinct impression that what is decisive for Hobbes is not good will in a Christian or Kantian sense but a sense of honor, a nonvoluntarist concept.[113] "That which gives to human actions the relish of justice," he says, "is a certain nobleness or gallantness of courage, rarely found, by which a man scorns to be beholden for the contentment of his life, to fraud, or breach of promise."[114] Surely, it is contempt for base actions rather than the moral quality of promising itself that Hobbes has in mind, though even in this case honor is only the motive for fulfilling promises, not the source of promises.

Indeed, one must be very careful of the concept of good will in Hobbes, even when he actually uses the phrase—as in the *Elements of Law*—for good will sometimes turns out to be a variety of power. Beginning by equating good will with "charity," Hobbes observes that "there can be no greater argument to a man, of his own power, than to find himself able not only to accomplish his own desires, but also to assist other men in theirs: and this is that conception wherein consisteth charity."[115] For Hobbes charity or good will is a kind of generosity *ex plenitudio potestatis:* it is what one can spare out of one's "superfluity," to use Pascal's term.[116] Hobbes goes on to discuss the most famous case of alleged good will—Socrates' "assisting" of Alcibiades—in a way that turns that will into something of near-Shakespearian bawdiness, mainly by playing with the words *conception* and *conceive* in the same way that he later shaped his ribald definition of sense perception in *Leviathan:* "There is no conception in a man's mind which hath not . . . been begotten upon the organs of sense."[117] The opinion of Plato concerning good will, or "honorable love," Hobbes argues, "delivered according to his custom in the person of Socrates," is that

a man full and pregnant with wisdom and other virtues, naturally seeketh out some beautiful person, of age and capacity to conceive, in whom he may, without sensual respects, engender and produce the like. And this is the *idea* of the then noted love of Socrates wise and continent, to Alcibiades young and beautiful...It should be therefore this charity, or desire to assist and advance others. But why then should the wise seek the ignorant, or be more charitable to the beautiful than to others? There is something in it savouring of the use of that time: in which matter though Socrates be acknowledged for continent, yet the *continent* have the passion they *contain*, as *much* and more than they that *satiate* the appetite; which maketh me suspect this *platonic* love for merely sensual; but with an honourable pretence for the old to haunt the company of the young and beautiful.[118]

So much for charity or good will. In the *Elements of Law* the concept is closer to that in Lucian's *Philosophies for Sale*[119] than to that in the *Critique of Practical Reason*.

Against this can be set the famous passage at the end of chapter 15 of *Leviathan*, on which some modern interpretations of Hobbes—particularly Howard Warrender's—rely so heavily:

The laws of nature oblige *in foro interno;* that is to say, they bind to a desire that they should take place: but *in foro externo,* not always. For he that should be modest, and tractable, and perform all his promises, in such time, and place, where no man else should do so, should but make himself a prey to others, and procure his own certain ruin, contrary to the ground of all laws of nature, which tend to nature's preservation...

And whatsoever laws bind *in foro interno,* may be broken, not only by a fact contrary to law, but also by a fact according to it, in case a man think the contrary. For though his action in this case be according to the law, yet his purpose was against the law; which where the obligation is *in foro interno,* is a breach.[120]

The second paragraph is almost Kantian in its insistence on good intention; but there are still difficulties. Among other things, Hobbes speaks of a desire that the natural laws should take place; but desire is not the same as intention, though his other term, *purpose*, comes closer. More significantly, Hobbes seems to hold that men should do what they ought to do only when it is safe to do so. This means that natural right, the right of self-preservation, can prevail even over natural law, which enjoins peace, unless the observation of that law will preserve natural right. But then, there is nothing over which natural right does not prevail in Hobbes, whereas in Kant man is entitled to preserve himself in order to be able to do his duty.[121] In any case, what is important about this passage, despite the ambiguities, can be seen by comparing it with a superficially similar one from Machiavelli's *The Prince:* "How we live is so far removed from how we ought to live, that he who abandons what is done for what ought to be done, will rather learn to bring about his own ruin than his preservation. A man who wishes to make a profession of goodness in everything must necessarily come to grief among so many who are not good. Therefore it is necessary. . . to learn how not to be good, and to use this knowledge, and not use it, according to the necessity of the case."[122]

The superficial resemblances to Hobbes are plain enough: both Machiavelli and Hobbes speak of the effort to carry out moral ideals in a state of nonsafety. But Hobbes states very clearly that a man can safely make the laws of nature "take place," then he is bound to do so and must always intend this, be ready to make this "endeavor." While Machiavelli speaks of "learning not to be good," Hobbes talks of men's natural right to all things, which is quite different, both insofar as it is justified only by self-preservation—but certainly not by the historical greatness that is of such weight in Machiavelli[123]—and insofar as by the law of nature "we are obliged to transfer to another, such rights, as being retained, hinder the peace of mankind."[124] Having a right to all things necessary for self-preservation may lead to not being good, but this is far from learning not to be good. Both Hobbes and Machiavelli think that what ought to be done is relative to the safety of circumstance, but Hobbes believes this in a way that preserves a large measure of the importance of willing, intending, and contracting, while Machiavelli does not. In general, Hobbes says that a man must will the carrying out of natural law whenever this is consistent with the preservation of natural right.

These comparisons of Hobbes with Machiavelli and Spinoza, instructive as they are, must yield to a more fundamental comparison of Hobbes with Kant—a comparison that shows, in a more precise way than any yet presented, why Hobbes's conception of will is both necessary to his notions of covenant, obligation, and justice and inadequate in explaining how those notions are in principle conceivable. It has been suggested that Hobbes never succeeded in distinguishing will from appetite, except insofar as will is the last appetite, though a last appetite is still an appetite. As a result, even though he urges in *Leviathan* that wills "make the essence of all covenants," that political legitimacy is derived from voluntary acts of consent, he was never able to show how an obligation can be derived from an appetite. His problem becomes clear enough if one substitutes his use of *will* in some key passages for his definition of it. Thus, "The last appetite makes the essence of all covenants" offers no notion of political obligation or authority, no idea that once a man has freely obligated himself to obey, "it is his duty not to make void that voluntary act of his own."[125] At the risk of some exaggeration it might be said that the only reason that Hobbes's system works at all is that he does not use the concept of will as his definition requires.

The solution to Hobbes's problem is at least suggested by Kant, who urges that the difficulty with Hobbesian arguments about the will is that they do not distinguish between a consciously arrived at maxim of action and an externally caused or determined "action-in-itself." Moral activity—including consenting, promising, obligating—cannot for Kant "lie in an object determining the will through inclination, nor yet in a natural impulse; it can lie only in a rule made by the will for the use of its freedom, that is in a maxim."[126] Kant insists that the will be understood as a faculty of determining oneself to action according to the conception of certain laws.[127] This definition means that while a man may be influenced by appetites, even last appetites, an act is not his own, not a moral cause, unless he consciously adopts this appetite as a self-imposed rule of conduct. Kant could even have urged that Hobbes's saying that there can be "no obligation on any man which ariseth not from some act of his own"[128] is unintelligible unless the act is really his, actually arises out of his own consciously and freely produced maxims; that if there are no maxims but only natural impulses and last appetites, then it would be, to quote Kant, "possible to trace the use of our freedom wholly to determination by natural causes."[129] But this, Kant would argue, would destroy responsibility, imputability, obligation, and other moral concepts that Hobbes himself uses constantly.

It would be perverse to say that Hobbes can be understood only by taking some of his terminology in a Kantian sense. Yet, it does seem that there is a tension between Hobbes's definition of will in terms of appetite and aversion and his use of voluntariness in explaining some of his fundamental moral conceptions. It can at least be argued that Kant provided a definition of will more congruent with Hobbes's own use of the term than any definition depending on appetite. Looking to Kant shows how a theory of will congruent with responsibility, consent, and obligation can be arrived at; for there is a great deal of force in Kant's notion that no conception of "ought" is conceivable as long as men are considered merely as parts of a system of nature who act according to laws—such as physical laws that cause appetites—but not according to the conception of laws.[130] It is, of course, still arguable that by obligation and justice Hobbes meant no more than non-self-contradictory social logic, that Hobbesian consent may sometimes mean a mere convergence of appetites in support of a power that will preserve that logic. But if that appetite-generated power fails—there being, on this view, no real moral obligation—what is left is the appetites themselves, with consequences that Shakespeare foresaw in *Troilus and Cressida:*

> Take but degree away, untune that string
> And hark, what discord follows! Each thing meets
> In mere oppugnancy. The bounded waters
> Should lift their bosoms higher than the shores
> And make a sop of all this solid globe.
> Strength should be lord of imbecility,
> And the rude son should strike his father dead.
> Force should be right; or rather right and wrong,
> Between whose endless jar justice resides,
> Should lose their names, and so should justice too.
> Then everything includes itself in power,
> Power into will, will into appetite;
> And appetite, an universal wolf,
> So doubly seconded with will and power.
> Must make perforce an universal prey,
> And last eat up himself.[131]

For Hobbes, the human race will not eat itself up if each man transfers authority and power to a sovereign beneficiary; then it will be true of each man that "he ought, and it is his DUTY, not to make void that voluntary act of his own."[132] Will has ceased to be a mere last appetite and has become a capacity for self-obligation. Since Hobbes uses the notion of voluntariness in a way that, say, Spinoza does not, it is perhaps reasonable to conclude by urging that those who insist on Hobbesian morality as simple non-self-contradiction might be better off with Spinoza; after all, if all of the problematical parts of Hobbes's voluntarism are lifted out of his system, what is left is the substance of political Spinozism. Those who would simply understand Hobbes might at least consider the possibility that there is a disjunction between his psychology and his ethical theory that is not overcome[133] and could not have been overcome except by adopting a notion of will that is more or less suggested by Bramhall but brought to complete adequacy only by Kant.[134]

On Finding an Equilibrium
between Consent and Natural Law
in Locke's Political Philosophy

I_N the *Second Treatise* Locke argues that "voluntary agreement gives...political power to governors for the benefit of their subjects" and that "God having given man an understanding to direct his actions, has allowed him a freedom of will, and liberty of acting."[1] At first sight Locke appears to have taken up and extended the social contract doctrine of Hobbes, but without reducing the will that makes "voluntary agreement" possible to a mere last appetite. On closer inspection, though, it turns out that Locke's theory of will is almost as problematical as Hobbes's. A further problem concerning Locke's voluntarism and contractarianism is that there is disagreement as to what extent he was really a contractarian at all. Locke is sometimes represented as a consent and social contract theorist, sometimes as a theorist of natural law, sometimes as a theorist of natural rights, particularly natural property rights. The problem is that all three characterizations are correct; the difficulty is to find an equilibrium between them so that none is discarded in the effort to define Locke's complete concept of right.

Sometimes all three of these criteria of right can work together rather than against each other. According to Locke one sets up, by consent and contract, a political system that guarantees the natural rights that one has as a consequence of natural law. The right to consent in politics can even be said to express the natural rights that natural law creates. Without a politics created by voluntary agreement there would be no actual "judge" to enforce the law of nature, and individuals would have to rely on self-help, which Locke calls "inconvenient." Without the law of nature there would be no criterion for determining what deserves to be consented to. Without natural rights natural law would lack definite and concrete content, such as natural property rights and rights of personal security. Thus, these three criteria can work as an ensemble in which none is superfluous or by itself altogether sufficient. Sometimes one of these criteria of right might oppose what would be permissible according to one of the others taken alone, as when Locke urges that a man cannot consent to give up the natural rights that natural law confers on him; and sometimes one of the criteria may qualify something that one of the others would have allowed, as when Locke says that consent can modify the way in which we enjoy natural property rights in society.[2] But none of these considerations makes it less necessary to find an equilibrium between consent and contract, natural law, and natural rights.

In Locke scholarship and interpretation, however, it is rare to find a disinterested search for a balance among the criteria of right that Locke so clearly used. Some commentators hold that Locke's natural law doesn't really work because natural law must be derived exclusively from reason, but Locke, to make his natural law a real law, needs divine rewards and punishments based on an immortality that only revelation but not reason can make certain. In this view Locke could not have believed in so incoherent a theory but was actually concerned with self-preservation and restless acquisitiveness; that is, he was really a covert Hobbist who deliberately perplexed his meaning and his readers.[3] Others hold that Lockean contractarianism represents a decline from the perfection of Lockean natural law and that there can be no motive to pass from a state of nature governed by such a natural law to a political order fashioned by consent.[4] Others assert that consent and natural law are both so undermined and subverted by Locke's theory of absolute and unequal natural property rights as to be reduced to a mere ideology,[5] while others urge that, on the contrary, consent in the form of majoritarianism is so weighty in Locke (qua "majority-rule democrat") that natural law and rights are rendered ineffective, even though, as it turns out, none of the forms that consent takes—tacit consent, majoritarianism, representative government—is an adequate expression of consent.[6] Still others say that since what is politically right is sufficiently determined by natural law and rights in Locke, consent and contract, even if truly present, are in a sense gratuitous additions to the natural concept of right.[7] Others will have it that it is precisely the law of nature, as the foundation of "the natural and original freedom and equality of men," that causes Locke to be "one of the most extreme and complete exponents of the idea of the social contract."[8] And some make a reasonable effort to balance the three criteria of right, only to add that Locke's political thought is not really "abstract" political philosophy in the strict sense at all and that it must therefore be treated in its historical context and not pressed too hard.[9]

To be sure, there are some who do try to show that consent, natural law, and natural rights all have claims to be part of Locke's complete concept of right; this is true especially of Hans Aarsleff, Raymond Polin, and Ernst Cassirer.[10] Cassirer in particular provides a good statement of Lockean right in his *Philosophy of the Enlightenment:*

> It was Locke who declared in his *Treatise on Government* that the social contract entered into by individuals by no means constitutes the only ground for all legal relations among men. All such contractual ties are rather preceded by original ties which can neither be created by a contract nor entirely annulled by it. There are natural rights of man which existed before all foundations of social and political organizations; and in view of these the real function and purpose of the state consists in admitting such rights into its order and in preserving and guaranteeing them thereby.[11]

Assuming at least for the moment that it is reasonable to treat Locke as a theorist seeking an equilibrium between contract and consent, natural law, and natural rights, four main questions arise: What is the exact nature of this balance? Does Locke provide a theory of volition adequate to account for consent as voluntary agreement? What is the nature of the natural law that Locke wants to balance against consent? And what sufficiently constitutes consent—representative government, majoritarianism, tacit consent? In examining these questions it becomes evident that it is precisely when Locke himself does not observe this equilibrium between his standards of right that he is most open to criticism.

Some writers urge that consent and contractarianism are not central in Locke because natural law is for him a sufficient standard of right, one that obviates the need for consensual arrangements.

"We are generally prone to think of Locke as the exponent of the social contract," says Sir Ernest Barker. "It would be more just to think of him as the exponent of the sovereignty of natural law."[12] It is of course true that if one bracketed out of Locke's system the obligations and rights to which consent and contract give rise, one would be left with a tolerably complete ethical doctrine based on natural law and rights, whereas in Rousseau, by contrast, one would be left with little, since for him obligations derive their whole force from mutual agreements and promises.[13] But surely natural law, though it is necessary for Locke, is not sufficient to define explicitly political rights and duties: there is a distinction to be drawn between the general moral obligations that men have under natural law and the particular political obligations that citizens have through consent and the social contract. This is clear not only in the *Second Treatise* but in the *Essay concerning Human Understanding* as well.

In book 2, chapter 28 of the *Essay* ("Of other relations") Locke draws a careful distinction between the natural law, to which all men as men are obliged to conform their voluntary actions, and the civil law, to which all men as citizens are obliged to adhere because they have created a human legislative authority by consent. "A citizen, or a burgher," Locke says, "is one who has a right to certain privileges in this or that place. All this sort depending upon men's wills, or agreement in society, I call instituted, or voluntary; and may be distinguished from the natural."[14] In a commonwealth, which is what human wills institute, men "refer their actions" to a civil law to judge whether or not they are lawful or criminal. Natural law, however, is not instituted by consent, even by a Grotian "universal" consent, as Locke explains best in his *Essays on the Law of Nature*.[15] Nor does it merely define "certain privileges in this or that place." It is rather the law "which God has set to the actions of men," and is "the only true touchstone of moral rectitude." But the natural law defines only general moral goods and evils, only moral duties and sins; it cannot point out what is a crime, in the strict legal sense, in a commonwealth, in "this or that place": "If I have the will of a supreme invisible lawgiver for my rule, then, as I supposed the action commanded or forbidden by God, I call it good or evil, sin or duty: and if I compare it to the civil law, the rule made by the legislative power of the country, I call it lawful or unlawful, a crime or no crime."[16]

To say, then, that the natural law is a complete and sufficient standard of political right for Locke is to conflate sin and crime, the duties of man and citizen, what one owes to God with what one owes to the civil magistrate. It is one thing to say, as Locke does in section 12 of the *Second Treatise*, that the "municipal laws of countries" are "only so far right, as they are founded on the law of nature, by which they are to be regulated and interpreted"[17] and quite another to say that natural law renders such municipal laws superflous, or that the latter can be reduced to the former. Locke does not say, with Hobbes, that the natural and the civil law "contain each other" and are "of equal extent."[18] It is true that for Locke all laws—whether divine, civil, or "of reputation"—are formally of one kind: all of them involve a "moral relation" or "conformity or disagreement" of men's voluntary actions "to a rule to which they are referred"; and all of them must have some kind of sanction, some means whereby "good or evil is drawn on us, from the will and power of the lawgiver."[19] But this is not grounds for saying that all laws have the same lawgiver or the same sanctions. Indeed, Locke makes clear that the giver of natural law is God, that of civil law the voluntarily instituted commonwealth, and that of reputation the public; the sanction in the first case is reward and punishment in a future life, in the second legal punishment, and in the third the public's "power of thinking well or ill."[20]

As a result, the kind of objection to Lockean contractarianism that one finds, for example, in T. H. Green ("a society governed by...a law of nature...would have been one from which political society would have been a decline, one in which there could have been no motive to the establishment of civil government")[21] is at best half- right. It is partly wrong because a society governed by a law of nature would have had a motive to establish civil government—a motive based not merely on a desire to distinguish between sin and crime, divine and civil law, what one owes as a man and as a citizen, but on a desire to set up some "known and impartial judge" to serve as "executor" of the law of nature, to avoid men's being the judges of their own cases. Locke, after all, states clearly that there are three good reasons for allowing the natural law to be politically enforced:

> *First*, [in the state of nature] There wants an *established*, settled, known *Law*, received and allowed by common consent to be the standard of right and wrong...For though the law of nature be plain and intelligible to all rational creatures; yet men being biased by their interest...are not

apt to allow of it as a law binding to them in the application of
it to their particular cases.

Secondly, In the state of nature there wants a *known and
indifferent judge*, with authority to determine all differences
according to the established law . . .

Thirdly, In the state of nature there often wants *power* to
back and support the sentence when right, and to give it due
execution.[22]

Green, though he is wrong in saying that there is no motive to
the establishment of civil government in Locke's state of nature, is
certainly right in saying that the transition from a society truly and
completely governed by natural law, if such a society could exist,
to one under political government would involve a decline. In
section 128 of the *Second Treatise* Locke argues that under the terms
of the law of nature every man "and all the rest of mankind are one
community, make up one society distinct from all other creatures."
If it were not for the "corruption" and "viciousness" of "degener-
ate men," Locke goes on, "there would be no need of any other"
society; there would be no necessity "that men should separate
from this great and natural community, and by positive agreements combine into smaller and divided associations."[23] If Green is
right in pointing out that voluntarily instituted political society in
some sense represents a decline, that does not mean that it is
unnecessary, that there is no motive for setting it up; for Locke, as
for Kant, the mere fact that it would be better if natural law were
universally observed, such that one could dispense with politics,
does not make politics unnecessary, given human life as it is.[24]

Indeed, there is an excellent motive for instituting a political
order, assuming that men do not naturally obey natural law
completely. That is that natural law does not itself set up or pull
down any government; it is men who do so. Natural law does not
translate itself into existence, as if it were a beneficiary of the
ontological argument: "The law of nature would, as all other laws
that concern men in this world, be in vain, if there were nobody in
the state of nature, [that] had a power to execute that law." A
government that violates natural law may objectively deserve
revolution by placing itself in a state of war with its subjects, by
using "force without right," which creates a state of war either in
the state of nature or in society.[25] But it is people who bring about
such an event, properly through the consent of the majority.
Natural law helps them decide whether a government is acting

legitimately, but it does not tell them which is their legitimate government. It is a criterion of right, but one that requires application. This Locke makes clear, first in general and abstract terms in the *First Treatise* and then, in quite specific political terms, in the treatment of a state's right to punish alien lawbreakers in section 9 of the *Second Treatise*.

In the *First Treatise*, in a passage as neglected as the rest of that able but tedious work, Locke argues that "since men cannot obey anything, that cannot command," and that "ideas of government," however perfect or right, cannot "give laws," it is useless to establish government, as a general idea, without providing a way whereby men can "know the person" to whom obedience is due. Even if, as Locke says, I am fully "persuaded"—perhaps by natural law injunctions—that I should obey political powers, that "there ought to be magistracy and rule in the world," I am still at liberty "till it appears who is the person that hath right to my obedience." Locke adds, anticipating Rousseau, that until one sees "marks" that distinguish him "that hath a right to rule from other men, it may be my self, as well as any other."[26] He then comes to the passage that matters most for present purposes, suggesting that even if natural law helps to determine what kinds of political action are legitimate, it nonetheless does not point to a particular legitimate ruler:

> Though submission to government be every one's duty, yet since that signifies nothing but submitting to the direction and laws of such men, as have authority to command, 'tis not enough to make a man a subject, to convince him that there is *regal power* in the world, but there must be ways of designing, and knowing the person to whom this *regal power* of right belongs, and a man can never be obliged in conscience to submit to any power, unless he can be satisfied who is the person, who has a right to exercise that power over him.

Since the person possessing that right will not be Sir Robert Filmer's heir of Adam, Locke urges, "all his fabric falls," and governments "must be left again to the old way of being made by contrivance, and the consent of men...making use of their reason to unite together into society."[27]

Sometimes, as in Locke's treatment of punishing aliens in the *Second Treatise*, it turns out that natural law is directly applied, though not by a person recognized by the alien as one having a magistrate's right to obedience. The magistrates of any community, Locke argues, cannot punish an alien offender against the state on the basis of the civil laws: "the legislative authority, by which they are in force over the subjects of the commonwealth, hath no power over him." But since the alien offender is in a state of nature with respect to the host state, and since the state of nature has a law of nature to govern it, those magistrates can certainly, as executors of the law of nature, enforce that law against the offender. A native offender, however, would be punished under the civil law to which he had in some way consented, and this law would be merely "regulated" by the natural law. As a result of these distinctions, Locke says (*Second Treatise*, section 87), it is "easy to discern who are, and who are not, in *political society together*": "those who are united into one body, and have a common established law and judicature to appeal to, with authority to decide controversies between them, and punish offenders, *are in civil society* one with another; but those who have no such common appeal, I mean on earth, are still in the state of nature."[28] Sometimes, then, the natural law is directly applied by an unrecognized person to a political end; but an alien is an exceptional case in the state, and the ordinary case of the citizen is to be determined by a civil law, applied by a properly recognized person, which would have to conform to the natural law.

Locke develops and completes these points in section 122 of the *Second Treatise*, where he says that merely submitting to the laws of a country and "enjoying privileges and protection" under those laws "makes not a man a member of that society." A man is bound "in conscience" to submit to the administration of a government whose subject he is not, perhaps because such a government can serve as a known and indifferent judge and give effect to natural law in an "inconvenient" world. But nothing can make a man a true member of a commonwealth except his "entering into it by positive engagement, and express promise and compact." This merely reinforces what was laid down earlier in the *Second Treatise* (section 15), where Locke had argued that "all men are naturally" in the state of nature and remain in it "till by their own consents they make themselves members of some political society; and I doubt not in the sequel of this discourse, to make it very clear."[29] This clarification, which comes in section 22, contains one of the fullest statements of Locke's views on the relation of natural law to consent: "The natural liberty of man is to be free from any superior power on earth, and not to be under the will or legislative authority of man, but to have only the law of nature for his rule. The liberty of man, in society, is to be under no other legislative power, but that established, by consent, in the common-wealth, nor under the dominion of any will, or restraint of any law, but what the legislative shall enact, according to the trust put in it."[30]

It seems, then, that natural law cannot be a sufficient standard of Lockean political right whenever men's depravity brings about less than perfect conformity to that law. In consequence, the "great and natural community" of men under a perfectly observed natural law must give way to "smaller and divided associations" whose civil laws must simply be regulated by natural law. Since natural law neither appoints nor removes civil magistrates, neither creates nor pulls down particular political structures, consent and promise and contract must provide this appointing and removing and creating and pulling down. When natural law is used directly in politics, and not simply as a criterion of right, it will be in marginal or exceptional cases, such as those of aliens or of rulers who place themselves in a state of war with their subjects. Thus, when Sir Ernest Barker claims that while "we are generally prone to think of Locke as the exponent of the social contract," it would in fact be more just "to think of him as the exponent of the sovereignty of natural law,"[31] he distorts the real issue: the social contract, for Locke, is necessitated by natural law's inability to be literally "sovereign" on earth, by its incapacity to produce "one society." Natural law and contractarianism, far from being simply antithetical in Locke, necessarily involve each other, at least given human imperfection and corruption.

It is not the case, however, that Locke placed as much weight on consent and contract in his earlier works as in his later ones, and these differences ought, in all fairness, to be taken into account. In his early *Essays on the Law of Nature* Locke minimized consent and contractarianism. In the sixth *Essay* Locke put forward his general theory, from which he departed little in later works, that "ultimately all obligation leads back to God," partly because of his divine wisdom and partly because of "the right which the creator has over his creation." However, even if all obligation ultimately leads back to God and to his justifiable punishments, it is still possible to distinguish between kinds of obligations. Obligations can consist, Locke writes,

in the authority and dominion which someone has over another, either by natural right and the right of creation, as when all things are justly subject to that by which they have first been made and also are constantly preserved; or by the right of donation, as when God, to whom all things belong, has transferred part of his dominion to someone and granted the right to give orders to the first-born, for example, and to monarchs; or by the right of contract, as when someone has voluntarily surrendered himself to another and submitted himself to another's will.[32]

Here, the notion of contract as a foundation of right is not only distinctly subordinated but is defined in terms of voluntary surrender and submission to another's will rather than in terms of the egalitarianism that leads to the social contract in the *Second Treatise*. A little later in the sixth *Essay* contractarianism is left out of account altogether, and Locke defines legitimate authority simply in terms of a delegation of power by the will of God: "all that dominion which the rest of law-makers exercise over others ...they borrow from God alone, and we are bound to obey them because God willed thus, and commanded thus, so that by complying with them we also obey God."[33] This is closer to St. Paul than to social contract theory.

It is not exclusively in the *Essays on the Law of Nature* that consent and contract play a small role. One of the papers from the Lovelace collection of Locke manuscripts, entitled "On the Difference between Civil and Ecclesiastical Power," like the *Essays* dates from the early 1670s. Also like the *Essays* it subordinates consent and contract to other considerations. Membership in a church, Locke says, "is perfectly voluntary" and may end whenever anyone pleases, "but in civil society it is not so." Civil societies, far from being purely voluntary, must rely on occasional coercion and "abridgement" of rights if they are to be effective; and they do not arise only through contractarianism, since "all mankind" are "combined into civil societies in various forms, as force, chance, agreement, or other accidents have happened to constrain them." This is an argument that Hume could have accepted and turned to anticontractarian advantage. Locke makes it plain that it is not voluntary consent that legitimizes such a civil society but rather its conforming itself to its appropriate and natural sphere, namely "civil peace and prosperity," to its avoiding what lies "without" civil happiness: salvation.[34] Here legitimacy is defined in terms of appropriateness of functions, not in terms of mode of origin.

In all of Locke's mature works, however, consent, contractarianism, voluntarily produced polities and obligations have a much greater weight, even if they do not displace or replace natural laws and rights. This is true not only of the *Second Treatise* but of such works as the *Third Letter for Toleration* (1692), a work in which Locke, exasperated with an opponent's claim that "civil societies are instituted by [God] for the attaining all the benefits which civil society or political government can yield," including salvation, finally exclaims, "If you will say, that commonwealths are not voluntary societies constituted by men, and by men freely entered into...that commonwealths are constituted by God for ends wich he has appointed, without the consent and contrivance of men...I shall desire you to prove it."[35]

The most familiar contractarian arguments are found in the *Second Treatise*. Sometimes—indeed, repeatedly—Locke contents himself with the bare claim that consent creates political right, as in section 102 ("politic societies all began from a voluntary union, and the mutual agreement of men freely acting in the choice of their governors, and forms of government") and in section 192 (rulers must put the people "under such a frame of government, as they willingly, and of choice, consent to"). Occasionally, however, he provides a more elaborate argument, particularly when he wants to distinguish legitimate political power from both paternal and despotic power.

> *Nature gives* the first of these, viz. *paternal power to parents* for the benefit of their children during their minority, to supply their want of ability, and understanding how to manage their property... *Voluntary agreement gives* the second, viz. *political power to governours* for the benefit of their subjects, to secure them in the possession and use of their properties. And *forfeiture gives* the third, *despotical power to lords* for their own benefit, over those who are stripped of all property.[36]

By this time the notion of a species of natural political authority—granted by God, as in the *Essays on the Law of Nature*—has given way completely to voluntarist and contractarian language.

It is never the case, at least not when Locke offers more than mere claims about consent, that consent and contract are treated as the whole of political right, that whatever happens to be produced by this process would *ex necessitatis* be correct. In Locke there is no general will that is always right.[37] This is perfectly clear, for example, in section 95 of the *Second Treatise,* which is one of Locke's best statements of an equilibrium between the naturally and the consensually right. Since men are naturally "free, equal and independent," no one can be subjected to the political power of anyone else "without his own consent." In giving up "natural liberty," and putting on the "bonds of civil society," men agree to "join and unite into a community" not for the purpose of being controlled by any objective to which a group may happen to consent but for the purpose of "comfortable, safe, and peaceable living amongst one another, in a secure enjoyment of their properties, and a greater security against any that are not of it." Security, of course, is authorized by natural law, which protects the innocent by allowing defense against wrongful attacks, while property is a natural right derived partly from God's giving the earth to men and partly from human labor.[38] A political order, created by consent, makes these things possible even given the "inconvenience" of some men's "corruption" and "depravity." In this passage there is an equilibrium between consent, natural law, and natural rights: it is because men are made free and equal by God, because they want to enjoy natural rights in the security of a political society in conformity with natural law, that they consent to become citizens, to conform their voluntary actions to the civil law as well as to the divine law and the law of reputation. Consent operates within a context.

If Locke had built his entire theory of right on consent alone as an exclusive standard, as Hume accused him of doing, he might have been open to the objections that Hume raises against him in his essay "Of the Original Contract" and that others have continued to bring forward. In that essay Hume urges that Lockean contractarianism is not only historically implausible and inaccurate but that it is needlessly cumbersome: since the real reason for obedience to government is that without such obedience "society could not otherwise subsist," it is useless to rest the duty of obedience on consent, on a "tacit promise" to obey. We must then ask, "Why are we bound to observe our promise?" For Hume the only possible answer is that observing promises is simply necessary because there can be "no security where men pay no regard to their engagements." Since actual usefulness is the measure of obedience in general, as well as of promises, it is useless and awkward to base one on the other: "we gain nothing by resolving the one into the other," since "the general interests or necessities of society are sufficient to establish both."[39]

Locke is not really open to this objection, formidable as it is, since he can ground the obligation of promises and of tacit consent not in social utility but in natural law: the keeping of faith, he says, "belongs to men, as men, and not as members of society."[40] We have a duty to keep promises faithfully because in breaking our word and in acting deceitfully we would harm other men and thereby violate natural law, which forbids harming others, particularly the innocent, except in self-preservation. Locke maintains that there is a natural duty to keep promises, including political ones; indeed, he often holds that the notion of a promise could not work without God and his natural laws. In the *Essays on the Law of Nature* in particular he argues that without natural law the faithful fulfillment of contracts is "overthrown," because "it is not to be expected that a man would abide by a compact because he has promised it. . . unless the obligation to keep promises was derived from nature"—that is, from the natural law as the will of God, backed by sanctions of infinite weight and duration. Much the same argument is put forward in the *Essay* (book 1, chapter 2), where Locke argues that it is "certainly a great and undeniable rule in morality" that men should keep their compacts and adds that a Christian will believe this because of his conviction that "God, who has the power of eternal life and death, requires it of us."[41] (A "Hobbist," however, will believe it only because "the public requires it, and the Leviathan will punish you if you do not.")[42] In the *Letter concerning Toleration* Locke bases his refusal to tolerate atheists on the notion that "promises, covenants, and oaths, which are the bonds of human society, can have no hold upon an atheist," that "the taking away of God. . . dissolves all."[43] This may not be a particularly effective argument, but at least it meets Hume's charge that Lockean promise and tacit consent have no grounding and hence must always lead back to utility. And it shows that, for Locke, natural law and consent support and even require each other: without natural law and its eternal sanctions men would have no sufficient motive to observe promises and covenants; but without the political societies that are held together by promises and oaths and covenants the natural law would not be enforced by a known and indifferent judge.

Even in his late works Locke does not invariably define political right in terms of consent or even of consent hedged round by natural law. At the very beginning of the *Second Treatise,* for instance, he defines political power as the right of making laws for the purposes of preserving property, defending the commonwealth from foreign injury, and upholding the public good—and this without even mentioning consent. In the *First Treatise,* in a passage reminiscent of the *Essays on the Law of Nature,* he suggests that men are equal and ought to enjoy the same rights and privileges until "the manifest appointment of God...can be produced to shew any particular person's supremacy, or a man's own consent subjects him to a superior."[44] Even here—since the rest of the *First Treatise* is designed to show that God has not appointed such a "particular person"—consent, though it comes second, wins out by a kind of default.

Although it can be shown decisively that Locke at least meant to give consent a great deal of weight as one standard of political right, this does not exhaust problems of interpretation. We are still left with the other questions posed earlier, the next of which is: Does Locke provide a conception of will and of voluntary action adequate to account for consent and voluntary agreement as one foundation of what is right?

That Locke himself, at least in his later writings, took voluntariness to be an essential component in the ideas of consent, contract, political obligation, and political legitimacy is quite clear. Some of the passages already cited could make this sufficiently plain—particularly those in which Locke calls the political rights and obligations of "a citizen or a burgher" dependent upon "men's will or agreement in society [and therefore] instituted or voluntary," and those in which he distinguishes between paternal and despotic power, which do not involve consent, and political power, which is created by voluntary agreement. There are other important passages, such as the one in *The Conduct of the Understanding* in which Locke draws a distinction between "natural agents," which are "observable in the ordinary operations of bodies one upon another"[45] (bodies which, like the tennis balls of book 2, chapter 21 of the *Essay,* are not taken by anyone to be "free agents"),[46] and the operations of "voluntary agents," that is, "the actions of men in society, which makes civil and moral history."[47] Clearly, Locke thought that the notion of voluntariness is essential in distinguishing between different kinds of powers, between natural history and civil history, between natural and free agents. But there has always been a question whether Locke provides in this section of the *Essay* an account of will and volition adequate to account for his apparent moral and political purposes. One of the main reasons for this questionability is that Locke completely recast the last half of book 2, chapter 21 in the second (1694) edition of the *Essay* without substantially revising most of the first half, much of which was then incongruent with the new part. To make matters more complicated, Locke inserted some further revisions of this chapter in the third and fourth editions of the *Essay* and in Pierre Coste's French version, and at his death left behind still other revisions that were never incorporated into the work.[48] That Locke was more dissatisfied with this chapter than with any other part of the *Essay* is clear not just from his many efforts to better it but from his letters to his friend William Molyneux. (Whenever the post-1690 revisions and recastings have an important bearing on Locke's argument, particularly on his view that legislative power is "derived from the People by a positive voluntary Grant," they will be pointed out.)[49]

It may be useful to recall that Hobbes, who is ordinarily taken to be the first great social contract theorist (though this may involve injustice to Suarez),[50] had got into difficulties in trying to represent political obligation as the consequence of voluntary actions. Though he held in chapter 40 of *Leviathan* that human wills "make the essence of all covenants," he also claimed, in chapter 6, that will is simply the last appetite in deliberation. If, as we have seen, his use of the notion of will is substituted for his definition of it ("the last appetite makes the essence of all covenants"), this does not add up to a coherent moral theory, since it tries to derive a concept of right from a fact of psychology. Hobbes's physiologico-psychological treatment of the concept of will as the last of any appetites renders nearly meaningless the idea that once a man has freely obligated himself to obey a political authority, "it is his duty not to make void that voluntary act of his own,"[51] since if the last part of this dictum really means "last appetitive act of his own," the notion of duty vanishes.

It sometimes looks as if Locke, despite his passing rejection of "Hobbism" in book 1, chapter 2 of the *Essay*, comes close to falling into these same difficulties. In the first twenty-seven sections of book 2, chapter 21 of the *Essay*—that is, in those sections that were not revised very much in the second, third, and fourth editions— his theory of volition has much in common with Hobbes's. The power that the human mind possesses to "order the consideration of any idea" or to "prefer the motion of any part of the body to its rest," Locke urges, "is that which we call the will," and the actual exercise of that power is called volition or willing. Locke agrees with Hobbes, in effect though not by name, that this power should not be called a faculty, since the notion of "faculties of the mind" has led to "a confused notion of so many distinct agents in us." It is useless and confusing, Locke continues, to ask whether this power is free or not; for the will is one kind of power, and freedom, which is simply "the power to think or not to think, to move or not to move," according to the preference of one's mind—is another kind of power. But one power cannot be a modification of another power. Therefore, it makes sense to ask whether a man is free but not whether his will is free; "liberty, which is but a power, belongs only to *agents,* and cannot be an attribute or modification of the will, which is also but a power." This is clearer, Locke adds, when one treats the will as a power than when one treats it as a faculty. If an advocate of free will speaks of faculties, he can conceal from himself the fact that he is demanding that the will be "a substance, an agent. . .since freedom can properly be attributed to nothing else," while if he treats will as a power and sees that freedom or liberty is another power, he cannot fall into this error.[52] In essence, will is the power to prefer something, liberty the power to do what one prefers.

However, Locke was apparently not content with this refutation of free will, for he added another less plausible one, saying that "a man in respect of willing" cannot be free because it is "unavoidable that the action depending on his will should exist or not exist." There is no being, Locke says, "capable of such a freedom of will, that it can forbear to will."[53] Of course, this is not what is at issue in the traditional free-will controversy: no advocate of free will ever urged that such freedom involved forbearing to will something but only that whatever choice was made not be determined or caused. (Surely, Leibniz was right when he urged in the *Nouveaux Essais* that "when one reasons about the freedom of the will. . .one doesn't ask whether a man can do what he wills, but whether there is enough independence in his will itself.")[54] Not only is Locke's argument in this connection unrelated to the real problem, but it tends to weaken the more effective arguments he had made earlier about the impossibility of conceiving one power as a modification of another power. In any case, he ends these early sections of book 2, chapter 21 by reverting to the theory of distinct powers of the mind, arguing that "the power of thinking operates not on the power of choosing, nor the power of choosing on the power of thinking,"[55] an argument perfectly congruent with the notion that one power cannot modify another but arguably incongruent with the idea (that he begins to develop after section 47) that the mind can "suspend" the power of willing while it rationally determines its own greatest good.

There is a hint of this later operation in section 29, where Locke writes: "to the question, What is it determines the will? the true and proper answer is, the mind." This seems to make intelligible the notion of obligating oneself reasonably and voluntarily to have duties as a citizen. For a mind would be required to understand the concept of citizenship or the concept of civic obligations; the mind could determine the will to enter into such obligations rather than allow the law of nature to be upheld by men's self-help without an indifferent judge. But this situation would come perilously close to one power—thinking—operating on, or modifying, another power—willing. Perhaps this is why Locke at least momentarily drops the notion that the "mind" determines the will and turns to the idea that it is "uneasiness" that does so. In asking what determines the mind in its determination of the will, one finds that the "motive for continuing in the same state or action, is only the present satisfaction in it"; but the motive for change "is always some uneasiness." It is this uneasiness that ultimately determines the will. Locke adds that it is important to be able to distinguish between will and "desire," since will is active but desire may be more or less passive and not produce any result: "whence it is evident that desiring and willing are two distinct acts of the mind."[56]

Whatever Locke's reason for trying to distinguish between will and desire—and it is at least conceivable that he did so because he wanted voluntary agreement to mean something other than desirous agreement—it is certain that he does not long succeed in keeping them distinct. Observing that it is not the "greater good in view" that determines the will but rather some pressing "uneasiness," Locke goes on to allow that this causal uneasiness may be called "desire," which is "an uneasiness of the mind for want of some absent good." The distinction between uneasiness and desire, and hence between willing and desiring, is rapidly crumbling. Then, in sections 33 and 34 Locke, perhaps forgetting that he had said in section 29 that the mind determines the will, suggests in a crucial passage that "good and evil, present and absent, it is true, work upon the mind. But that which immediately determines the will, from time to time, to every voluntary action, is the uneasiness of desire, fixed on some absent good: either negative, as indolence to one in pain; or positive, as enjoyment of pleasure... The greater good... does not determine the will, until our desire, raised proportionately to it, makes us uneasy in the want of it."[57] By this point the distinction between uneasiness and desire has been conflated in the phrase "uneasiness of desire." Since uneasiness simply becomes desire, and uneasiness determines the mind, and the mind determines the will, it is ultimately desire that determines the will. Locke treats desire largely as determined by pain and pleasure, so that the determination of the will must in the end turn on pain and pleasure.

If Locke had stopped here, as he did in effect in the first edition of the *Essay*, Lockeanism would be mired in problems fully comparable to those of Hobbes. After all, if a Hobbesian volition is an appetite and a Lockean volition is a desire or an uneasiness, it is equally difficult to derive a voluntarist and contractarian theory of right and obligation from either of them. As the reformulation "the last appetite makes the essence of all covenants" throws Hobbes's problems into high relief, so too Locke's contractarian utterances lose most of their intelligibility if "voluntary agreement gives ...political power to governors"[58] is translated into "uneasy or desirous agreement gives...political power to governors." Locke plainly intended *voluntary* in the *Second Treatise* to mean something more than a restless desire for some absent good; but his account of volition in the early sections of book 2, chapter 21 of the *Essay* seems not to allow for that something more.

The fact that Locke intended *voluntary* to mean something more than a restless desire for some absent good does not, of course, mean that such restless desire is excluded from his political system. On the contrary, Lockean men in the state of nature are in an uneasy and uncertain condition precisely because of an absent good that they desire: an impartial judge who can enforce natural law. These men are moved by their uneasiness to make an agreement that institutes civil society and does away with the inconvenience of the state of nature. So a restless desire for an absent good is certainly present in the transition from the state of nature to society. Still, the notion of voluntary agreement seems to involve more than simple restlessness and desire: Locke's claim that "voluntary agreement gives...political power to governors for the benefit of their subjects" is meant to distinguish legitimate rule from patriarchy and despotism; legitimacy is not a question of restlessness. It is not extravagant to claim that when Locke uses the notion of voluntariness he is sometimes, at least implicitly, treating human will as a "moral cause" that can produce moral effects, such as a political obligation that is not also a natural obligation under natural law. For example, in section 81 of the *First Treatise* Locke says that even if a man is persuaded that there ought to be government and law, perhaps so that natural law can be enforced, that does not settle the question of whom he is obligated to obey: "a man can never be obliged in conscience to submit to any power, until he can be satisfied who is the person, who has a right to exercise that power over him." Since natural law—for Locke as for Suarez before him—does not appoint persons who have a natural enforcing authority, "governments must be left again to be made...by the consent of men"—that is, by the voluntary agreement that gives political power to governors. Unless men know who the persons are who are entitled to govern by virtue of consent and voluntary agreement, there is no political "obligation to obedience": no obligation until consent and voluntary agreement show "not only that there is a power somewhere in the world, but the person who by right is vested with this power."[59] Apparently voluntariness refers not just to the psychological facts of restlessness and desire, though those who are not excluded, but to a kind of moral causality that produces political power by right, that produces political obligations as distinguished from natural moral obligations.

If Locke does not at least occasionally understand human will as a moral cause, then what he says about political obligation to a person being conventional does not make sense. If a political obligation is not simply a moral obligation, and if there is no natural authority, then there is no legitimate government unless men's wills institute rightful power. Thus, will must create political right; for, as Locke says in the *Essay*, political laws and rights "depend upon men's wills, or agreement in society" and are therefore "instituted, or voluntary and may be distinguished from the natural."[60]

Fortunately for Locke, at least as a contractarian and voluntarist, his notion of will begins to undergo a metamorphosis after section 47 of book 2, chapter 21. In section 48 Locke is already urging that while "for the most part" some "great" and "pressing" uneasiness is "ready to determine the will," this is "not always" the case.

For the mind having in most cases, as is evident in experience, a power to *suspend* the execution and satisfaction of any of its desires; and so all, one after another; is at liberty to consider the objects of them, examine them on all sides, and weigh them with others...This seems to me the source of all liberty; in this seems to consist that which is (as I think improperly) called *free-will*. For, during this suspension of any desire, before the will be determined to action...we have opportunity to examine, view, and judge of the good or evil of what we are going to do; and when, upon due examination, we have judged, we have done our duty, all that we can, or ought to do, in pursuit of our happiness; and it is not a fault, but a perfection of our nature, to desire, will, and act according to the last result of a fair examination.[61]

Earlier Locke had, in a rather Hobbesian way, construed freedom or liberty to consist in a man's power to do what he prefers to do, or wills. In this passage, however, it is the mind's power to suspend "the prosecution of this or that desire" that constitutes liberty: the mind, in a rational sense of the word, seems now to be ascendant. This power of suspension may even, though not quite properly, be called free will. Locke reinforces this position in section 49, arguing that every man as an intelligent being is necessarily "determined in willing by his own thought and judgment...else he would be under the determination of some other than himself, which is want of liberty." Here liberty seems to be not merely the power of suspension but the capacity to be determined by thought and judgment, and this is certainly congruent with a man's being able, say, to commit himself to civic obligations because he understands what he is doing and accepts it; but it is not so congruent with Locke's earlier claim that the power of thinking "operates not" on the power of choosing. Locke moves even further in this new rationalist direction when he declares, in section 69, that "without understanding, liberty (if it could be) would signify nothing" because "the being acted by a blind impulse from without, or from within, is little odds."[62] Finally, he sums up his altered theory of volition in a key passage from section 53:

This, as seems to me, is the great privilege of finite intellectual beings...That they can suspend their desires, and stop them from determining their wills to any action, till they have duly and fairly examined the good and evil of it...This we are able to do; and when we have done it, we have done our duty, and all that is in our power; and indeed all that needs. For, since the will supposes knowledge to guide its choice, all that we can do is to hold our wills undetermined, till we have examined the good and evil of what we desire.[63]

Having established that the will is only ordinarily determined by uneasiness but may be determined by the knowledge that guides choice, Locke is able to treat moral and political principles which one understands as kinds of knowledge that may (and ought to) determine one's will. Setting aside his quasi-Hobbesian opinion that good and evil are relative only to our pleasures and pains (section 43), Locke insists that "we should take pains to suit the relish of our minds to the true and intrinsic good that is in *things*" and that we can do this by reflecting on this intrinsic good and suspending our desire for a lesser good until we have "made ourselves uneasy in the want" of such a good. If there is no intrinsic good beyond present earthly life, then it is reasonable that a man's will should be determined by the desire for present pleasures, whatever their intrinsic character. Such a person's motto might well be, "Let us enjoy what we delight in, 'for tomorrow we die.' " But to a man who reflects on the probability of an eternal life governed by God's laws, "the measures of good and evil that govern his choice are mightily changed." He goes on, "Morality, established upon its true foundations, cannot but determine the choice in any one that will but consider...The rewards and punishments of another life, which the Almighty has established, as the enforcements of his law, are of weight enough to determine the choice, against whatever pleasure or pain this life can show, when the eternal state is considered but in its bare possibility, which nobody can make any doubt of."[64]
Apparently, then, it is possible to suspend the will's being determined by a present pleasure and to govern one's choices by a rational consideration of greater and lesser goods. Here, in the revised version of the *Essay*, Locke's theory of will moves away from uneasiness as something causal and toward a more or less Kantian notion of will as the capacity to bring oneself to act according to the conception of a law that one understands and uses in shaping one's conduct.[65] It is a notion of will already present in the earlier *Second Treatise*, where Locke had insisted that "the freedom then of man and liberty of acting according to his own will, is *grounded on* his having *reason*, which is able to instruct him in that law he is to govern himself by, and to make him know how far he is left to the freedom of his own will."[66] On this point the 1694 revised *Essay* simply catches up with the 1690 *Treatise*.

The knowledge of God's eternal rewards still causes uneasiness in the want of them, but as they are intrinsically good, it is reasonable to desire them. This much Locke makes clear in section 57, which contains the best statement of his conviction that men are responsible for their voluntary actions because they have a capacity to act better or worse. "And here we may see how it comes to pass that a man may justly incur punishment...For, though his will be always determined by that which is judged good by his understanding, yet it excuses him not; because, by a too hasty choice of his own making, he has imposed on himself wrong measures of good and evil...The eternal law and nature of things must not be altered to comply with his ill-ordered choice." The last sentence is decisive, showing why Locke had to argue in his revisions that the mind can suspend the operation of the will and avoid imposing on a man "wrong measures of good and evil." For as he insists in book 2, chapter 28 of the *Essay*, a moral relation involves "the conformity or disagreement men's voluntary actions have to a rule [such as natural law] to which they are referred."[67] It is clear that divine or natural law is the law Locke has in mind in speaking of "the eternal law and nature of things" that men must not violate, for they could not have such a responsibility if their wills were inevitably determined by whatever uneasiness happened to be most "pressing" and "great" at a given moment. It is true that men must feel uneasiness in the want of God's eternal rewards before their wills can be determined by such a want; but there must be a reason for preferring that "remote" good to some present one, namely the "intrinsic" superiority of those eternal rewards. But to be able to appreciate this superiority one must think, suspending immediate desire as something causal. As Locke urged in a letter to William Molyneux, it is "the result of our judgment" that ultimately determines a man, who could not be free "if his will were determined by anything but his own desire, guided by his own judgment."[68]

On the whole, Locke largely avoids Hobbes's difficulties with the question of will, at least in the recast sections of book 2, chapter 21, where he speaks of suspending the will, of letting it be determined only by intrinsic goods, of its being "of little odds" when it is not determined by the understanding. Problems do remain, however, not the least of which is the question put by A. C. Fraser, the editor of the standard edition of the *Essay*: "are our determinations to suspend our desires naturally necessitated by uneasiness, or is this 'suspending' not a voluntary determination at all; and if not an act of will, what is it?"[69] This is an important question that never gets a perfectly clear answer. In addition, Locke occasionally treats the freedom that makes responsibility and obligation possible as something that philosophy alone cannot demonstrate, as something that only revelation can make intelligible. For example, in the *Second Reply to the Bishop of Worcester* Locke says that since God has "revealed that there shall be a day of judgment," revelation must serve as "foundation enough, to conclude men are free enough to be made answerable for their actions." Locke appears to say that this is knowable only through the "light of revelation" and concludes by remarking that "how man is a free agent" surpasses his "explication or comprehension."[70]

Apart from a few passages such as this, Locke's theory of will does not exclude the possibility of determining oneself to action in accordance with the conception of a law—whether divine, civil, or of reputation—that we understand. It leaves open the possibility of obligating ourselves in a reasonable sense; and that is all that is necessary to make the voluntarist and contractarian elements of the *Second Treatise* relatively intelligible.

It should already be clear that Locke set a high value on natural law as a standard to which men ought to conform their voluntary actions, even if he did not think that, given an imperfect world, it could ordinarily be directly "sovereign." At the very least, natural law provides a sanction in the form of divine rewards and punishments that gives one a motive to observe obligations based on promise and contract. As we have seen, contractarianism is important to Locke, and his theory of volition usually allows for the notion of voluntary consent. However, some Locke critics argue that his natural law theory is not very coherent. One even maintains that since Locke was a philosopher of "rank and sobriety," he must have recognized this incoherence and therefore could not possibly have taken his own natural law theory seriously.[71]

Most of the charges of incoherence in Locke's theory of natural law revolve around the question of whether that law can be derived from reason alone. In his most famous, if not most truly representative, passage on natural law Locke certainly encourages the belief that natural law simply is reason itself: section 6 of the *Second Treatise* urges that even a state of nature has "a law of nature to govern it," and that reason, "which is that law," teaches all who will consult it that men ought not to "harm each other" in their lives, health, liberty or possessions. The reason for this, Locke goes on, is that men are the "workmanship" of an omnipotent and "infinitely wise" God, that they are "his property, whose workmanship they are, made to last during his, not one anothers pleasure."[72] (Here, Locke's theory that labor creates natural property rights is carried to its most extreme point: God is entitled to govern what he has produced.)[73] The content of natural law is derived from what is necessary to men's "lasting" during God's pleasure: thus, natural law forbids suicide and commands men to "preserve the rest of mankind" whenever their own security is not at stake. The law of nature generally "willeth the peace and preservation of all mankind," and anything that can reasonably be represented as conducive to that peace and preservation constitutes one of the articles of natural law.[74]

As is evident in the rest of Locke's writings, however, he was not usually content simply to identify natural law with reason; indeed, even in the *Second Treatise* (section 135) he says that all men must conform their actions to "the law of nature, i.e. to the will of God."[75] Locke's reason for shifting the emphasis from reason to divine will is never made clear in the *Second Treatise*—where it would not have been advantageous to enlarge on the difficulties of natural law theory—but is taken up at length in the *Essay*, in *The Reasonableness of Christianity*, in the *Essays on the Law of Nature*, and in the unpublished manuscript entitled *Of Ethick in General*.

In the first of the *Essays on the Law of Nature* Locke states his reasons for believing that natural law is a "decree of the divine will" rather than a mere "dictate of reason."

> [Natural law] appears to me less correctly termed by some people the dictate of reason, since reason does not so much establish and pronounce this law of nature as search for it and discover it as a law enacted by a superior power and implanted in our hearts. Neither is reason so much the maker of that law as its interpreter, unless, violating the dignity of the supreme legislator, we wish to make reason responsible for that received law which it merely investigates; nor indeed can reason give us laws, since it is only a faculty of our mind and part of us.[76]

In this case Locke is mainly showing that reason is a faculty or power, that the content of a rule cannot be derived from the existence of a capacity. This is, at least from the point of view of his philosophy, a good argument and one that he never stated with any greater force in his later works.

Most of what Locke says about natural law is contained in the *Essay* (book 2, chapter 28) and in *The Reasonableness of Christianity*. In the *Essay* Locke states his familiar view that good and evil are "nothing but pleasure or pain," that moral good and evil involve "the conformity of our voluntary actions to some law, whereby good or evil is drawn on us, from the will and pleasure of the lawmaker." After subdividing law into the divine, the civil, and that of reputation, Locke defines divine law as that "which God has set to the actions of men, and whether promulgated to them by the light of nature, or the voice of revelation." In this instance, then, Locke is resolutely avoiding putting forth a purely rational natural law, instead speaking indefinitely of a divine law that comprises both reason and revelation.[77] (That he knew exactly what he was doing is shown by his letter to James Tyrrell of August 1690: "You say, that to show what I meant, I should, after divine law, have added in a parenthesis, *which others call the law of nature*, which had been so far from what I meant, that it had been contrary to it, for I meant the divine law indefinitely, and in general, however made known or supposed.")[78] After recalling the doctrine of the *Second Treatise* that God has a right to give laws to men because "we are his creatures," Locke concludes by saying that the divine law is "the only true touchstone of moral rectitude." It is of course intrinsically reasonable and just (*pace* Descartes and his belief that God's will creates the rightness of norms),[79] but the "formal cause" of its being a true law is indeed God's will: what duty is, Locke argues in book 2, chapter 2 of the *Essay*, "cannot be understood without a law, nor a law be known and understood without a lawmaker, or without reward and punishment."[80] In the manuscript entitled *Of Ethick in General*, written at roughly the same time as the *Essay*, Locke enlarges on this point. Let philosophers "discourse ever so acutely of temperance or justice," he says, "but show no law of a superior that prescribes temperance, to the observation or breach of which law there are rewards and punishments annexed, and the force of morality is lost, and evaporates only into words, disputes, and niceties." Those who provide mere definitions of virtues and vices, he argues, "mistake their business" and are only "language-masters," so long as they do not prove the existence of a "superior power" who has the right to obligate men. "To establish morality, therefore, upon its proper basis, and such foundations as may carry an obligation with them, we must first prove a law, which always supposes a lawmaker: one that has a superiority and right to ordain, and also a power to reward and punish according to the tenor of the law established by him. This sovereign lawmaker who has set rules and bounds to the actions of men is God, their Maker."[81]

In *The Reasonableness of Christianity*, which contains Locke's most problematical utterances on natural law, special new difficulties arise. In the works just discussed the question was whether reason alone can supply a content for natural law, as section 6 of the *Second Treatise* had suggested. On this point Locke's final opinion appears to be that even a perfectly rational moral principle would not be a real law unless it were willed by a superior being who has a right, by virtue of having created everything, to govern his creation as he sees fit, and that even if reason helps us find that law, it does not constitute that law.

What is remarkable about *The Reasonableness of Christianity* is that Locke vacillates in a confusing way on the question of whether reason alone can demonstrate a "science" of ethics. After observing that before the advent of Christ "human reason unassisted failed men in its great and proper business of morality," that it never "from unquestionable principles, by clear deductions, made out of an entire body of the 'law of nature,'" Locke switches temporarily to the view that a science of ethics can be proven either through purely rational demonstration or through revelation. Whoever wants his moral opinions, "however excellent in themselves," to pass for actual natural laws, Locke says, either must show that he "builds his doctrine upon principles of reason, self-evident in themselves, and that he deduces all the parts of it from thence, by clear and evident demonstration," or must "show his commission from heaven, that he comes with authority from God, to deliver his will and commands to the world."[82] What is extraordinary here is that Locke presents these as alternatives, apparently equally valid; but according to his usual principles even a demonstration of the rationality of a principle would not make it obligatory: if rationality alone were sufficient, God's will, and his right to govern, would be superfluous.[83] This is probably why Locke, despite the fact that in *The Reasonableness of Christianity* he appears to believe that the moral philosophers had simply failed to demonstrate a rational ethics that remained in principle demonstrable, finally reverted to his more characteristic view that even if reason could be shown to require some definite practical conduct, obligatoriness would still be necessary: "Those just measures of right and wrong, which...philosophy recommended, stood on their true foundations...But where was it that their obligation was thoroughly known and allowed, and they received as precepts of a law; the highest law, the law of nature? That could not be, without a clear knowledge and acknowledgement of the law-maker, and the great rewards and punishments, for those that would, or would not obey him."[84]

While Locke thought that the revelation of God's existence through miracles was something that the "many" who could not "know" (and therefore had to believe) could use as a grounding for natural law,[85] he also thought that God's existence could be rationally demonstrated and that such a demonstrably extant God qua creator would have a right to govern, insofar as such a right is contained in Locke's idea of creation.[86] Ultimately, Locke had some reason for defining the divine law loosely, as either reason or revelation, in book 2, chapter 28 of the *Essay*. What matters most is that for natural law to be a real law, God must rightfully will it; it matters less whether the few know this through reason—through the concept of God as creator—or the many know it through revelation and miracles. The only thing that is truly confusing in *The Reasonableness of Christianity* is that Locke keeps hinting that if men were better at reasoning, they might hit upon a purely demonstrable rational ethics "in a science like mathematics," but that "the greatest part of mankind want leisure or capacity for demonstration."[87] However, the real problem is that such an ethics would lack a "formal cause," or a legislator. Either reason or revelation may discover such a legislator in God, but in neither case does reason alone constitute the content of ethics.

Apart from this one problem—and Locke was obsessed with the demonstrability of ethics, though he never produced such a demonstration—his natural law theory is relatively coherent. Its content, though not constituted by reason, is always reasonable, since God is as all-wise as he is omnipotent; that content defends God's creation against the voluntary wrongdoing of men and is backed up by sanctions of "infinite weight and duration" in another life.

With this last point we come to the most serious attack ever leveled against Locke as a natural law theorist. Leo Strauss in *Natural Right and History* observes that most commentators on Lockean natural law, such as J. L. Gough, are content to say that it contains "logical flaws" but that they do not go nearly far enough. In Strauss's opinion "Locke cannot have recognized any law of nature in the proper sense of the term." Since he grants that this conclusion "stands in shocking contrast to what is generally thought to be his doctrine," he tries to support it by a close and sometimes brilliant exegesis of a number of Lockean texts. But the substance of his argument, stated in his own words, is this:

> [Locke] says, on the one hand, that, in order to be a law, the law of nature must not only have been given by God, but it must in addition have as its sanctions divine "rewards and punishments," of infinite weight and duration, in another life. On the other hand, however, he says that reason cannot demonstrate that there is another life. Only through revelation do we know of the sanctions for the law of nature or of "the only true touchstone of moral rectitude."

As a result, Strauss says, Locke's measures of right and wrong "do not have the character of a law," for they lack sanctions that reason can demonstrate, and therefore "there does not exist a law of nature."[88]

Strauss gains an unfair advantage by calling the law of nature, as distinguished from revelation, the "only true touchstone of moral rectitude" in Locke, whereas Locke in fact said that it is divine law, comprising both rational natural law and revelation, that constitutes this touchstone. Since Locke never said that reason can demonstrate anything more than the probability of immortality, Strauss distorts Locke by speaking as if Locke first said that a purely rational natural law alone constitutes the "only true touchstone of moral rectitude" and then said inconsistently that reason cannot demonstrate immortality. Strauss's substitution of the phrase "law of nature" for "divine law" looks like a small alteration, but in fact it is a major one that alone makes his argument possible. He is doing exactly what Locke criticized Tyrrell for doing in 1690. What is more, even if Locke's theory of natural law were as inadequate as Strauss says it is, there would still be no grounds for saying that Locke himself could not have believed it: only Strauss's conviction that Locke was deliberately "perplexing his sense," providing an esoteric and an exoteric doctrine, would lead necessarily to that conclusion. As Locke himself argued in his *First Letter to the Bishop of Worcester*, it cannot be said that because a writer is obliged to use "imperfect, inadequate, obscure ideas, where he has no better," he is deliberately trying to "exclude those things out of being, or out of rational discourse" by making them obviously implausible.[89]

If it is the requirements of Strauss's mode of interpretation rather than anything in Locke that make him say that Locke could not have believed in his own natural law theory, his philosophical objection still identifies some problems. Here, a great deal turns on the word *demonstration*. Actually, Strauss was not by any means the first to object to Lockean natural law on the grounds that the immortality of the soul, on which eternal rewards and punishments would be visited, could not be demonstrated by Locke; Tyrrell had made the same objection in 1690, and Locke at least tried to meet it. In his reply to Tyrrell Locke said that while he thought that demonstration in religion and morality could be taken much farther than it had been, nonetheless one sometimes had to settle for something less: "The probability of rewards and punishments in another life, I should think, might serve for an enforcement of the divine law."[90] Even if, Locke wrote in the *Essay*, the immortality of the soul cannot be demonstrated, the "bare possibility, which nobody can make any doubt of," of another life governed by divine rewards and punishments makes it a good bargain to conform one's voluntary actions to the divine law: "if the good man be in the right, he is eternally happy; if he mistakes, he is not miserable, he feels nothing."[91] If Locke did not believe that the immortality of the soul was demonstrable by reason unaided by revelation, he did at least think that such immortality was probable and that a Pascalian wager on that point was reasonable; but Strauss, by not even mentioning Locke's theory of probability, strives to create the impression that Locke's theory of immortality is utterly groundless.

Locke did, of course, think that immortality could be proved by revelation and that nothing in genuine revelation can contradict reason. In the *Essay* (book 4, chapter 18) Locke grants that the notion that "the dead shall rise, and live again" though true is "beyond the discovery of reason" and that only revelation and faith can uphold it. He adds that while everything that God has revealed "is certainly true" and that "no doubt can be made of it," nonetheless nothing that is "contrary to, and inconsistent with, the clear and self-evident dictates of reason, has a right to be urged or assented to as a matter of faith."[92] But it is mainly in the *Second Reply to the Bishop of Worcester* and in *The Reasonableness of Christianity* that Locke treats immortality with care. "God has revealed that the souls of men shall live forever," he urges in the *Second Reply*, and "the veracity of God is a demonstration of the truth of what he has revealed." The fact that "a proposition divinely revealed" cannot be demonstrated by "natural reason" alone does not make it "less credible than one that can"; apparently it is sufficient that there be no manifest conflict between reason and what is revealed.[93] And in *The Reasonableness of Christianity* Locke points out at length all of the passages from Scripture that suggest the probability of "immortality and eternal life" and characterizes such an eternal life as "the reward of justice and righteousness only." Then, in a central passage that reinforces his view of divine rewards and punishments as the main sanction of the divine law, he points out the connection between those sanctions and immortality: "Life, eternal life, being the reward of justice or righteousness, appointed by the righteous God...it is impossible that he should justify those who had no regard to justice at all whatever they believed. This would have been to encourage iniquity, contrary to the purity of his nature; and to have condemned that eternal law of right which is holy, just and good...The duties of that law...are of eternal obligation."[94]

Locke, then, is certain that the divine law, as the only true touchstone of moral rectitude, requires immortality and sanctions; that reason alone, though it must not conflict with revelation, is not something out of which a complete "science of ethics" can be deduced. This is probably why he always put off writing a "book of offices," saying in a well-known letter to his friend Molyneux that "the gospel contains so perfect a body of ethics, that reason may be excused from that inquiry, since she may find man's duty clearer and easier in revelation, than in herself."[95] He might have added that without divine will and sanctions there would be no absolute obligation to do even that which is "conformable to right reason," that it is not simply clearer and easier to pass from reason to revelation but necessary as well.[96]

Ultimately, Locke's theory of natural law is problematic only if one thinks that he began by saying that such a law is derived from reason alone and later changed his argument. However, apart from the passage in the *Second Treatise* on a natural law that simply is reason, Locke's writings generally state that the divine law depends on both reason and revelation. Locke is unlike, say, Grotius in his effort to rationalize natural law: Locke could not have accepted even as a Grotian hypothesis the notion that the truths of morality are exactly like those of logic and mathematics, for obligation would be lacking.[97] Still, taken on its own terms, Locke's natural law is tolerably coherent. Perhaps the phrase "divine law" should always be used when discussing Locke's ultimate moral norm. But since he himself often uses the idea of natural law, it is safe to employ that term so long as one remembers that when Locke is being strict, the natural law is only a part of the divine law; revelation is needed as well to provide a complete touchstone of moral rectitude.

It is clear that Locke treats contract or consent or voluntary agreement as one standard of political right, that he sometimes provides a theory of volition that makes this possible, and that he enunciates a natural law theory that provides both a context within which voluntary agreement can operate and a sanction that gives men a sufficient motive to observe their agreements. Some might still want to deny, however, that the ways in which Locke says that consent can be politically expressed are full and adequate. In other words, some might want to treat Locke as a genuine but unsuccessful contractarian.

It is traditional to grant that Locke took consent and contract seriously, if not as exclusive criteria of right. As T. H. Green and others have pointed out, the most obvious difference between Locke and Hobbes is that in Hobbes there is at most one act of consent in the political lifetime of a polity—the act of establishing the state—whereas in Locke not only the foundation but the ordinary operation of the state rests at least in part on consent.[98] As a consequence, Locke had to deal at length with problems that Hobbes could treat briefly, if at all. Must consent be active and take the form of positive declarations and actions? May it be passive and consist in accepting and benefiting from the security offered by the state? Does inheritance of property under a regime bind a person to observe its laws? Hobbes, of course, was aware of all these difficulties; but since there was only one act of consent in his system, he did not have to consider at length what kinds of consent really constitute consent.[99] (In Locke's view, there is not even one act of real consent in some Hobbesian states. In a "commonwealth by acquisition," fashioned by a conqueror, there might be voluntary—in Hobbes's sense of the word—submission at sword point; nonetheless, Locke insists that "where there is no resistance there is a general submission, but there may be a general submission without a general consent which is an other thing." For Locke real consent requires choice, as John Dunn convincingly argues.)[100]

Locke, in contrast to Hobbes, not only had to explain both the original legitimacy of society, as distinguished from government, on the basis of consent and the ordinary operation of government in terms of consent; he also had to explain the difficult question of the origin of money in terms of universal consent. This issue throws an interesting light on his idea of property, itself originally justified by labor and by God's having given the world to men in order to preserve them. The relative egalitarianism of Locke's original theory of property—based on the fact that one has a property in that with which he mixes his labor, provided nothing is wasted, and that "as much" which is "as good" is left for others— is very much modified by his theory of money, which holds that because money cannot spoil, no one can object to a man's amassing a great deal of it. Furthermore, in his view money is justified by the fact that men have agreed to "disproportionate and unequal possession of the earth" by having, through a "tacit and voluntary consent," discovered a way that a man "may fairly possess more land than he himself can use the product of, by receiving in exchange for the overplus, gold and silver, which may be hoarded up without injury to any one, these metals not spoiling or decaying in the hands of the possessor." Thus, the theory of justification by consent is sometimes used in contradistinction to what is naturally justifiable in terms of natural law and rights, of God's gifts and men's labor.[101]

It would have been more logical, and would have better preserved a true equilibrium between consent, natural law, and natural rights, if Locke had said that money, while merely conventional and more convenient than trading goods, ought to remain strictly proportional to naturally justifiable property. Thus, a man should be allowed to possess no more money (which could, in vastly unequal quantities, do the harm that natural law forbids) than would represent or stand for the value of property justified under the original criteria: nonspoilage and "as much" that is "as good" left for others. What is interesting is that if one insists on an equilibrium between standards of right in Locke, the defects of his system can be seen to be self-correcting. After all, according to Locke's own theory of natural law and rights a socially harmful degree of acquisitiveness can be condemned. Locke himself provided the grounds for criticizing his theory of money long before it became fashionable to treat this problem as if it were the main one in his philosophy.[102] What he can be criticized for is not keeping his criteria in constant balance, for occasionally allowing one criterion—consent—to justify things—such as limitless quantities of money—that do violence to the other criteria.

If consent is truly an important standard in Locke, one that he occasionally takes too far, even by his own lights, it is nonetheless hard to show how certain political approximations to consent really amount to consent in his system. Locke's problem is to show that representative government, majoritarianism, and tacit consent adequately express the meaning of consent. It is, of course, widely believed that he did not solve this problem very well. Plamenatz, for example, says:

> The case against Locke is that he failed in his own purpose. If a man's consent is his deliberate and voluntary agreement, and if nothing but a man's consent can make it his duty to obey government, then most people at most times and in most places have no duty of obedience. This was a conclusion that Locke rightly wanted to avoid. He therefore...went to the other extreme, and gave the name consent to almost any action that creates an obligation to obey...If you begin by assuming that only consent creates a duty of obedience, you are only too ready to conclude that whatever creates that duty must be consent.[103]

Some of this criticism, trenchant as it is, is overstated. It is not only consent, for example, that Locke says creates a duty of obedience. The general duty arises from natural law; consent only tells us which persons to obey. On the whole, though, this passage is a fair representation of what critics think is wrong with Locke.

Locke apparently did not consider representation to be a problem in consent theory, to judge from the number of times he speaks of personal consent and indirect consent through representatives as virtually equivalent: levying taxes, he says in the *Second Treatise,* requires the consent of the majority, "giving it either by themselves, or their representatives chosen by them." This virtual equivalence is scattered throughout the *Second Treatise:* "No government can have a right to obedience from a people who have not freely consented to it: which they can never be supposed to do, till either they are put in a full state of liberty to chuse their government and governors, or at least till they have such standing laws, to which they have by themselves or their representatives, given their free consent."[104] Despite some exaggeration, this passage illustrates that Locke was not concerned with the kind of argument found later in Rousseau: that personal will can never be represented, since "to deprive your will of all freedom is to deprive your actions of all morality"; that one cannot will for someone or on behalf of someone.[105] Locke does not even concern himself with a possible distinction between representation and strict agency or between actual and virtual representation; indeed, he devotes much more time to the problem of the representation of rotten boroughs than to the general theory of representation as an expression of consent.

Majoritarianism is treated mainly in sections 96, 97, and 98 of the *Second Treatise*, though an important passage in section 140 does show that Locke is not really more concerned with the general theory of majoritarianism than with that of representation. Though everyone who enjoys the state's protection should pay taxes to maintain that state, he urges, "still it must be with his own consent, i.e. the consent of the majority, giving it either by themselves, or their representatives chosen by them."[106] For Locke, apparently, one could give one's "own" consent simply as part of a majority (if one were fortunate enough not to belong to the minority) or through representatives or even through a majority of representatives, though such a majority would be twice removed from one's "own" consent.

Locke modifies the notion that such consent is always requisite when he says, in section 98, that if the consent of the majority is not accepted as if it were the act of the whole, "nothing but the consent of every individual can make anything to be the act of the whole." He adds that unanimous consent is "next impossible ever to be had," and that unless people accept majoritarianism, society will be "immediately dissolved again." Whether this is true or not, it arguably does not defend the notion of every man's own consent. In section 97 Locke goes further suggesting that everyone's insisting on his own consent leads to anarchism: "What appearance would there be of any compact. . . if he were no farther tied by any decrees of the society, than he himself thought fit, and did actually consent to?"[107] Locke, then, is no partisan of Thoreau's claim that "a man more right than his neighbors constitutes a majority of one already."[108]

Locke ordinarily argues that personal consent must take the form of being part of a majority because of the "inconvenience" of unanimity; but he does offer one justification for majoritarianism in terms of an analogy that he derives from physics:

When any number of men have, by the consent of every individual, made a *community*, they have thereby made that *community* one body, with a power to act as one body, which is only by the will and determination of the *majority*. For that which acts any community, being only the consent of the individuals of it, and it being necessary to that which is one body to move one way; it is necessary the body should move that way whither the greater force carries it, which is the *consent of the majority:* or else it is impossible it should act or continue one body, one community...[109]

It is at least arguable that if Locke believed that men's consent is an expression of their natural equality, of the natural rights they have by virtue of natural law, he ought to have considered the special character of a theory of unanimous consent more carefully.[110] Only if everyone, without exception, agrees to a given measure is it certain that no one's rights will be violated. Rousseau saw this clearly enough, and a number of contemporary contractarians have attempted to construct workable theories of unanimous consent.[111] It can be pointed out, though, in Locke's defense, that he needed unanimity less than Rousseau did: after all, Rousseau believed that the obligations that bind men to society are obligatory only because they are "mutual,"[112] while Locke could rely on natural law and rights as well. In Rousseau the general will must always be right, since that is all there is.

Of course, Locke devotes the bulk of his consent theorizing to neither representation nor majoritarianism. It is the notion of tacit consent that looms much the largest. One need not, perhaps, dwell on those passages in which Locke suggests that the use of roads and other state facilities constitutes tacit consent to uphold that state; these obligations are not all of one kind, given his distinction between citizens and aliens. "Submitting to the laws of any country, living quietly, and enjoying privileges and protection under them, makes not a man a member of that society." But the voluntary inheritance of property under an established regime is the surest sign of a binding tacit consent.

Every man being, as has been shewed, *naturally free...* it is to be considered, what shall be understod to be a *sufficient declaration of* a man's *consent, to make him subject* to the laws of any government...Nobody doubts but an *express consent-* ...makes him a perfect member of that society, a subject of that government. The difficulty is, what ought to be looked upon as a tacit consent...And to this I say, that every man, that hath any possession, or enjoyment, of any part of the dominions of any government, doth thereby give his *tacit consent*.[113]

Express consent, then, is no problem for Locke, and tacit consent is demonstrated mainly by the inheritance of property under the laws of a given commonwealth. Here, the original egalitarianism of Locke's first theory of property is weakened further: a man can will his property to his heir who has neither labored for it nor left "as much" that is "as good" for others; yet the inheritance is legitimate if the heir accepts the property "with the condition it is under." In the end, then, consent modifies property as being naturally justifiable beyond recognition. That is, only the first holder of property labored for it; yet he may bequeath money, itself authorized by universal consent, to his heirs, provided they accept it with its conditions by their own consent. Thus, most property is justified by a combination of universal and private consent rather than by Locke's original, equitable criteria. In his theory of personal tacit consent, at least with respect to inheritance, Locke again upsets his own equilibrium, weakening the claims of natural law and rights, just as his theory of money justified by universal consent had weakened them.

It is certainly possible to deal with representation, majoritarianism, and tacit consent at greater length. But for present purposes it is enough to point out that if Locke had always kept the "only true touchstone of moral rectitude" in mind when he talked about the forms consent can take, he might have been more careful to ask whether a man's own will can be represented, whether personal will is really defended in a theory of majoritarianism argued for in terms of convenience, and whether tacit consent through inheritance does not simply reinforce the damage to natural law and rights done by the theory of money. If it is true that, given his views on natural law and rights, on the notion that men can and should conform their voluntary actions to what is intrinsically right, Locke ought to have been more careful in treating the question of what constitutes consent, that does not mean that he is not a theorist of contract and consent. It simply means that he is not wholly successful or consistent as a contractarian. The important thing is that Locke's system can reasonably be seen as self-correctible. It is possible to imagine, for example, a Lockean theory of money that would preserve what he says about the greater convenience of currency than plums and nuts and that would at the same time preserve a proportionality between what could be justified in terms of labor and of leaving for others "as much" that is "as good." And this can be done without treating Locke as either a purveyor or a victim of false consciousness, though it is only fair to add that he himself did not perform the self-correction that a completely coherent position requires.[114]

In the end, Locke's political system is rather impressively defended. He provides a theory of natural, or rather divine law that, taken as a whole, is intelligible, even if one might not want to derive the validity of such law from divine will, and even if one might wish that he had not occasionally argued as if such a law could be derived from reason alone. He shows that the general moral obligations under such a law need to be given political specificity through consent and contract, through finding a person whom it is a citizen's duty to obey. He sketches a theory of volition that ultimately allows for voluntary adherence to natural law and for voluntary agreement as the definition of consent, at least when the mind can suspend some pressing uneasiness. And he suggests that consent is in harmony with natural law and rights because that law and those rights make all men morally equal and necessitate the voluntary creation of superiors who are not superior. As Richard Aaron put the matter nearly fifty years ago: "The [Lockean] social contract theory was closely linked with that of the law of nature. In one sense the former is the corollary of the latter. In nature all men are equal, but in political society some are rulers and others are ruled. This difference needs to be explained and is explained by the theory of the social contract."[115] If Locke had more carefully preserved the equilibrium between the criteria of right that he had set out to keep in balance, consent and contract would be a more obvious corollary of the only true touchstone of moral rectitude. At least the defects of Locke's system can be remedied with his own concepts, and in a Lockean spirit.

{ 4 }

A Possible Explanation
of Rousseau's General Will

I_N treating Rousseau as a contractarian and a voluntarist new problems come into view. In the case of Hobbes the difficulty is that he did not develop a theory of moral personality or of the will as a kind of moral causality that would account for consent as the foundation of political obligation and the legitimacy of the state. In short, the problem with Hobbes is one of a radical disjunction between psychological theory and moral theory, though his psychology is consistent enough in itself, losing coherence only when juxtaposed with his moral philosophy.[1] And while Locke often avoids most of these problems, he occasionally does not.[2] In the case of Rousseau the problem is rather different. The unstable and paradoxical character of the idea of volition makes difficulties for him as well, causing him to vacillate between the moral and the psychological sense of willing. But in Rousseau there is a further problem: even when he accepts the idea of will, he still vacillates. Sometimes the will is seen as the source of duty and legitimacy and sometimes simply as a manifestation of "particularism" and egoism. It is Rousseau's effort to entertain and expel the idea of will simultaneously that gives his political philosophy its unusual cast.

This simultaneous entertaining and expelling, or to use Hegelian language "canceling and preserving,"[3] is doubtless what leads Rousseau to the notion of the general will, to a will that is not merely capricious and egoistic. However, it is arguable that the idea of a general will—at least when it is a corporate or collective will—is a philosophical and psychological contradiction in terms, that will is a conception understandable only in terms of individual actions.[4] The problem cannot be glossed over by attempting to reduce the general will to a "common ego," as does T. H. Green, or to an analogical forerunner of Kant's pure practical reason.[5] Why, then, did Rousseau make so problematical an idea the center of his political theory, and why has that idea continued to receive serious attention?

The general will has continued to be taken seriously because it is an attempted amalgam of two extremely important traditions of political thought, which may be designated ancient cohesiveness and modern voluntarism. As has already been suggested, political thought since the seventeenth century has been characterized by voluntarism, by an emphasis on individual will and consent as the standard of political legitimacy.[6] Rousseau ordinarily upheld much of this tradition, sometimes even exaggerating his agreement with a voluntarist and contractarian such as Locke: the English philosopher, he says, had treated political matters "with exactly the same principles as myself."[7] In *Lettres écrites de la montagne,* number six, speaking of contract and consent Rousseau says that a state is made one by the union of its members; that this union is the consequence of obligation; and that obligation can follow only from voluntary conventions. He admits that the foundation of obligation had divided political theorists: "according to some, it is force; according to others, paternal authority; according to others, the will of God." All theorists, he says, establish their own principle of obligation and attack that of others. "I myself have not done otherwise," Rousseau declares, "and, following the soundest element of those who have discussed these matters, I have settled on, as the foundation of the body politic, the contract of its members." He concludes by asking, "What more certain foundation can obligation among men have, than the free agreement of him who obligates himself?"[8]

While voluntarism took care of legitimacy, it could say nothing about the intrinsic goodness of what is willed. It is, of course, possible to assert that whatever is willed is right simply because it is willed.[9] But this was not enough for Rousseau; and it was here that he made a stand for a particular kind of will. He wanted will to take a particular form; he wanted voluntarism to legitimize what he conceived to be the unity and cohesiveness, the generality, of ancient polity, particularly of Sparta and of republican Rome.[10] His political ideal was the ancient polity, now willed by moderns who were as concerned with reasons for obligation as with perfect forms of government. Against the alleged atomism of earlier contract theory Rousseau wanted the generality—the nonindividualism, or rather the preindividualism—of antiquity to be legitimized by consent. Here, he created the paradox of insisting on the willing of the essentially nonvoluntaristic politics characteristic of antiquity: the philosophical paradox of willed nonvoluntarism. If this paradoxical concept of the general will as a will that is sometimes the corporate "will" of a whole society and sometimes the individual will to stop being willful is rather difficult to defend, it can at least be unraveled with interesting implications for all voluntaristic and perfectionist theories, not to mention democratic theories, which are always hard pressed to fuse what is wanted with what is intrinsically good.[11] This treatment helps to clear up some of the usually insoluble paradoxes in Rousseau and to make his thought clearer, if not less problematical.

Jean-Jacques Rousseau was a severe critic of modern political life—of its lack of a common morality and virtue, of its lack of patriotism and civic religion, of its indulgence in "base" philosophy and morally uninstructive arts.[12] At the same time, he was a great admirer of the more highly unified political systems of antiquity, in which, as he thought, morality, civic religion, patriotism, and a simple way of life had made men "one," wholly socialized, and truly political.[13] And he thought that modern political life divided man against himself, leaving him, with all his merely private and antisocial interests, half in and half out of political society, enjoying neither the amoral independence of nature nor the moral elevation afforded by true socialization.[14]

Why Rousseau thought the unified ancient political systems preferable to modern ones is not hard to understand. He conceived the difference between natural man and political man in very sharp terms. While for most contract theorists political life is merely not natural (and this position was held largely to do away with arguments for natural political authority), for Rousseau it was positively unnatural, even antinatural, a complete transformation of the natural man. The political man must be deprived of his natural powers and given others "which are foreign to him and which he cannot use without the help of others." Politics reaches perfection when natural powers are completely dead and extinguished and man is given "a partial and corporate existence."[15]

The defect of modern politics, in Rousseau's view, is that it is insufficiently political; it compromises between the utter artificiality and communality of political life and the naturalness and independence of prepolitical life and in so doing causes the greatest misfortunes of modern man: self-division, conflict between private will and the common good, a sense of being neither in one condition nor another. "What makes human misery," Rousseau says in *Le bonheur public,* "is the contradiction which exists between our situation and our desires, between our duties and our inclinations, between nature and social institutions, between man and citizen." To make man one, to make him as happy as he can be, "give him entirely to the state, or leave him entirely to himself. . .but if you divide his heart, you will rip him apart; and do not imagine that the state can be happy, when all its members suffer."[16] Above all, in Rousseau's view, the imperfect socialization of modern man allows private persons and corporate interests to control other private persons, leading to extreme inequality and personal dependence. Only generality of laws based on an idea of common good can abolish all private dependence, which was for him perhaps the supreme social evil. What he wanted was that socialized men might be "perfectly independent of all the rest, and extremely dependent on the city," for only the power of the state and the generality of its laws "constitutes the liberty of its members."[17]

Ancient polities such as Sparta, Rousseau thought, with their simplicity, their morality or politics of the common good, their civic religion, moral use of fine and military arts, and lack of extreme individualism and private interest had been political societies in the proper sense: in them man was "part of a larger whole" from which he "in a sense receives his life and being."[18] Modern "prejudices," "base philosophy," and "passions of petty self-interest," by contrast, ensure that "we moderns can no longer find in ourselves anything of that spiritual vigor which was inspired in the ancients by everything they did."[19] This spiritual vigor may be taken to mean the avoidance, through identity with a "greater whole," of "that dangerous disposition which gives rise to all our vices": self-love. Political education in an extremely unified state will "lead us out of ourselves" before the human ego "has acquired that contemptible activity which absorbs all virtue and constitutes the life and being of little minds."[20] It follows that the best social institutions "are those best able to denature man, to take away his absolute existence and to give him a relative one, and to carry the *moi* into the common unity."[21] These social institutions in ideal ancient polities were always for Rousseau the creation of a great legislator, a Numa or a Moses. They did not develop and perfect themselves in political experience but were handed down by the lawgiver.[22]

If Rousseau thought the highly unified ancient polity and its political morality of common good superior to modern fragmented politics and its political morality of self-interest, at the same time he shared with modern individualist thought the conviction that all political life is conventional and can be made obligatory only through individual consent. Despite the fact that he sometimes treats moral notions as if they simply arose in a developmental process during the course of socialization,[23] Rousseau often falls back on a kind of moral a priorism, particularly when speaking of contract and obligation, in which the wills of free men are taken to be the causes of duties and of legitimate authority. Thus, in an argument against obligations based on slavery in the *Contrat social*, Rousseau urges that "to deprive your will of all freedom is to deprive your actions of all morality,"[24] that the reason that no notion of right or morality can be derived from mere force is that "to yield to force is an act of necessity, not of will."[25] In the *Discourse on Inequality*, in a passage that almost prefigures Kant, he insists on the importance of free agency, arguing that while "physics" (natural science) might explain the "mechanism of the senses," it could never make intelligible "the power of willing or rather of choosing," a power in which "nothing is to be found but acts which are purely spiritual and wholly inexplicable by the laws of mechanism."[26] It is this power of willing rather than reason that distinguishes men from beasts. In the unpublished *Première version du contrat social* Rousseau even says, "Every free action has two causes which concur to produce it: the first [a] moral [cause], namely the will which determines the act; the other physical, namely the power which executes it."[27] Thus Rousseau not only requires the idea of will as moral causality; he actually uses such a term.

Confirmation of this view of will is given in *Émile*, where Rousseau argues, through a speech put into the mouth of the Savoyard Vicar, that "the motive power of all action is in the will of a free creature," that "it is not the word freedom that is meaning-less, but the word necessity." The will, Rousseau goes on, is "independent of my senses": "I consent or I resist, I yield or I win the victory, and I know very well in myself when I have done what

I wanted and when I have merely given way to my passions." Man is, he concludes, "free to act," and he "acts of his own accord."[28] To be sure, the pre-Kantian voluntarism of *Émile*, and *Inequality* as well, is not the whole story; even in the *Lettres morales* (1757), which were used as a quarry in the writing of *Émile*, the relation of will to morality is complicated and problematical. The opening of the fifth *Lettre*—"the whole morality of human life is in the intention of man"[29]—seems at first to be a voluntarist claim, almost prefiguring Kant's notion that a "good will" is the only "unqualifiedly" good thing on earth.[30] But this *intention* refers not to the will of *Émile* but to conscience, which is a "divine instinct" and an "immortal and heavenly voice." Rousseau, after a striking passage on moral feelings ("if one sees . . . some act of violence or injustice, a movement of anger and indignation arises at once in our heart"), goes on to speak of feelings of "remorse" that "punish hidden crimes in secret"; and this "importunate voice" he calls an involuntary feeling ("sentiment involontaire") that "torments" us. That the phrase *involuntary feeling* is not a mere slip is proven by a deliberate repetition of the word *involuntary:* "Thus there is, at the bottom of all souls, an innate principle of justice and of moral truth [which is] prior to all national prejudices, to all maxims of education. This principle is the involuntary rule ['la règle involontaire'] by which, despite our own maxims, we judge our actions, and those of others, as good or bad; and it is to this principle that I give the name conscience." Conscience, then, is an involuntary moral feeling—not surprisingly, given Rousseau's view that "our feeling is incontestably prior to our reason itself."[31] And so, while the fifth *Lettre morale* opens with an apparent anticipation of *Émile*'s voluntarism, this is only an appearance. It proves that it is not simply right to find in Rousseau a predecessor of Kant. Rousseau's "morale sensitive" is not easy to reconcile with rational self-determination, for if Rousseau says that "to deprive your will of all freedom is to deprive your actions of all morality," he also says that conscience is a moral feeling that is involuntary.

The fact remains, however, that while *Émile* was published, the *Lettres morales* were held back. Perhaps Rousseau anticipated the judgment of Bertrand de Jouvenel that "nothing is more dangerous" than the sovereignty of a conscience that can lead to "the open door to subjectivism": "the good, as I see it, is the objective good."[32] And in *Émile* Rousseau certainly insists on the moral centrality of free will. Human free will, moreover, does not derogate from Providence but magnifies it, since God has "made man of so excellent a nature, that he has endowed his actions with that morality by which they are ennobled." Rousseau cannot agree with Hobbes that human freedom would lessen God by robbing him of his omnipotence: "Providence has made [man] free that he may choose the good and refuse the evil...What more could divine power itself have done on our behalf? Could it have made our nature a contradiction and have given the prize of well-going to one who was incapable of evil? To prevent a man from wickedness, should Providence have restricted him to instinct and made him a fool?"[33]

For Rousseau, then, caused or determined volition is not a necessity of proper theology; in this respect unlike Hobbes he was able to avoid having to treat will as determined and was also able to understand will as a moral causality with the power to produce moral effects. Rousseau very definitely thought that he had derived political obligation and rightful political authority from this power of willing: "civil association is the most voluntary act in the world; since every individual is born free and his own master, no one is able, on any pretext whatsoever, to subject him without his consent." (Here, as often in Locke, consent is understood as a political way of expressing natural freedom and equality.) Indeed, the first four chapters of the *Contrat social* are devoted to refutations of erroneous theories of obligation and right: paternal authority, the "right of the strongest," and obligation derived from slavery. "Since no man," Rousseau concludes, "has natural authority over his fellow men, and since might in no sense makes right, convention remains as the basis of legitimate authority among men."[34]

For Rousseau, however, contract theory may have been more a way of destroying wrong theories of obligation and authority than of creating a comprehensive theory of what is politically right. While for some theorists a notion of obligation by consent is of central importance, for Rousseau it is not a complete political theory. Any political system that "confines itself to mere obedience will find difficulty in getting itself obeyed. If it is good to know how to deal with men as they are, it is much better to make them what they ought to be."[35] That was Rousseau's criticism of all contract theory: it dealt too much with the form of obligation, with will as it is, and not enough with what men ought to be obligated to and with will as it might be.

His criticism of Hobbes is based on this point. Hobbes had, indeed, established rightful political authority on consent, rejecting paternal authority and (arguably) obligation based on either divine or natural law; he had made law and therefore morality the command of an artificial "representative person" to whom subjects were "formerly obliged" through transfer of natural rights by consent.[36] But Hobbes had done nothing to cure the essential wrongness, in Rousseau's view, of modern politics: private interest was rampant, and indeed paramount, in Hobbes's system (could one not decide whether or not to risk one's life for the Hobbesian state?). The essential error of Hobbes, Rousseau thought, was to have read back into the state of nature all the human vices that half-socialization had created and thus to see culturally produced depravities as natural and Hobbesian absolutism rather than the creation of a feeling of the common good as the remedy for these depravities. "The error of Hobbes and of the philosophers," Rousseau declares in *L'état de guerre*, "is to confound natural man with the men they have before their eyes, and to carry into one system a being who can subsist only in another."[37] Rousseau thought that a perfectly socialized state such as Sparta could elevate men and turn them from "stupid and limited animals" into moral and intelligent beings.[38] He must have thought Hobbesian politics incomplete, a system that "confines itself to mere obedience," one that does not attempt to make men what they ought to be but that, through mere mutual forbearance,[39] undertakes no improvement in political life. "Let it be asked," says Rousseau, "why morality is corrupted in proportion as minds are enlightened." Hobbes might well have an enlightened view of obligation, to the extent that he bases it on consent, but he says nothing about the moral corruption caused by private interest and individual will. The result is that while Hobbes knew "quite well what a *bourgeois* of London or of Paris is like," he never saw a natural man.[40]

Rousseau had another objection to traditional contractarianism, an objection that he nevertheless kept under control in the *Contrat social:* namely, that a social contract might simply be a fraud imposed on the poor by the rich with a view to legitimizing a ruinous inequality. In the *Discourse on Inequality* Rousseau suggests that the rich man, "destitute of valid reasons" that he can use to justify his unequal possessions and fearful of being plundered by the many, "conceived at length the profoundest plan that ever entered the mind of man: this was to employ in his favor the forces of those who attacked him...and to give them other institutions as favorable to himself as the law of nature was unfavorable." He goes on to say: " 'Let us join,' he said, 'to guard the weak from oppression, to restrain the ambitious, and secure to every man the possession of what belongs to him: let us institute rules of justice and peace, to which all without exception may be obliged to conform; rules that may in some measure make amends for the caprices of fortune, by subjecting equally the powerful and the weak to the observance of reciprocal obligations.'" Such an argument, Rousseau continues, would have worked quite well with "barbarous" men who were "easily seduced"; "all ran headlong to their chains, in hopes of securing their liberty." Only the rich, who had something to lose, saw the danger involved, since they had "feelings...in every part of their possessions."[41]

Even in the *Première version du contrat social,* which Rousseau himself suppressed, his hostility to contractarianism is in evidence. "This pretended social treaty dictated by nature is a veritable chimera," he wrote, "since the conditions of it are always unknown or impracticable." The social contract "only gives new power to him who already has too much," while the weak party to the agreement "finds no asylum where he can take refuge, no support for his weakness, and finally perishes as a victim of this deceitful union from which he had expected his happiness." This leads Rousseau to claim, in chapter 5 of the *First Version,* that it is the "utilité commune" rather than contract or the general will that is "the foundation of civil society."[42]

It is worth noting that in the published version of the *Contrat social,* where Rousseau wants to rely on contractarian arguments, he very much mitigates the radicalism of this view. Indeed, in the definitive version he confines himself to the moderate observation that since "laws are always useful to those who have property, and harmful to those who have nothing," the social state "is advantageous to men only in so far as they all have something and no one has any more than he needs." In this work Rousseau emphasizes the benefits of the social contract, provided that conditions are roughly equalized for all parties to the agreement: "since each gives himself entirely, the condition is equal for all; and since the condition is equal for all, it is in the interest of no one to make it burdensome to the rest."[43] But in the *Contrat social* the notion that a social contract is a rich man's confidence trick is distinctly subordinate.

Rousseau, in any case, held both the idea that the closely unified political systems of antiquity as he idealized them were the most perfect kinds of polity and the notion that all political society is the conventional creation of individual wills through a social contract, at least when conditions could be equalized. Holding both of these ideas created problems, for while the need for consent to fundamental principles of political society, for creation of a mere political construct through will and artifice, is a doctrine characteristic of what Michael Oakeshott has called the "idiom of individuality,"[44] the ancient conception of a highly unified and collective politics was dependent on a morality of the common good quite foreign to any insistence on individual will as the creator of society and as the basis of obligation. Rousseau sometimes recognized this distinction, particularly in the *Économie politique*. As Hume put it, both accurately and amusingly: "The only passage I meet with in antiquity, where the obligation of obedience to government is ascribed to a promise, is in Plato's *Crito;* where Socrates refuses to escape from prison, because he had tacitly promised to obey the laws. Thus he builds a *Tory* consequence of passive obedience on a *Whig* foundation of the original contract."[45]

Not being a systematic philosopher, as he often pointed out, Rousseau never really reconciled the tensions between his contractual theory of obligation and his model of political perfection. To make Rousseau more consistent than he cared to be, one must admit that his ancient ideal model, as the creation not of a contractual relation of individual wills but of a great legislator working with political education and a common good morality, is not obligatory on citizens, is not founded in right. It is true that Rousseau sometimes spoke as though ancient systems were constructed by mutual individual consent; but he did not usually speak in those terms. Even though, for him, all political society, ancient or modern, is artificial in the sense that it is not the original condition of man, contract theory involves an additional element of artifice: the notion that a society must be created by the will of all its members. Rousseau rarely spoke as though ancient polity had been artificial in this sense; he usually said that ancient systems were created not by contract but by the genius of legislators like Moses and Lycurgus. Moses, for example, "had the audacity to create a body politic" out of "a swarm of wretched fugitives"; he "gave them customs and usages." Lycurgus "undertook to give institutions" to Sparta; he "imposed on them an iron yoke."[46] It is really only in the *Contrat social* that Rousseau makes much reference to consent or contract in ancient politics; the usual emphasis, as in the *Économie politique* and *Gouvernement de Pologne*, is on great men, political education, and the absence of a highly developed individual will.[47] As Rousseau put it in an early prize essay called *Discours sur la vertu du héros:* "Men...do not govern themselves by abstract views; one does not make them happy except by forcing them to be, and one has to make them feel happiness in order to make them love it. There is a job for the talents of the hero; it is often through main force that he puts himself in a position to receive the blessings of the men whom he has earlier constrained to bear the yoke of the laws, in order to submit them finally to the authority of reason."[48]

Rousseau may have made errors in analyzing the unified spirit of ancient politics by recognizing the desirable effects of a morality of the common good without recognizing that the very absence of a notion of individual will as supreme had made that morality, and thereby that unity, possible. Nevertheless, Rousseau consistently held that modern calamities caused by self-interest must be avoided and that the political systems created by ancient legislators were better than any modern ones. It did not always occur to Rousseau that both the merely self-interested will which he hated, and the will necessary for consent to conventional society, were part of the same individualistic idiom of modern political thought and perhaps inseparable. Still, he always thought that mere will as such could never create a proper political society. Whatever the confusions over naturalness, will, or the presence or absence of either or both in any political idiom, the problem of political theory, above all in the *Contrat social,* is that of reconciling the requirements of consent, which obligates, and perfect socialization, which makes men one. Men must somehow choose the politically perfect, somehow will that complete socialization that precludes self-division. Will, though the basis of consent, cannot be left as it is in some contract theory, with no proper object. If it is true that will is the source of obligation, it is also true that merely self-interested will is the cause of everything Rousseau hated in modern civilization.[49] And perfect political forms, whatever Rousseau might have said about their being given, must now, in the *Contrat social,* be willed.

Setting all the contradictions and vacillations aside, there are two important elements in the two views that Rousseau held simultaneously: first, that the importance of ancient polity had to do with its unity and its common morality and not with its relation, or lack of it, to contract theory; second, that individual consent (whatever this might do to the "legitimacy" of Sparta) is needed for obligation, which in turn is needed because the state is conventional. It is impossible to make every element of Rousseau both consistent and true to the political principle that he tried to establish: that will is not enough, that perfect polity alone is not enough, that will must be united to perfection, and that perfection must be the standard of what is willed. This synthesizing may be the source of that odd idea the general will: a fusion of the generality (unity, communality) of antiquity with the will (consent, contract) of modernity. (Or perhaps it is more accurate to say that it is one of the sources of that idea, for the actual term *general will* comes from seventeenth-century French theology, specifically the inquiry pursued by the main Augustinians of the Grand Siècle— Arnauld, Pascal, Malebranche—as to whether God has a general will to save all men or only a particular will to save the elect. But Rousseau, following Montesquieu, gives the term an almost wholly secular turn: the city steps into God's place.)[50] What makes Rousseau without doubt the most utopian of all great political theorists is his insistence that even a perfect political system be willed by all who are subject to it. "Undoubtedly," he says, "there is a universal justice derived from reason alone; but this justice, to be admitted among us, must be mutual...conventions and laws are necessary, therefore, to unite rights with duties, and to accomplish the purposes of justice." Though "that which is good and conformable to order is such by the nature of things, independent of human conventions," those conventions are yet required.[51]

Rousseau's political thought is a noble attempt to unite the best elements of contract theory, of individual consent, with his perfect, unified ancient models, which, being founded on a morality of common good, had no private wills to reconcile to the common interest and thus no need of consent, no need of contract. It is this perhaps unconscious and certainly unsystematic attempt to fuse two modes of political thought—to have common good and individual will—that gives Rousseau's political thought the strange cast that some have thought contradictory, a vacillation between individualism and collectivism.[52] But it is not merely that. The questions for Rousseau were more specific and more subtle: How can a man obey only his own free will, the source of obligation, in society? How is it possible to purify this will of mere private interest and selfishness, which create inequality, destroy virtue, and divide man against himself? How is it possible to insure that this individual will will want only what the common good requires? The problem is really one of retaining will while making it more than mere will in order to provide society with a common good and a general interest, as if it enjoyed a morality of the common good—a morality that Rousseau sometimes recognized as the real foundation of ancient unity.

Looked at from this point of view, all of the paradoxes and problems in Rousseau's political philosophy become comprehensible. One sees why will must be retained and why it must be made general; how general laws will promote the common good but why it is not law but legislative will that is final; why a great legislator can suggest perfect political forms but cannot merely impose them. Above all, this point of view helps explain the greatest paradox in all of Rousseau: the paradox created by the fact that in the original contractual situation the motives needed by individuals to relinquish particular will and self-interest and to embrace a general will and the common good cannot exist at the time the compact is made but can only be the result of the socialization and common morality that society alone can create.[53] This is doubtless what Rousseau had in mind when he said that "the general will is always right, but the judgment which guides it is not always equally enlightened." As a result the legislator must help men to "bring their wills into conformity with their reason," and the bringing together of the legislator's genius with the people's inalienable right to consent will "effect a union of understanding and will within the social body." Actually, Rousseau had his doubts about the possibility of this union, doubts that occasionally led him to ask quite radical questions about the plausibility of social contract and consent theory: "for a new-born people to be able to appreciate sound political principles, and to follow the fundamental rules of political necessity, the effect would have to become the cause; the social consciousness to be created by the new institutions would have to preside over the establishment of those same institutions; and men, before laws existed, would have to be as the laws themselves should make them."[54]

If Rousseau did not ordinarily allow this opinion, which could have led him to be a persuasive anticontractarian, to affect his conviction that the people's moral right to consent to the fundamental laws under which they live is inalienable, even if they lack the intellectual capacities that ideally ought to accompany that moral right, he often tried to enlarge and deepen contractarianism, saying in a characteristic passage from the *Première version du contrat social* that "there is a great deal of difference between remaining faithful to the state solely because one has sworn to do it, or because one takes it to be divine and indestructible."[55]

It is certain that if either an ideal of social perfection, such as Sparta, or a notion of conventional society created by will and artifice were enough for Rousseau, he would never have insisted on a combination of will and perfect socialization, on a general will. There would, in fact, be no paradox at all if perfection were only a formal question, if the state were founded on a morality of the common good, and obligation were not a central problem. A great legislator like Moses or Lycurgus could create the best forms, and obedience would be only a matter of corresponding to a system naturally and rationally right. But Rousseau said that in order to will good laws a newborn people must be able to "appreciate sound political principles" that cannot merely be given to them but must be willed. Why is it that "the social consciousness to be created by the new institutions would have to preside over the establishment of those same institutions" unless somehow the people must understand and will the system?[56] There would be no paradox of cause and effect—the central problem of sound politics—in Rousseau if men did not have both to will and to will a perfection that presupposes a transcendence of mere will and the attainment of all the advantages of a morality of the common good without actually having that morality, which would destroy obligation, or at least not take it into account.

It remains to show that the attempted fusion of individual will and common-good morality is comprehended in the notion of the general will.[57] Rousseau begins the *Contrat social* not with the concept of general will but with a fairly traditional contractarian view of the origin of society. Men being naturally, if not by nature, perfectly independent, and society being made necessary only by the introduction of property, men unite by contract to preserve themselves and their property.[58] In this conventional society there is an area of common interest, "for if the opposition of private interests made the establishment of societies necessary, it is the agreement of these same interests that made it possible." It is "what these several interests have in common," Rousseau urges, "that constitutes the social bond." It is only on the "basis of this common interest that society must be governed."[59]

Rousseau does not talk in these rationalistic, contractarian terms for very long. Soon he declares that society's common interest is not merely what a lot of private interests have in common. A perfect society is a complete transformation of these private interests; only when "each citizen is nothing, and can do nothing, without all the rest" can society "be said to have reached the highest attainable peak of perfection." In other words, when society is much like highly unified ancient society, perfection is reached; only "in so far as several men conjoined consider themselves as a single body" can a general will operate.[60]

This transformed society must be governed on the basis of common interest, which has become something more than traditional common interest; only general laws, the creation of a general will (sovereignty), can govern the common interest. Laws must be perfectly general because the general will that makes them "loses its natural rectitude when directed toward any individual and determinate object." The sovereign (the people when active, when willing fundamental law) must make such a law: "the people subject to the laws should be their author; only those who are forming an association have the right to determine the conditions of that society." But if fundamental law is the creation of a general will, how does such a will come about? It cannot be the sum of individual wills, for "the particular will tends by its nature to partiality," and this partiality has been the source of modern "calamities." Law must be willed by those subject to it, for will is the source of obligation. Yet, mere wills can never yield generality, and law must be perfectly general, which can happen only "when the whole people legislates for the whole people." If general laws composed with a view of the common good were enough, there would be no problem; but even the most general laws must be willed. How can a self-interested multitude "by itself execute so great and difficult a project as a system of legislation?"[61] How can a genuine general will that creates general conditions for society arise?

It is on this point that Rousseau is uncharacteristically weak; he is always able to say what a general will must exclude, but he cannot say what it is. This should come as no surprise, for strictly speaking, the ideas of generality and will are mutually exclusive. Will, whatever its crudity as a psychological construct, is characteristically a concept of individuality, of particularity; it is only metaphorically that will can be spoken of as general. No act of philosophic imagination can conjure up anything but a personal will. What can be imagined, and what Rousseau admired in ancient society, is not really a general will but a political morality of the common good in which individual will is not suppressed but simply does not appear in contradistinction to, or with claims or rights against, society. What gave ancient polity its unity was not the concurrence of many wills on central points of common interest but rather a moral idiom in which extreme socialization was natural and in which there was little notion of will and artifice.

There are a number of revealing passages in which Rousseau observes that something like a political morality of common good rather than a general will is necessary for unity and communality. For example, at the end of book 2 of the *Contrat social* he discusses "the most important of all" laws, "which preserves the people in the spirit of its original institutions," that is, "manners, morals, customs and, above all, public opinion...a factor with which the great legislator is secretly concerned when he seems to be thinking only of particular regulations." Here, Rousseau is speaking not of consent or will but of a kind of political education that will promote a sense of the common good. And he gave other indications that he knew that unity was the consequence of thinking about political relations in terms of such a good rather than in terms of canceling out of private wills "all the mutually destructive pluses and minuses" so that a "general will remains as the sum of the differences."[62] Indeed, in the *Économie politique* he says that if men "were early accustomed to regard their individuality only in its relation to the body of the state, and to be aware, so to speak, of their own existence merely as a part of that of the state, they might at length come to identify themselves in some degree with this greater whole." If children are educated in state laws that promote only a common good and a common morality, "they will learn to cherish one another mutually as brothers, to will nothing contrary to the will of society."[63] There are similar passages in the *Gouvernement de Pologne* and in the *Projet pour la Corse*, in which the idea of a morality of the common good, reinforced by political education and legislation, is set forth with little or no reference to consent or will.[64]

Much of the time, however, and particularly in the *Contrat social*, Rousseau speaks not of the common good but of a tension between particular will and general will and of reconciling these wills.[65] Indeed, the whole concept of political virtue is entirely tied up with this reconciliation of wills, as Rousseau demonstrates in the *Économie politique*. There, he says that the "first and most important rule of legitimate or popular government" is "to follow in everything the general will," but that in order to follow the general will it must be known and clearly distinguished from individual or particular will; "this distinction is always very difficult to make, and only the most sublime virtue can afford sufficient illumination for it." A few pages later he says that "if you would have the general will accomplished, bring all particular wills into conformity with it; in other words, as virtue is nothing more than the conformity of the particular wills with the general will, establish the reign of virtue."[66] The argument is circular: the conformity of particular to general will creates virtue, and virtue is necessary to bring particular will into conformity with general will. This circularity is not due to the fact that Rousseau had no clear conception of virtue; on the contrary, ancient polities were models of virtue as he described them.[67] The circularity is caused by his trying to make virtue as unity, as communality, dependent on reconciliation of particular to general will, whereas, as Rousseau himself recognizes in the same treatise, virtue as conformity to a common good morality is the creation of great legislation and political education. Rousseau's vacillation on the true source of unity and communality—reconciliation of wills or absence of will— is the cause of the circularity of his concept of virtue. Moreover, this circularity reflects the same kind of cause-effect paradox as the one that exists in the original contractual situation. In both cases Rousseau knew perfectly well what he admired: the virtue of ancient society and the perfection of laws in ancient politics. It is only when he tries to describe the possibility of these attributes in terms of reconciled will that he falls down. Nor is this surprising, for he did sometimes recognize that the very absence of the problematic notion of will as supreme had constituted the greatness of antiquity.[68] All the paradoxes, circularities, and vacillations in Rousseau are caused by his attempt to fuse moral-political idioms that are incompatible on fundamental points.

An illustration of this point is Rousseau's treatment of Brutus in the *Histoire des moeurs*. In that fragment Rousseau, observing that "it will always be great and difficult to submit the dearest affections of nature to country and virtue," cites Brutus' execution of his treasonous sons as an example of this submission, not ever mentioning that this was no case of submitting particular will to a general will but more likely a case of a common-good morality at work, coupled with the traditional rights of the Roman pater-familias.[69] Yet, in other works written at about the same time he makes no reference to submission of will in Roman society, speaking only of legislation and political education.[70] Nonetheless, despite these vacillations it is easy to see why he attempted a fusion of political idioms. Even though perfect socialization was Rousseau's ultimate ideal, consent and will as the source of obligation were too important to be summarily discarded. Thus the general will, however problematic, was a necessity.

"Actually," says Rousseau in the *Contrat social* "each individual may, as a man, have a private will contrary to, or divergent from, the general will he has as a citizen." This could not, of course, be the case in a state with a common-good morality reinforced by legislation and education, such as the system sketched in the *Économie politique*. The passage from the *Contrat social* shows that in that work, which is the most contractarian of Rousseau's writings and the closest he comes to a systematic political theory, neither mere will nor perfection wins out. In the *Contrat social* there is the possibility that a private person, already a concept of modern individualism, may regard "the artificial person of the state as a fictitious being" and that this "may make him envisage his debt to the common cause as a gratuitous contribution." It seems clear that if Rousseau were not trying, however unsystematically, to reconcile will with perfect socialization, these problems could not exist: the new state could not be considered a fictitious being, for it would educate men to think otherwise; people would not think of their political role as a contribution, because they would naturally be part of a greater whole; and there would be no conflict between man and citizen, because the distinction would not exist. The paradox that a man must be "forced to be free" if his particular will does not conform to the general will indicates that Rousseau tried to gain the advantages of a common-good morality through reconciliation of wills, and this only because will is necessary to obligation.[71]

There is in this, Rousseau's most systematic political work, little postulation of a political morality of the common good as the source of the much-desired unity. Rather, there is a constant attempt to bring particular will into conformity with general will through the efforts of a great legislator. What the great legislator in his wisdom knows to be good supplies the absence of a common-good morality. The difference between the great legislator of ancient politics and Rousseau's ideal legislator corresponds exactly to the difference between giving a perfect form to a nonvoluntaristic and highly unified polity (antiquity) and making people will perfect forms (modernity). In the contractual period "all stand equally in need of guidance." Individuals "must be obliged to bring their wills into conformity with their reason"; that is, they must will that which is in itself rationally best. The combination of individual consent and the legislator's guidance "will effect a union of understanding and will within the social body."[72] What is rationally best, to avoid that self-division caused by half-socialization, is the perfectly united and communal polity of antiquity. The legislator, who effects the bringing of will into conformity with reason not by force but through persuasion and religious devices, supplies the defect of a common-good morality and simply gets each individual to will something like the laws that would have resulted from such a morality.

Michael Walzer is thus wholly correct in saying that while Rousseau denies the legislator "the right to coerce the people," he "insists on his right to deceive the people." But it is not so clear that Walzer is correct when he says that the legislator's persuasive activity "raises the most serious questions about Rousseau's fundamental argument, that political legitimacy rests on will (consent), and not on reason (rightness)."[73] The whole point of generalizing will, of course, is to make it "right"; but a general will is precisely what men do not have until they are transformed into citizens, partly through the "deceit" of Numa, Moses, and Lycurgus. Surely, Rousseau was making a heroic effort to draw will and reason, consent and rightness together, for will avoids willfulness by taking reason—or at least generality—as its object. The will and reason that Walzer holds apart, then, are the very things that Rousseau was trying to fuse. (Whether a generalized will is still will is another, though important, question.)

What Rousseau ultimately posits, in any case, is not a general will, which is hard to conceive, but a will to the generally good, which is conceivable as political perfection requires both truly general laws and consent to them. Rousseau did not, could not, abolish will; but he prescribed the form that it must take, and this form is clearly derived from the generality and unity of ancient politics as Rousseau saw it, but without a morality of common good, which would not have accounted for obligation.

Moreover, not only the form of laws is derived from ancient models; the conditions under which good laws and indeed good states are possible are little more than idealizations of ancient political circumstances. A people is "fit for legislation," according to Rousseau, if it has no old laws; if it is free from threats of invasion and can resist its neighbors; if it is small enough that its "individual members can all know one another"; if it can get along without other peoples; if it is "neither very rich nor very poor" and can be self-sufficient; and if it "combines the firmness of an old people with the docility of a new one."[74] Most of these conditions are abstracted from Rousseau's idealized version of ancient city-states, particularly Sparta. Not only the form of a good political system, then, but also the actual conditions that could make such a system possible are derived from Rousseau's models of perfection.

So far, we may understand Rousseau to have said: (1) a perfect state—that is, a perfectly socialized, united, and communal state—would have perfectly general laws—that is, laws reinforcing Rousseau's vision of a common good; (2) but in order to be obligatory laws, especially the most general laws, must be willed by everyone subject to those laws, and they must be made obligatory, for society is merely conventional; (3) therefore, will must take the form of general laws; (4) but will tends to the particular, and law, though the creation of will, must somehow be general; (5) moreover, for particular wills to appreciate the necessity of general laws, effect would have to become cause; (6) therefore, a great legislator is needed whose instruction can supply the defect of a morality of the common good, the only morality that would naturally produce general laws; (7) but this legislator is impossibly rare, and furthermore he cannot create laws, however general and good, for sovereignty is inalienable; (8) thus, the legislator must have recourse to religion and use it to gain the consent of individuals to the general will; (9) but now consent is something less than real consent, since it is based on an irrational device; (10) finally, the whole system is saved for individual will by the fact that "a people always has a right to change its laws, even the best," that legislative will rather than law itself is supreme, and that the entire social system can be abolished by will, for "there is not, and cannot be, any sort of fundamental law binding on the body of the people, not even the social contract."[75]

Rousseau's contractarianism, then, ultimately reduces itself to two main elements: the need for a great legislator to create a general will and the extreme limitations put on this legislator by the fact that this general will is and must still be will. Both elements are the consequence of his attempting to unite all the requirements of voluntarism with all the advantages of perfect socialization. The legislator may formulate and propose general laws that will produce such socialization, and he can get them "willed" through religious devices; but the sovereign cannot be permanently bound even by perfect laws, and he can change these laws and even dissolve society. Thus, neither perfection nor will has all the claims in Rousseau; but will can finally, even if only in a destructive way, be triumphant, for if a people "is pleased to do itself harm, who has a right to prevent it from doing so?"[76]

Not that this destructive will, this willful will, was Rousseau's aim: on the contrary, he seems to have hoped that at the end of political time men would finally be citizens and would will only the common good by virtue of what they had learned; at the end of political time they might actually be free and not just forced to be free. Political society would finally, at the end of its political education, be in a position to say what Émile says at the end of his domestic education: "I have decided to be what you made me."[77] At this point there would be a "union of will and understanding" in politics, but one in which understanding is not the possession only of a Numa or a Lycurgus. At this point too agreement and contract would really mean something: the general will would be enlightened as well as right, and contract would go beyond the use of religious devices as well as beyond the confidence tricks of the rich. It would *become* true that, in Judith Shklar's felicitous phrase, the general will "conveys everything" that Rousseau "most wanted to say," that it is "a transposition of the most essential individual moral faculty to the realm of public experience."[78] But before the faculty can be enlightened as well as right in the realm of public experience, time and education are needed. Just as, in *Émile*, children must be taught necessity, utility, and finally morality, in that inescapable order, so too in the *Contrat social* a union of will and understanding comes on the scene only at the end. That Rousseau had some such educational parallel in mind is almost certainly indicated in his remarks about the "firmness of an old people" and the "docility of a young one." Whether peoples should be treated as having political infancies is a delicate question, not least for Rousseau himself. After all, his union of will and understanding requires time and shaping, but his fierce independence—plain in the "Stoic" passages of *Émile*, which insist that "there is only one man who gets his own way, he who can get it single-handed"—seems to repulse that shaping.[79] This is plainer still in the rather pathetic passages from the late *Rêveries du promeneur solitaire*, in which Rousseau insists,

> I have never been truly fit for civil society, where all is constraint, obligation, duty; and...my independent nature always made me incapable of those subjections which are

necessary to whoever wants to live with men. So far as I act freely I am good and I only do good; but as soon as I feel the yoke, be it of necessity or of men, I become rebellious or rather restive, and then I am nothing. When I have to do what is contrary to my will, I don't do it at all, whatever happens; I don't even do my own will, because I am weak. I abstain from acting.[80]

Here, *will*—which Jean Starobinski has called a "volonté de liberté immediate"[81]—is as particular as it can very well be. Nonetheless, a city with a general will remains one of Rousseau's models, and by no means the least important.

It is not meant, by analyzing Rousseau in this way, that he was always perfectly consistent in desiring that particular wills should consent to that which an ancient morality of the common good would require; in fact, he vacillated on several points, notably in his treatment of civil religion, in which he allowed any tolerant sect to exist so long as it did not claim exclusive truth or refuse to subscribe to the basic articles of civic religious policy.[82] In this Rousseau is as close to Locke's *Letter concerning Toleration* as he is to a defense of the actual religious policies of antiquity; indeed in his *Lettre à Voltaire*—written in 1756, before his notion of civil religion was formulated—he argued that "all human government is of its nature limited to civil duties, and whatever the sophist Hobbes may have said about this, when a man serves the state well he owes no one an accounting of the way in which he serves God."[83] Rousseau, in fact, insisted in the *Contrat social* that each socialized man should somehow "obey" no one but himself, and thought that he had found a solution to this problem by making the conditions of society (laws) perfectly general and equally applicable to all. Thus, the conditions being equal for all and willed by all, "it is in the interest of no one to make [social requirements] burdensome to the rest"; and since society cannot wish to hurt all its members by enacting bad general laws, society need offer its members no guarantees. But this system is essentially modified (1) by the fact that a will to general laws cannot be attained with mere wills as they are—the cause-effect problem again—but only through the influence of a great legislator; (2) by Rousseau's assertion that there is no real limit to the extent of undertakings possible between the sovereign and its members; (3) by the idea that the sovereign is the sole judge of how many powers of individuals must be socialized; and (4) by the notion that an ideal society should be very highly socialized indeed.[84] It is modified above all by book 4, chapter 2 of the *Contrat social*, which shows perhaps more clearly than anything else in Rousseau that consent is no longer a question of mere volition and that the general will is rather like a modified common-good morality.

> The constant will of all the members of the state is the general will; that is what makes them citizens and free. When a law is proposed in the assembly of the people, what the voters are being asked is not precisely whether they do or do not approve of the proposal, but whether or not it is in conformity with the general will, which is their own. Each, when casting his vote, gives his opinion on this question; and the declaration of the general will is found by counting the ballots. Thus when an opinion contrary to my own prevails, this proves nothing more than that I was mistaken, and that what I thought to be the general will was not.[85]

The meaning of this usually confusing passage, which is paradoxical precisely because it uses voluntarist language in a way that seems to make some people's wills not count, can be understood if the phrase *common good* is substituted for *general will*; then it can be seen how general will is constant will and how citizens are being asked not whether they approve a proposal but whether it is in conformity with a common good, a good comprising their own highest good. The substitution, however, can be only temporary, since Rousseau did not use the idea of the general will through mere inadvertence.

With all of these modifications in mind, it is clear that while Rousseau's theory of society and law really is, as he insisted, an attempt to preserve liberty, that liberty is conceived in a particular way: it is obedience to self-imposed law, which must, of course, be general law.[86] Liberty, then, comes down to freeing the individual from all private dependence by making him "very dependent on the city" and its general and equally applied laws. But though liberty is obedience to self-imposed law, proper law cannot be created without modification of will by a great legislator; thus, the idea of liberty is, like other elements of Rousseau, a fusion of the idioms of individual will and of highly unified society. It is because of these modifications that Rousseau's political philosophy cannot be so easily assimilated to traditional constitutionalism, or to Kant's theory of law, as some have suggested.[87] It is legislative will and not law itself that is supreme in Rousseau. Nor can Rousseau be easily assimilated to the German romantic tradition of the early nineteenth century, for he would never have replaced general will with the historical evolution of national spirits; he was certain that history in itself cannot justify anything.[88] This unassimilability to other traditions proves that those who view Rousseau as a unique and rather isolated figure are probably correct; he was, in his own words, one of those few "moderns who had an ancient soul."[89]

The object of this study has been to elucidate the concept of the general will and to clear up some of the paradoxes in the *Contrat social* by analyzing what Rousseau thought about will and contract on the one hand and about perfect political systems on the other. It has not been a central object to attack Rousseau as unsystematic, to reproach him for not adequately reconciling two modes of political thought, or to improve his ideas by making them more consistent. No series of conceptual ambiguities can detract anything from Rousseau's status as the greatest of political psychologists and the most eloquent critic of the psychological destruction wrought by inequality.[90] Nonetheless, it is evident that there is a serious conceptual problem in Rousseau's political thought. Voluntarist theories are usually composed of two parts: a theory of will as a kind of moral causality and a theoretical standard of right to which will ought to conform, arbitrary willfulness usually being rejected as a standard of right. In Locke or in Kant the standard of right to which will must conform—a fairly conventional natural law in the first case, a rather unusual one in the second—does not contradict voluntarism, once the problem of reconciling free will and absolute standards has been put aside. But in Rousseau, who ordinarily rejected natural law,[91] the standard to which will must conform—ancient perfection or its equivalent—is itself nonvoluntaristic; therefore, will and the standard to which it must conform are contradictory. The standard that gives will its object is the very negation of voluntarism. It is for this reason that Rousseau's political system is somewhat paradoxical. The idea of general will, the paradox of cause and effect in the original contractual situation, the circularity of the concept of virtue—all these are due to his attempt to fuse the advantages of a politics founded on will with one founded on reason and perfection. For Rousseau, men must will the kind of society in which they live, for "to deprive your will of all freedom is to deprive your actions of all morality," and this deprivation destroys the obligation men have to obey.[92] Yet, mere will can yield only particularity and inequality and can never produce social perfection.

To retain the moral attributes of will but to do away with will's particularity and selfishness: that is the problem of Rousseau's political thought. It is a problem that reflects Rousseau's difficulty with making free will and rational authority coexist in his moral and political thinking. Freedom of the will is as important to the morality of actions for Rousseau as for any traditional voluntarist; that is clear in every period of his thought, and not least in the magnificent *Lettre à M. de Franquières* (1769), in which Rousseau urges his correspondent to abandon a materialism and a determinism that are fatal to morals:

> Why do you not appreciate that the same law of necessity which, according to you, rules the working of the world, and all events, also rules all the actions of men, every thought in their heads, all the feelings of their hearts, that nothing is free, that all is forced, necessary, inevitable, that all the movements of man which are directed by blind matter, depend on his will only because his will itself depends on necessity; that there are in consequence neither virtues, nor vices, nor merit, nor demerit, nor morality in human actions, and that the words "honorable man" or "villain" must be, for you, totally void of sense...Your honest heart, despite your arguments, declaims against your sad philosophy. The feeling of liberty, the charm of virtue, are felt in you despite you.[93]

Rousseau was nevertheless suspicious of the very faculty that could moralize. That is why he urged, in the *Économie politique*, that "the most absolute authority is that which penetrates into a man's inmost being, and concerns itself no less with his will than with his actions."[94] Can the will be both morally autonomous and subject to the rationalizing influence of authority? That was the point that Rousseau never altogether settled. Even Émile, the best-educated of men, chooses to continue to accept the guidance of his teacher: "Advise and control us; we shall be easily led; as long as I live I shall need you."[95] How much more, then, ordinary men need the guidance of a great legislator when they embark on setting up a system that will not only aid and defend but also moralize them. The relation of volition to authority is one of the most difficult and inscrutable problems in Rousseau; the general will is dependent on "a union of understanding and will within the social body," but that understanding, which is provided by authority, weakens the idea of will as an autonomous authorizing faculty.[96]

This notion of the relation of educative authority to will appears not just in Rousseau's theories of public or national education— particularly in the *Économie politique* and the *Gouvernement de Pologne*—but also in his theory of private education in *Émile*: in educating a child, Rousseau advises the tutor, "let him think he is master while you are really master." And then: "There is no subjection so complete as that which preserves the forms of freedom; it is thus that the will itself is taken captive."[97] One can hardly help asking what has become of will when it has been taken captive, and whether it is enough to preserve the mere forms of freedom. On this point Rousseau appears to have been of two minds: the poor who agree to a social contract that merely legitimizes the holdings of the rich "preserve the forms of freedom," after all, and yet Rousseau dismisses this contract as a fraud. It cannot simply be the case—as John Charvet argues in his remarkable study of Rousseau—that Rousseau was not "worried by the gap which opens up between the appearance and the reality of freedom."[98] And yet Charvet has a point, since according to Rousseau will is taken captive (*Émile*) and penetrated by authority (*Économie politique*); but Rousseau criticizes neither this captivity nor this penetration, despite the Rousseauean dictum that depriving the will of freedom deprives actions of all morality. So it is again clear why a general will would appeal to him: capricious willfulness would be canceled, will rationalized by authority preserved.

At a higher level of generality it can be said that Rousseau's difficulties arise from a vacillating attitude toward the nature and genesis of moral ideas. Sometimes, like the older contractarians, he treats men as morally complete prior to socialization, or at least he holds that if contractarianism were to work, men would have to know in creating society what they can know only at the end of the socializing process. More often he treats moral conceptions as if they arise by degrees as that process unfolds: "When, through a development whose course I have shown, men begin to cast their eyes on their fellow men, they also begin...to learn ideas of fitness, of justice and of order; the fineness of morality begins to become sensible to them, and conscience becomes active: then they have virtues..."[99]

Perhaps a species of moral à priorism is essential to genuine and full contractarianism: after all, if society must be legitimized at its outset, the source of that legitimacy—the wills of individuals—must in some sense be prior to society. But this is exactly the point on which Rousseau had his doubts, sometimes treating the capacity to make moral judgments and decisions as something all but innate, sometimes treating it as a learned ability that comes from the political education afforded by great legislators.

It is not useful, however, to "bracket out" either of these strains in Rousseau in an effort to make him more consistent: such a bracketing out is, after all, precisely the operation that he himself did not perform. In any case, one can see how a purely noncontractarian Rousseau would look by examining the wonderfully cogent and consistent *Économie politique*. However, the fact remains that he saw fit to call his principal political work *Du contrat social*, and it is hard to believe that there was no reason for this.

To project the question on a grander scale, there is in Rousseau's political thought an intuitive attempt to reconcile the two greatest traditions of Western political philosophy: that of will and artifice and that of reason and nature, in Michael Oakeshott's phrase. General will is surely rationalized will. Yet, it is not self-rationalized will, in a Kantian sense, but will rationalized by the standards and conditions of idealized ancient polity.

Whatever Rousseau's means in undertaking a fusion of two great modes of political thinking, and however unsuccessful his attempt to make general will a viable concept, one must always, while analyzing and even criticizing the result, grant the grandeur and importance of the effort. If it were possible to have the best of both idioms, the result would be a political philosophy that would synthesize almost everything valued in the history of Western political philosophy.

⊸⊰ 5 ⊱⊸

On Kant as the Most Adequate
of the Social Contract Theorists

*K*_{ANT'S} political philosophy is often taken to be part of the social contract tradition that began with Hobbes and was developed by Locke and Rousseau. In many ways this view is quite correct, since Kant always said that an ideal state, or a true republic, must conform to the Idea of the social contract, that "the act through which a people constitutes itself a state, or to speak more properly the Idea of such an act, in terms of which alone its legitimacy can be conceived, is the original contract by which all (*omnes et singuli*) the people surrender their outward freedom in order to resume it at once as members of a common entity, that is, the people regarded as the state (*universi*)."[1] Despite the obvious influence of Rousseau, the word *Idea* in this passage separates Kant from the contractarian tradition even while linking him with it, for in Kantian political philosophy the notion of the contract becomes hypothetical, as does so much else in his system, including freedom and the will. The social contract is an idea of reason that provides a standard for judging the adequacy of states and their laws, but it has nothing to do with actual agreement or with an actual promise to obey. Here, indeed, Kant means Idea in quite a strict sense: as he says in *The Conflict of the Faculties,* the notion of a state that corresponds to the Idea of a social contract "may be called a Platonic Ideal (*respublica noumenon*) which is not an empty figment of the imagination, but the eternal norm for all civil constitutions whatsoever."[2] That this ideal is not meant to require actual consenting and promising Kant makes quite plain in his important *Theory and Practice:* "an original contract...is in fact merely an *idea* of reason, which nonetheless has undoubted practical reality; for it can oblige every legislator to frame his laws in such a way that they could have been produced by the united will of a whole nation, and to regard each subject, in so far as he can claim citizenship, as if he had consented within the general will."[3] Kant says the same thing in a slightly different way in the *Handschriftlicher Nachlass*, where he urges that the social contract is "not a principle explaining the origin of the civil society" but one "explaining how it ought to be." It is not a principle that actually establishes the state through historical consent but one that provides "the idea of legislation, administration, and public legal justice."[4]

To be sure, Kant does not always keep this ideal so abstract. Sometimes he puts it in a clearly political form that also obviously owes a great deal to Rousseau: "What the people (the mass of subjects) cannot decide with regard to themselves or their fellows also cannot be decided by the sovereign regarding them." Kant uses this principle to show that a people could not "throw away" freedom by agreeing, for example, to the existence of a hereditary nobility that does not merit its rank: "it is impossible that the general will of the people would consent to such a groundless prerogative, and therefore neither can the sovereign make it valid."[5] Kant's ideal or hypothetical contractarianism, then, has a great deal in common with the Rousseauean notion that the people as sovereign could reasonably agree to universally applicable laws that bear equally on all citizens but not to particular privileges.[6]

In reformulating the social contract as an Idea of reason that shows what a people could reasonably agree to, Kant is obviously trying to avoid a number of difficulties. Above all, the reformulation allows him to meet Hume's anti-Lockean historical objection that states ordinarily arise through force and violence, not through agreement or promise.[7] Here, Kant simply agrees with Hume; and he can afford to, since the Idea of the contract is a standard only for judging present legislation and administration. He also avoids theories of a right of revolution based on breaches of the social contract by rulers. Since for Kant the ruler's authority is derived not from consent or a promise to obey but from his being the executor of a public legal justice—which, as a context for morality, is dictated by practical reason itself—he is able to say that, imperfect legality being better than "anarchy," subjects must obey even if a ruler violates the Idea of the contract. One cannot stop with this seeming endorsement of political quietism, however, since Kant also holds that the people are sovereign, though perhaps only in the sense that all law must be such that they could consent to it. He also holds that it is the ruler's duty to make the state conform more and more to the Idea of the contract and that the results of inherently unjust revolutions that bring the state closer to this Idea, even by removing a lawful ruler, should not be overturned, since this would involve regression.[8] For the moment it is sufficient to point out that Kant was trying to rescue what he conceived as the essential element of contractarianism—the notion that all laws must be such that rational men could consent to them—from charges of historical unreality as well as from what he apparently took to be anarchistic implications of the doctrine in some forms, such as Locke's theory of a right of revolution.[9]

Kant also had a good moral reason for treating contract and consent as Ideas of reason. He speaks of what a people could not will, could not consent to. It is clear, however, that a people could, in the abstract, consent to anything. This had been Rousseau's objection to traditional contractarianism: it could be used to legitimize authoritarianism, as in Hobbes.[10] But a moral being could not consent to laws that would violate morality or its political-legal preconditions. This is why Kant insists, in *The Conflict of the Faculties*, on political principles "akin in spirit to the laws of freedom which a people of mature rational powers would prescribe for itself, even if the people is not asked literally for its consent."[11] As an Idea of reason to which laws must conform, this hypothetical consent—which insists on laws of freedom, on maturity, on rationality—can restrict abuses in a way that actual consent might not. Thus, Kant does not have to struggle, like Rousseau, to get the particular will to generalize itself, to think as a citizen and not as a man, because consent can be treated as a standard.[12]

It is important to try at the outset to clarify the relation of Kant's political philosophy in general to his moral philosophy in general, for he clearly subordinates politics to morality while at the same time basing politics on "right," not on utility or happiness. As he said in his letter to Jung-Stilling (March 1789), "The laws...must be given not as arbitrary and accidental commandments for some purposes that happen to be desired but only insofar as they are necessary for the achievement of universal freedom."[13] As is well known, Kant often insisted that the only unqualifiedly good thing on earth is a good will[14]—a will that acts on the basis of maxims that can be universalized in a way that does not violate the dignity of men as "ends in themselves."[15] Every element of this definition—the concept of will, the idea of universality, the problem of persons as ends—is directly relevant to Kant's political philosophy. That is, if a good or moral will is the only unqualifiedly good thing on earth—which does not, of course, mean that everything else is therefore worthless—then politics, among other qualified goods, must be instrumental to morality. A merely powerful and stable, even glorious state that pursues moral evil cannot be praiseworthy. This is doubtless why Kant urges, in *Eternal Peace*, that "true politics cannot take a single step without first paying homage to morals." If, he grants, there exists "no freedom and no moral law based upon it, and if everything which happens. . . is simply part of the mechanism of nature," then it is appropriate to manipulate men as natural objects in order to govern them; but if right is to be the "limiting condition of politics," morality and politics must be conceded to be "compatible," capable of coexistence.[16]

While it is quite clear that Kant invariably ranks morality, or acting dutifully from duty, above mere legality, or acting dutifully for any reason that will produce the desired external conduct[17]—here prudence, fear, benevolence, sympathy, or love of order would suffice—something more needs to be said about the relation between morality and legality. If a good will, or morality, is the only unqualified good, then politics and public legal justice can only be instrumental to the possibility of that good will. And instrumentality, for Kant, is quite important: as he says in the *Critique of Practical Reason*, "Whatever diminishes the obstacles to an activity furthers this activity itself."[18] In Kant, though, there are different ways of being instrumental to morality. Happiness, for example, though it is something that cannot directly and in itself be a duty, let alone something from which the concept of a duty can be derived, may indirectly become a duty if it can be seen as supportive of morality. It may, Kant allows in *Practical Reason,* be a duty to provide for our own happiness partly because some of the elements of happiness—skill, riches—can provide "means for the fulfilment of our duty," partly because the absence of happiness in the form of poverty may tempt us to transgress our duty. "But it can never," Kant adds, "be an immediate duty to promote our happiness, still less can it be the principle of all duty."[19]

Legality, and rightful politics generally, cannot be instrumental to morality in this way, because law and morals commonly require the same things: they both prohibit murder, fraud, and so forth. Only the incentive of obedience to the demands of practical reason differs in morality and legality; as Kant says in the *Rechtslehre*, "Jurisprudence and ethics are distinguished...not so much by their different duties as by the difference in the legislation that combines one or the other incentive with the law."[20] On the difference between moral and legal incentives Kant speaks quite clearly: "What is essential in the moral worth of actions is that the moral law should directly determine the will. If the determination of the will takes place in conformity indeed to the moral law, but only by means of a feeling, no matter of what kind, which has to be presupposed in order that the law may be sufficient to determine the will, and therefore not for the sake of the law, then the action will possess legality but not morality."[21]

Legality and morality, then, are concerned with duties, for example the duty not to kill. Happiness, on the other hand, might well involve killing, though Kant would add that since the good will is never extinguished, even in evil men, there would be a conflict between this *Schadenfreude* and a knowledge of its wrongness.[22] As a result, happiness cannot be instrumental to morality in the same way that political or public legal justice is. Happiness can indirectly become a duty; adherence to the law established by the political order is in itself and directly a duty, whatever one's incentive may be. But political-legal justice is still only instrumental to morality because politics can operate on the basis of any incentive to obedience. A good political order, Kant says in *Eternal Peace*, is possible "even for a people of devils, if only they have intelligence, though this may sound harsh."[23] If it is possible for devils it is certainly possible for, say, Benthamites trying to maximize their utility function. (It is not, of course, even conceivable to Kant that public legal justice should try to moralize men; law is precisely external, and morality is nothing unless internal duty alone is the incentive of obedience.)[24]

For Kant there is a duty to enter into a "juridical state of affairs," because moral freedom involves both the "negative" freedom of the will from "determination by sensible impulses" and the "positive" freedom of a will that is determined by pure practical reason itself—by what ought to be, by respect for persons as objective ends. Negative freedom is thus instrumental to, or the condition of, positive freedom.[25] If this is the case, and if public legal justice can remove or control some of the objects that cause human will to be shaped by impulse—if politics can control, for instance, a fear of violence that would lead one to violate the categorical imperative—then politics is supportive of morality because it advances negative freedom. This point is well made by Kant himself in the first appendix to *Eternal Peace,* and in a way that has the incidental merit of showing that Kant, like Hobbes before him, took the problem of possible dangers to the "first performer" of moral actions seriously. By putting an end to outbreaks of lawlessness, government, or public legal justice, "genuinely makes it much easier for the moral capacities of men to develop into an immediate respect for right." Every man believe that he would conform his conduct to what is right if only he could be certain that everyone else would do likewise; and "the government in part guarantees this for him." By creating a coercive order of public legal justice, "a great step is taken *toward* morality (although this is still not the same as a moral step), towards a state where the concept of duty is recognized for its own sake."[26]

None of this should be construed to mean that Kant set too low a value on legality; indeed, one of the principal charges against his political theory is that he assessed it at too high a rate, even when it conflicts with what morality appears to demand. It was Kant, after all, who said that "if public legal justice perishes it is no longer worthwhile for men to remain alive on this earth."[27] But this high valuation does not lower the superior claims of morality in his system. Kant even derives the notion of God from human moral knowledge. "So far," he insists in the *Critique of Pure Reason,* "as practical reason has the right to serve as our guide, we shall not look upon actions as obligatory because they are the commands of God, but shall regard them as divine commands because we have an inward obligation to them."[28] The idea of God, he adds in the *Fundamental Principles of the Metaphysic of Morals,* is derived from "the idea of moral perfection, which reason frames *a priori* and connects inseparably with the notion of a free will."[29] In view of the supremacy of morality it is perhaps best to say that in Kant politics and public legal justice set up a context supportive of negative freedom in which men obey duties demanded by reason on the basis of any incentive that will produce appropriate external conduct.

What is then most necessary in politics is liberty: a liberty that, by constraining others in giving me rights, will both remove impediments to morality and allow the unrestricted enjoyment of those things that morality does not forbid.[30] What is essential is a harmony of my external freedom with that of others according to a universal law. One of Kant's finest statements of this view is in the *Critique of Pure Reason:* "a constitution allowing the greatest possible human freedom in accordance with laws which insure that the freedom of each can co-exist with the freedom of all the others (not one designed to provide the greatest possible happiness. . .), is at all events a necessary idea which must be made the basis not only of the first outline of a political constitution but of all laws as well."[31] The doctrine of liberty in Kant has two sides: the restrictive and the permissive. Liberty restricts what others can do to me by the exercise of their wills—things that might make it more difficult for me to be moral—and it permits what is morally indifferent.

Kant's whole system, including the quasicontractarian politics, works if his moral philosophy works, since politics only creates a context for morality, or at best insures that moral laws will be obeyed for nonmoral reasons—that is, that moral ends will be realized through "legal" incentives. Thus, there is in Kant no problem of political obligation through consent, contract, or promise as there is in Hobbes and Rousseau. Objective moral law is ultimate, and politics not only creates a context for it but even enforces part of it, at least insofar as external conduct is concerned. Men are thus obliquely obliged to the political order without explicit voluntary acts.

This is true despite the fact that Kant is the one member of the contractarian school who arrives at a conception of will adequate to account for the possibility of consent, promise, and obligation as intelligible ideas and who could have developed a theory of political obligation based on consent and promise. Nonetheless, political obligations exist in Kant not by virtue of consent, promise, and the like but by virtue of obeying dictates of duty commanded by the categorical imperative for nonmoral reasons. When Kant says in the *Rechtslehre* that state laws must be conceived as the product of a hypothetical general will of the whole people as sovereign, this must be understood within a context of natural law. As a believer in his own version of natural law, Kant could not hold that consent, or even the Idea of consent, was the sole standard of right. In his *Rechtslehre,* indeed, he defines natural laws as "those to which an obligation can be recognized *a priori* by reason without external legislation," whereas positive laws are those that "would neither obligate nor be laws without actual external legislation."[32] The public legal order will certainly make and enforce positive laws; it will also enforce, though it will not make, some natural laws—for example, against murder and theft—though it cannot require that men abstain from violating politically enforced natural laws for moral reasons (out of duty itself). But consent, or rather the Idea of it, can be important in Kant only in the context of natural law. In general, for Kant those laws are legitimate that could have been consented to by a mature, rational people *and* that are congruent with natural law.

This *and* is not very satisfactory; someone might say that the effort to represent Kant as a contractarian, even an ideal contractarian, is doomed if natural law alone shapes the really important things in the Kantian political order. Or someone might at least say that whether Kant is any kind of contractarian at all turns on a correct reading of his moral philosophy, since "true politics cannot take a single step without first paying homage to morals." If the core of Kant's ethics is identified as the teleological notion that "a rational nature exists as an end in itself," and that such a rational nature (man) is an objective end that is the source of the categorical imperative,[33] then murder and all lesser crimes are ruled out on grounds of counterpurposiveness; and public legal justice, as a reflection of morality so conceived, may be thought of mainly as enforcing objective ends through mere legal motives. But if, in the manner of Lewis White Beck, the notion is stressed that Kant agrees with Rousseau that "obedience to a law that one has prescribed is the only real freedom," and that in Kant's hands Rousseau's "doctrine of self-government" is "deepened into a moral and metaphysical doctrine,"[34] it can be said that the moral law is made, not found, and that by reasonable analogy state law is also made by agreement and not found in objective ends. In short, the extent to which Kant is a contractarian in politics might be thought to depend on whether he is a contractarian in morals, given that politics pays "homage" to morals.

Even on the strongest teleological reading of Kant's ethics—one in which objective ends constitute morality and shape politics— contract could still have a place in Kant's politics.[35] For Kant citizens of a republic arguably would not consent to adventuristic wars, since they might be ruined by those wars. Thus, republican citizens would dissent from war out of the "legal" motive of self-love.[36] It may be, then, that a republic under the Idea of the contract yields, from purely legal motives, a political state of affairs that coincides with some moral requirements, such as eternal peace. This would merely reflect Kant's claim that morality and law share duties or ends or purposes but differ over motives. Since rational beings would have to acknowledge social practices, a contractarian republic might be more likely than other forms of government to bring legality closer to morality, even if the content of that morality were found in objective ends, not made by agreement. On this view, even if Kant's moral thought were not "deepened Rousseau," quasi-Rousseauean ideal contractarianism could still figure in the political-legal realm.

The distinction between legality and morality is, of course, one of the most important in Kant. Nonetheless, he does seem to hope that politics and morality will, at some point in the future, draw closer together—not in the sense that a moral incentive could ever become the motive for obedience to public legal justice but in the sense that, as the world is increasingly republicanized, as states more adequately embody the Idea of the original contract, politics will no longer demand what morality positively forbids. As men come closer to enlightenment, Kant suggests, they will alter the structure of politics more and more until the state is finally republican—that is, such that every organ of it treats men as free, autonomous, and legally equal persons, and everyone either consents to law through a representative system or lives under laws worthy of consent.[37] As the process of rational historical evolution produces universal republicanism, the political-legal context provided by states will violate morality less often. In a "cosmopolitical" order of eternal peace in which states voluntarily enter into a permanent equilibrium striking a balance between the "intrinsically healthy resistance" of states and absolute chaos, states will no longer require their citizens to be spies, poisoners, and traitors.[38] As states become more republican, as a world order of an equilibrium of republican states emerges, Kant argues in the *Idea for a Universal History*, politics at the national and international level will increasingly become simply that uniform context that gives men the opportunity to have the kind of will they ought to have. The political order will then be parallel to the moral order, though never identical to it. All of these points Kant makes clear in his late and unaccountably neglected *The Conflict of the Faculties*:

> The profit which will accrue to the human race as it works its way forward will not be an ever-increasing quantity of *morality* in its attitudes. Instead, the *legality* of its attitudes will produce an increasing number of actions governed by duty, whatever the particular motive behind these actions may be... Violence will gradually become less on the part of those in power, and obedience towards the laws will increase... and this will ultimately extend to the external relations between the various peoples, until a cosmopolitan society is created.[39]

At the end of time—and Kant calls this the last, though most important, human problem to be settled—politics and morality may finally be able to coexist.

Even if politics and morality are one day able to live together, however, legality will still be merely instrumental to morality; and since Kant excludes utilitarian and "eudaemonistic" defenses of politics, a political order can be no better than the moral order it makes more nearly possible. What is essential is to try to meet some of the chief objections to Kant's moral philosophy, then to see whether his political and legal ideas are at least congruent with this moral system. On this last point there are some well-known problems: whether there can ever be a duty to disobey political laws on moral grounds (a particularly difficult question for a natural law theorist); whether forcing men into a political-legal order does not treat them as means to a merely utilitarian end—security; whether revolution could be justified if it brings the state closer to republicanism and the Idea of the social contract, and so forth.

When it comes to meeting objections to Kant's moral philosophy as such, leaving politics temporarily out of account, there are even greater difficulties. Among these objections perhaps the most serious is Hegel's contention that Kantian morality is abstract, formal, and without content; that politics cannot be viewed as instrumental to a mere empty formalism, and one that makes will and freedom only hypothetical at that; that if freedom is to be preserved as something real, and if *will* is granted a content other than bare universality and the self-satisfaction of following duty for duty's sake, then it is necessary to posit and defend an ethics, amounting to custom seen as the actualization of rational will, that goes beyond mere good will and establishes something objective— the state—as distinguished from the subjectivism of Kantianism.[40] Hegel's objections can be rejected as politically inspired; he increasingly saw Kantianism as symptomatic of the kind of spiritual disease that led to the French Revolution, if not as an actual cause of it.[41] Nonetheless, his objections are only a particular and peculiar version of a wholly nonpolitical charge that is harder to meet, namely that even if Kant's moral philosophy is not exclusively formal and contentless, what content it does have is imported from the outside, or at least is arbitrarily assumed; that the successive formulations of the categorical imperative, which begin with the mere form of universality but end with the notion of respect for the dignity of men as ends-in-themselves, are not all really "the same" (as Kant says they are) without these outside importations and arbitrary assumptions. The non-Hegelian forms of this objection are the hardest to meet; but if they can be met, then Kant is largely vindicated, because the other objections can be met with greater confidence. For example, it is sometimes urged that there are two quite different and perhaps incompatible theories of will in Kant;[42] but since the coherence of his theory of will is one of the main elements of his superiority as a voluntarist over Hobbes, Locke, and Rousseau, this charge must be rebutted.

If Kant's moral philosophy can be defended along its main lines, and if it can be shown that a Kantian political-legal order is instrumental to morality, or rather to morality's duties or ends as distinguished from morality's incentives, and if a republic under the Idea of the social contract is the political-legal order most instrumental to or most congruent with morality, then the whole Kantian system is successful. Thus, the real question concerning Kant's political philosophy is: How successful is his moral philosophy?

Kant proposes to build his moral philosophy on the notion of a good will: that is, on the notion of a kind of moral "causality," itself uncaused by nature, that is the source of man's freedom and responsibility.[43] In insisting on the will as a kind of moral causality Kant obviously bears a relation to the voluntarists who came before him, and particularly to Rousseau, who had urged in the *Discourse on Inequality* that while "physics" might explain in part the mechanism of the senses and even the formation of ideas, "in the power of willing or rather of choosing, and in the feeling of this power, nothing is to be found but acts which are purely spiritual and wholly inexplicable by the laws of mechanism." With this much Kant could agree; but he could not accept Rousseau's opposing free agency to understanding, nor could he allow Rousseau's dictum that "if I am bound to do no injury to my fellow-creatures, this is less because they are rational than becaus they are sentient beings."[44] Here, in Kant's view, Rousseau spoils what began well—that is, with free will. On Rousseau's view, Kant believes, men would have no duties to each other if they did not feel the pleasures and pains of others as sentient beings. But duty would then be contingent on having a feeling, such as sympathy, which would reduce it to an epiphenomenon of a psychology whose content might differ from day to day and minute to minute. Kant wanted to preserve and defend Rousseau's notion of will as uncaused causality but to remove Rousseau's distinction between reason and will; he wanted to show how a truly free will would be determined by practical reason itself. All of this he made clear in an important passage from the *Fundamental Principles of the Metaphysic of Morals:* "Everything in nature works according to laws. Rational beings alone have the faculty of acting according to the conception of laws, that is according to principles, i.e. have a *will.* Since the deduction of actions from principles requires reason, the will is nothing but practical reason...The will is a faculty to choose that only which reason independent of inclination recognizes as practically necessary, i.e. good."[45]

What Kant is saying, in effect, is that Rousseau ruined his own distinction between physics and free agency by relating a good will to a nonrational sympathy for sentient beings—to the involuntary, prerational *morale sensitive* of the *Lettres morales*[46]—because sympathy and sentience are both, as "pathological" feelings, part of nature, caused by nature. It is not possible to escape Rousseau's laws of mechanism by drawing a line between free agency and reason. In Kant's view duty cannot be deduced out of sympathy, feelings of pleasure and pain, or happiness simply because, however one revolves these psychological notions, a concept of "ought" cannot be extracted from them. Why this is so Kant makes particularly plain in a passage from the *Critique of Pure Reason* that is the foundation of his whole moral position.

That our reason has causality, or that we at least represent it to ourselves as having causality, is evident from the *imperatives* which in all matters of conduct we impose as rules upon our active powers. "Ought" expresses a kind of necessity ...which is found nowhere else in the whole of nature. The understanding can know in nature only what is, what has been, or what will be...When we have the course of nature alone in view, "ought" has no meaning whatsoever.[47]

It is for this reason, Kant urges, that writers such as Hume made such serious mistakes in explaining how concepts of duty, virtue, and so on are in principle conceivable. Hume had held in the *Treatise of Human Nature* that an action or sentiment or character is "virtuous or vicious" because "its view causes a pleasure or uneasiness of a particular kind," that to have a sense of virtue "is nothing but to feel a satisfaction of a particular kind from the contemplation of a character," and that this very feeling "constitutes" our praise or admiration. It is true that by pleasure or satisfaction of a particular kind Hume meant not aesthetic or physical pleasure but a pleasure caused "only when a character is considered in general, without reference to our particular interest."[48] But this qualification could not, in Kant's view, save the theory. Those who think that "a certain moral sense" connects virtue with feelings of pleasure and vice with "mental unrest and pain," he urges, simply reduce all morality to a desire for happiness. "In order to represent a vicious man as tormented by psychic anxiety as a result of being aware of his transgressions, they must first represent him as fundamentally morally good ...Therefore they must represent him as already virtuous who is pleased with the consciousness of dutiful action. Hence the concept of morality and duty must precede any thought of this satisfaction and cannot be derived from it."[49]

In this connection Kant's strictures against deriving the concept of morality from feelings of happiness or pleasure ought to be mentioned. As is well known, Kant is sometimes represented as being opposed to human happiness, and there are even a few passages in his work that lend force to this view, for example, his saying that "the majesty of duty has nothing to do with the enjoyment of life."[50] Even in less extreme statements, however, he is quite strict: it is every man's own special feeling of pleasure and pain that determines in what he is to find his happiness, and even in a single person the content of happiness will change as his wants and feelings change; therefore happiness cannot furnish objective principles of conduct or indeed any principles at all.[51] Here Kant actually agrees with Hobbes that felicity is relative to the pleasures and pains of individuals, though without agreeing with Hobbes's solution to this problem.

Elsewhere in Kant's writing, however, it is clear that he is not opposed to happiness itself but only to efforts to derive the concept of morality from it. The best statement of this view is found in his *Theory and Practice*. Man is not expected to renounce his natural aim of attaining happiness, Kant argues, for "he simply cannot do so." All that is necessary is that one "abstract" from considerations of happiness when a question of duty is involved, that one not make happiness "a *condition* of his obeying the law prescribed to him by reason."[52] Taking this passage into account, and recalling that for

Kant happiness may indirectly become a duty if it is instrumental to duty itself, there is ultimately no reason to say that Kant is hostile to happiness.

Kant, then, wants to ground morality in the notion of a free will's obeying laws given by reason, not in happiness, pleasure, or utility. Indeed, one of the main aspects of Kant's superiority to earlier voluntarists is that his conception of will, of voluntariness as an essential component of morality, is far more adequate and coherent than theirs. Here, of course, a certain irony emerges: while Kant is not a contractarian in the literal sense—that is, he does not base political duties on explicit voluntary acts such as consent and even modifies the Idea of consent by insisting on natural law—he was in the best position of any voluntarist to be a literal contractarian had he wanted to be one. Kant's theory of will would have served the strict contractarians extremely well and would have provided Hobbes and Locke with better notions of willing than appetite and uneasiness.[53] But Kant himself uses the idea of a good or free will only in relation to morality and reduces the contract to an Idea of reason that regulates and judges a politics that can only be instrumental to that morality.

Turning from these considerations to the conception of the will itself in Kant, it is clear that he was able to avoid most of the confusions over the notion of will that had introduced a degree of incoherence into the voluntarist and contractarian tradition by defining the will as "a faculty of determining oneself to action in accordance with the conception of certain laws," as "a kind of causality belonging to living beings insofar as they are rational."[54] A being that is capable of acting according to the conception of laws, Kant suggests, is an intelligence or rational being, and "the causality of such a being according to this conception of laws is his will."[55] Freedom, he argues, is the capacity of this will-as-causality to be efficient—to produce moral effects—independent of "foreign causes" determining that will.[56] For Kant, then, the will is a kind of noumenal causality that is itself independent of natural causality.

There are many difficulties involved in this position. For example, freedom and will become only "necessary hypotheses" that explain our merely practical conviction that something could and ought to have been done by us, though it was not done, because we are in part noumenal beings belonging to a "world of intelligence" who can produce moral effects through our free causality.[57] And such a noumenal world becomes only a point of view—not a "constitutive" principle of "theoretical" reason, but one that we are obliged to adopt to explain our notions of freedom and duty.[58] Waiving all these problems momentarily, it seems that if Kant can make this concept of will intelligible and plausible, he is also able to avoid the reduction of will to appetite, to impulse, to uneasiness, and is thus able to explain rationally the traditional distinctions initiated by Plato in the *Gorgias* between duty and pleasure, virtue and happiness. Kant's definition of will insists on consciousness, on understanding the conception of a law, on determining oneself independent of external causes such as sensations. On this view a notion such as moral responsibility is at least intelligible: after all, if one is the free cause of something of whose character he is conscious, the effect can reasonably be imputed to him; whereas if his will is simply the "last appetite in deliberation," in the words of Hobbes, then he may be the efficient cause of an effect but not, so to speak, the moral cause of it. Kant insists on will as the undetermined causality of a rational being who understands the conception of the laws according to which he acts, whereas objects in physical nature act according to laws but not according to the conception of them. Kant is thus able to rescue a rational foundation for a distinction between morality and psychology.

Nietzsche once said of Kant that he is "in the end an under-handed Christian."[59] By this he meant that Kant had attempted to salvage the doctrine of free will, responsibility, and the like in an underhanded way—that is, by making those notions necessary but hypothetical. There is a certain truth in this charge, putting aside the elements of accusation and malice, for Kant does begin with what he takes to be the ordinary moral conceptions with which everyone operates ("criticism can and must begin with pure practical laws and their actual existence").[60] He goes on to suggest that he is supplying not new moral principles but simply a "transcendental deduction" of common moral concepts—that is, an explanation of how those concepts are in principle possible, as distinguished from pleasure, utility, or custom. In explaining the possible objectivity of moral ideas, Kant does not feel entitled to use the traditional ideas of freedom, will, and autonomy in traditional ways, as if those ideas were unproblematical and "constitutive" principles of theoretical reason having the same status as the principles of empiricism. As he says in *the Fundamental Principles of the Metaphysic of Morals*, "freedom is only an idea of reason, and its objective reality in itself is doubtful; while nature is a concept of the understanding which proves, and must necessarily prove, its reality in examples of experience." However, if the idea of a free will as a noumenal or intelligent quasicausality is given up, all morality will become empirical. Kant argues that"for practical purposes the narrow footpath of freedom is the only one on which it is possible to make use of reason in our conduct...Philosophy must then assume that no real contradiction will be found between freedom and physical necessity of the same human actions, for it cannot give up the conception of nature any more than that of freedom."[61]

Kant proposes to rescue a nonempirical, non-"pathological" morality by preserving some traditional moral ideas in a hypothetical form. His most effective version of this is to be found in the incomparable part 3 of the *Fundamental Principles of the Metaphysic of Morals*, where, after defining the will in terms of autonomy, of its capacity to be a law unto itself, Kant begins to introduce his hypothetical qualifications. Every being that "cannot act except under the *idea* of freedom," he says, is "in a practical point of view" really free, just as if a "theoretically conclusive" proof of free will were possible. This freedom cannot be proved to be "actually a property of ourselves or of human nature," but it must be presupposed "if we would conceive a being as rational and conscious of its causality in respect of its actions, that is, as endowed with a will."[62]

If a rational being is to be possessed of a causality that is itself not causally determined, Kant urges, he must draw a distinction between "a world of sense and the world of understanding." With respect to "mere perception and receptivity of sensations," he argues, man belongs to the "world of sense"; but insofar as he is capable of initiating rational "pure activity," he must count himself as belonging to "the intellectual world." He goes on, "a rational being...has two points of view from which he can regard himself, and recognize laws of the exercise of his faculties...first, so far as he belongs to the world of sense, he finds himself subject to laws of nature (heteronomy); secondly, as belonging to the intelligible world, under laws which, being independent of nature, have their foundation not in experience but in reason alone."[63]

If man belonged solely to the world of understanding, Kant continues, then all of his actions would conform to the principle of "autonomy of the free will"; if he were solely a creature of sense, then only a will determined by desires and inclination would be possible. Since, however, beings such as men, who are partly rational, recognize themselves as "subject to the law of the world of understanding, that is, to reason," this law is an imperative for them. A semirational being has duties because his will ought to and could conform to reason, but is affected (though not determined) by desire and inclination. What makes categorical imperatives of morality possible, Kant insists, is that the idea of freedom "makes me a member of an intelligible world, in consequence of which, if I were nothing else, all my actions *would* conform to the autonomy of the will; but as I at the same time intuit myself as a member of the world of sense, they *ought* so to conform."[64]

Kant ends his treatment of the foundations of morality by reaffirming the hypothetical though necessary character of a "world of understanding," of freedom, of a faculty of willing. The conception of an intelligible or noumenal world is, he grants, only a "point of view which reason finds itself compelled to take outside the appearances [of the phenomenal world] in order to conceive itself as practical." Freedom too is "a mere idea" that holds good "only as a necessary hypothesis of reason in a being that believes itself conscious of a will."[65] Here, despite this cautiousness Kant is going farther than in the *Critique of Pure Reason*, where he dares affirm only that freedom is not in principle impossible or contradictory, once a distinction is drawn between the noumenal and the phenomenal world.[66] But sometimes, as in the preface to the *Metaphysic of Morals*, he is willing to be less cautious, to say that in practice freedom and will prove their reality. "In the practical exercise of reason...the concept of freedom proves its reality through practical basic principles. As laws of a causality of pure reason, these principles determine the will independently of all empirical conditions...and prove the existence in us of a pure will in which moral concepts and laws have their origin."[67] At the end of the *Critique of Judgment* Kant even affirms that while God, freedom, and the immortality of the soul are the problems to whose solution all metaphysics is dedicated, of these three only freedom "proves its objective reality" because of the moral "causality implied in it"; that from the idea and the reality of freedom "an inference can be drawn to the real existence of both God and the soul—being that otherwise would be entirely hidden from us."[68] Kant's reasons for this view are many; but these passages at least show that, so far as moral practice is concerned, he sometimes set aside his emphasis on the purely hypothetical nature of the will's freedom in order to derive a "religion within the limits of reason alone" from that free will and the moral laws that it legislates and follows.

All of the foregoing remarks cannot, of course, serve as a complete characterization of Kant's concept of will and its relation to freedom and a world of intelligence; but they do provide a sufficient indication to suggest why he is able to avoid the problems that beset most voluntarists. Since Kant's very avoidance of them is of the greatest interest to a critical understanding of the philosophical foundations of social contract theory—if only to show what kind of theory of will would make the doctrines of consent and promise and obligation completely coherent—it is useful to turn, though briefly, to Kant's clearing up of a number of errors about the will, above all in *Religion within the Limits of Reason Alone*, but also in the *Critique of Practical Reason*.

Voluntarist theories before Kant had suffered from defects of various kinds, even though the main social contract theorists— Hobbes, Locke, and Rousseau—had had to make will the foundation of consent and promise and thereby of political obligation. Hobbes never succeeded in distinguishing will from appetite, except insofar as will is the last appetite in deliberation; but a last appetite remains an appetite. As a result, even though he urged in *Leviathan* that wills "make the essence of all covenants," that political legitimacy is derived from voluntary acts of consent taking the form of covenants, he was never able to show how an obligation can be derived from an appetite.[69] His problem, as we have seen, becomes clear if his definition of will is substituted for the word itself in some key passages: for example, "The last appetite makes the essence of all covenants" offers no notion of political obligation, no idea that once a man has freely obligated himself to obey, "it is his duty not to make void that voluntary act of his own."[70] The only reason that Hobbes's system works is that he appears not to use the concept of will as his definition requires.

Kant, particularly in *Religion within the Limits of Reason Alone*, provides a solution to Hobbes's problem, albeit one that rests on a distinction between a noumenal and a phenomenal world that Hobbes could never accept, though it might be argued that some of Hobbes's uses of the will seem to necessitate a free causality—in explaining obligation, for example.[71] The problem with Hobbes, a reading of Kant suggests, is that of not distinguishing between a consciously produced maxim of action and an externally caused or determined action-in-itself. Moral activity, Kant says, "cannot lie in an object *determining* the will through inclination, nor yet in a natural impulse; it can lie only in a rule made by the will for the use of its freedom, that is, in a maxim."[72] Kant could even have urged that Hobbes's saying that there can be "no obligation on any man which ariseth not from some act of his own"[73] is unintelligible unless the act is really his, unless it actually arises out of his own consciously produced maxims. If there are no maxims but only natural impulses, "it would be possible to trace the use of our freedom wholly to determination by natural causes";[74] but this would destroy responsibility, imputability, obligation, and other moral concepts that even Hobbes would want to maintain.

Kant makes much the same point in the *Critique of Practical Reason*. "*Good* or *evil* always implies a reference to the *will*, as determined by the *law of reason* to make something its object; for it is never determined directly by the object and the idea of it, but is a faculty of taking a rule of reason for the motive of an action . . . Good and evil, therefore, are properly referred to actions, not to the sensations of the person."[75] Kant could, doubtless, represent this distinction between mere action and the maxim of an action as necessary to Hobbes's moral convictions; he did not do this explicitly, but his distinction does help to point out what is problematical in Hobbes's theory of will and perhaps even shows why some commentators on Hobbes, despairing of finding a real theory of morality and obligation in *Leviathan*, speak as if the sole reason for obedience in Hobbes's system is fear of violent death and not consent or promise.[76]

It is not, however, only such Hobbesian problems with voluntarism that Kant attempts to resolve; he also tries to meet difficulties suggested by Stoicism and by moral positions such as Leibniz's, which insist simultaneously on the meritoriousness of voluntary actions and the impossibility of good will owing to human imperfection. Kant's criticism of Stoicism—which he certainly admired, at least as compared with Epicureanism—throws a great deal of light on the importance of will in his system and is indirectly related to the argument against a Hobbesian reduction of will to appetite. The Stoics, Kant says, were right in emphasizing the dignity of human nature, in attempting to derive moral laws from reason, and in insisting on independence from inclination; but since they had no conception of will, they could only "call out wisdom instead of folly," could only recommend a "heroic" struggle against impulse. But inclinations themselves, Kant says, are at least morally indifferent and sometimes even good—that is, if they are directed to an end commanded by reason. Genuine moral evil, he insists, consists in the fact that a man "does not *will* to withstand those inclinations when they tempt him to transgress.''[77] For Kant, Stoicism suffers from the fundamental problems of Hobbesianism, but in reverse: for Hobbes there is no real will because all will is reduced to appetite, while for Stoicism there is no real will because only wisdom should be directly causal. Both positions leave will out of account; but without it there can be no freedom, no responsibility, no duty. Inclination certainly cannot serve Kant as the foundation of morality, but no more can wisdom taken independently of a good will: even admirable qualities of mind can be used to serve moral evil unless the will is good.[78] The Stoics, Kant says, did not admit the possibility of willing evil but saw evil as resulting merely from being overcome by inclination; but this stance makes inclination universally causal, destroys the autonomy of the will, and leaves behind only "heteronomy" and "wisdom," neither of them adequate.

Kant's argument against the Leibnizian view of the will is related to the argument against Hobbes in that for Leibniz human imperfection, which he calls "metaphysical evil," is the cause of a bad will, just as for Hobbes appetites and aversions determine the will. Against both Kant argues for will as an uncaused causality. His refutation of the notion that human imperfection or limitation leads necessarily to moral evil is important not only in itself but also to his doctrine of the strict and full accountability of all men for their actions, regardless of what their character may seem to cause them to do; and this enters later into his theory of legal punishment, which is based on the idea that punishment must be deserved. The refutation is thus doubly interesting.

In his *Theodicy*, with respect to the importance of free will as a moral causality, Leibniz has taken up two positions that, when combined, did not add up to a coherent voluntarist theory. On the one hand he had argued, in a manner of which Kant could have approved, that "an inevitable necessity...would destroy the freedom of the will, so necessary to the morality of action: for justice and injustice, praise and blame, cannot attach to necessary actions." On the other hand, the requirements of his theology led him to assert in the same book that while "free will is the proximate cause of the evil of [guilt and] punishment," it is nonetheless true that "the original imperfection of creatures, which is already presented in the eternal ideas, is the first and most remote cause."[79] Clearly, the two parts of Leibniz's argument taken together at once affirm and deny the reality of free will.

Kant was both eager and able to overturn this kind of view: eager for obvious reasons and able because, for one thing, his theological position did not require or indeed allow him to think of men as imperfect though eternal ideas in the mind of God. On the contrary, Kant commonly derived the idea of God from the notion of moral perfection and even urged that men would have no knowledge of God were it not for their knowledge of the moral law that is "within" them.[80] In any case, against the Leibnizian position Kant argues that "through no cause in the world can [man] cease to be a freely acting being. For whatever his previous deportment may have been, whatever natural causes may have been influencing him...his action is yet free and determined by none of these causes; hence it can and must always be judged as an *original* use of his will." However evil a man's character may appear to be, Kant says, it was not only his duty to be better in the past, it is even now his duty to make himself better. To do so must be within his power, Kant insists; if it is not, then he is not a noumenal causality, and nothing can be imputed to him. Hence, Kant concludes, we must not inquire into the temporal origin of a deed but only into its rational origin; we must inquire whether it was in principle still possible for a man to have acted better.[81]

Kant's doctrine of the will—taking together the exposition of the necessary hypotheses of freedom and a noumenal world of intelligence and the objections to the Hobbesian, Stoic, and Leibnizian versions of willing—is forceful and compelling and does in fact avoid or overcome most of the traditional defects of voluntarism. Furthermore, it does this without mounting ridiculous attacks on empiricism. There remains, however, one final problem in Kant's theory of will that must be looked at briefly. In his very late *Metaphysic of Morals* he appears to operate not with a single conception of will as the capacity to determine oneself to action according to the conception of laws but with two notions of will. The first (*Willkür*) he defines as consciousness of the capacity of one's action to produce an object in accordance with a concept; the second (*Wille*) he defines as a *Willkür* whose "internal ground of determination" is found in the reason of the subject. In connection with these definitions he makes a number of familiar remarks: that a will determined by impulse is an "animal will," that human will is "affected but not determined by impulses."[82] But it is at least arguable that in the distinction between *Willkür* and *Wille* Kant is not talking about two kinds of will but only about a single will as it is differently motivated by different grounds. *Willkür* in itself is an uncaused consciousness of a capacity to produce objects, an uncaused causal faculty; while *Wille* is simply a *Willkür* determined by reason. In Kant's claim that the *Wille* is simply "practical reason itself"[83] it seems that *Wille* is only a certain kind of *Willkür*, one that is not merely free of causality (the negative concept of freedom) but one in which "pure reason is itself practical" (the positive concept of freedom). Ultimately, there is only one will in Kant: the consciousness of a capacity to be an uncaused cause; but this will becomes free in the positive sense of conforming to reason only when it goes beyond mere freedom from causality to self-determination through reason. In the end, Kant's concept of will turns out to be the most coherent of any in the voluntarist tradition, one that in some ways would have stood Hobbes, Locke, and Rousseau in good stead. But it must be granted that most objections to Kantianism are not to the Kantian concept of the will but to the alleged formalism and contentlessness of Kantian ethics. Since for Kant politics and legality are justified only to provide a context for moral endeavor and to realize some moral ends through legal incentives, the most essential thing in explaining Kantian politics is to show that Kantian ethics has a nonempirical content that politics and law can make more nearly possible on earth.

The most common and serious objection brought against Kant's moral philosophy—and by implication against as much of his political theory as supports that philosophy—is that it is merely formal, that it has no content, even that it can justify the universalization of anything, however intrinsically evil. Kant did, of course, insist in all of his major ethical works on the importance of the universal form of the moral law, on abstracting all "matter" from that law: as he argues in the *Critique of Practical Reason*, the moral law is the sole determining principle of a pure will, but since this law is merely formal, "it abstracts as a determining principle from all matter—that is to say, from every object of volition."[84] Nevertheless, the various formulations of the categorical imperative (above all in the *Fundamental Principles*) increasingly insist on what can only be seen as a moral content: the dignity of persons as ends-in-themselves, as members of a "kingdom of ends," who can never be used as means only to some arbitrary purpose.[85] How can the formal aspect of Kantian ethics be linked with this quite definite moral content, a content that shapes even Kant's politics, without doing violence to him?

The most formidable response to this question is provided by Hegel. He begins by praising Kant for giving prominence to "the pure unconditioned self-determination of the will as the root of duty" but then goes on quickly to say that to adhere to the "moral" position without passing on to "ethics" is to "reduce this gain to an empty formalism. If the definition of duty is taken to be the absence of contradiction, formal correspondence with itself . . . then no transition is possible to the specification of particular duties . . ." Kant's idea of universalization of moral maxims, Hegel continues, contains "no principle beyond abstract identity and the 'absence of contradiction.'" But, he insists, "a contradiction must be a contradiction of something." If property is shown to be valid independently of mere universality and noncontradiction, or if life is shown to be a good, "then indeed it is a contradiction to commit theft or murder." In Hegel's view Kant never shows that any particular moral content is valid; he only shows that certain kinds of action would be wrong if a certain content were presupposed. In Kant, Hegel argues, we follow duty not for the sake of real content but only for "duty's sake." As a result, we never know what is in itself good but know only that some action of ours would contradict a content that is no content.[86]

While it is not possible to be perfectly confident of any answer to this general objection—which was also made, in a somewhat different form, by J. S. Mill in *Utilitarianism*[87]—it is arguable that when Kant inveighs against including any matter in the moral law, he is trying above all to exclude "empiricism" in morality, to exclude sensible impulses of happiness and pleasure as motives for obedience to that law. A free will, he says in the *Critique of Practical Reason*, is determined simply by the moral law, "not only without the coöperation of sensible impulses, but even to the rejection of all such, and to the checking of all inclinations so far as they might be opposed to that law."[88] It is quite possible that in his zeal to exclude these sensible motives he overstates a certain part of his case in such a way as to make, for example, the dignity of persons as ends-in-themselves appear to be a matter that also had to be excluded from moral consideration. Yet the categorical imperative of treating persons as ends-in-themselves, as dignities, is represented by Kant as merely a different formulation of the first version of that imperative, which requires only that moral maxims be formally universalizable.[89] It must then be the case that Kant did not view respect for the dignity of persons as ends-in-themselves as a sensible impulse, as a motive resting on "pathological" feelings of happiness or pleasure. As John Rawls has urged, it is a mistake to treat Kantianism as a formal doctrine in which only universality matters: "That moral principles are general and universal is hardly new with him; and . . . these considerations do not in any case take us very far. It is impossible to construct a moral theory on so slender a basis, and therefore to limit Kant's doctrine to these notions is to reduce it to triviality. The real force of his view lies elsewhere."[90]

There is a good reason for taking this view, apart from the bare fact that it seems to be necessary in order to defend Kant's insistence that all of the versions of the categorical imperative are really the same. That reason is that Kant himself, in a number of works including the *Fundamental Principles of the Metaphysic of Morals,* the *Critique of Judgment,* the *Tugendlehre,* the *Anthropology,* and even the *Critique of Practical Reason* seems to allow for and even insist on the possibility of an unconditioned and uncontingent, nonarbitrary, objective end that is not dependent on happiness, pleasure, or utility—that is, persons as ends-in-themselves.[91] The relation of this unconditioned or objective end to the rest of Kant's ethics is certainly problematical, and no truly adequate treatment can be offered here. At least it can be said that the real question is not whether there is a content in Kantian moral theory (to which politics, for example, might be instrumental) but to what extent Kant succeeds in showing that there is a content that is not arbitrary but that is a necessary end of reason that extorts respect from us.

The most familiar version of Kant's doctrine that men are ends-in-themselves is probably the one that forms the whole middle section of the *Fundamental Principles of the Metaphysic of Morals.* He begins with an argument about two kinds of ends, "relative" ones and "objective" ones. Ends generally serve the will as the "objective ground of its self-determination." The arbitrary ends that a rational being proposes to himself "at pleasure" are only relative, since these ends change as his desires and interests change; but if there exists "something whose existence has *in itself* an absolute worth," something which, as an end-in-itself, can be a "source of definite laws," then *this* end could be the "source of a possible categorical imperative." These reflections lead Kant to the claim—and at this point it is only a claim—that "man and generally any rational being exists as an end in himself, not merely as a means to be arbitrarily used by this or that will, but...must be always regarded at the same time as an end."[92]

Kant begins to try to make good this claim by saying that if there is to be a categorical imperative, it must be one that "being drawn from the conception of that which is necessarily an end for everyone because it is *an end in itself,* constitutes an objective principle of the will. . ." This principle, he goes on, must be built on the notion that "rational nature exists as an end in itself." Kant's proof of this is, strictly speaking, intersubjective rather than objective: men necessarily conceive their own existence as an end-in-itself, but every other rational being regards its existence in the same way, "so that it is at the same time an objective principle from which as a supreme practical law all laws of the will must be capable of being deduced." In view of this Kant reformulates the categorical imperative, which heretofore had insisted only on willing one's maxims as universal laws, to read: "So act as to treat humanity, whether in thine own person or in that of any other, in every case as an end withal, never as means only."[93]

After adducing some examples, Kant goes on to say that the notion of men as ends-in-themselves is not merely derived from experience, for it does not "present humanity" as an arbitrary and contingent end (self-proposed "at pleasure") that may or may not be adopted but as the "supreme limiting condition of all our subjective ends." At this point he introduces a distinction between objective and subjective principles that is probably the cause of criticisms such as Hegel's: "The objective principles of all practical legislation lies. . .in the rule and its form of universality which makes it capable of being a law. . .; but the subjective principle is in the end; now by the second principle, the subject of all ends is each rational being inasmuch as it is an end in itself. Hence follows the third practical principle of the will. . .the idea of the will of every rational being as a universally legislative will."[94] This formulation appears to put the objective principle above the subjective one; since, however, it is the subjective end (men as ends-in-themselves) that provides universal maxims with a nonarbitrary content, the subjective element of this formulation is essential if criticisms like Hegel's and Mill's are to be met.

Kant next relates his argument to what he had said earlier about the will. The reformulated categorical imperative is a "law of one's own giving," a law legislated by one's own will but not in terms of a mere interest, such as happiness. The moral laws to which a man is subject, he urges, are given by his own will—a will, however, that is "designed by nature to give universal laws." A will that determines itself by laws that recognize objective ends is autonomous, Kant says, while one that makes merely contingent ends the maxims of its action is heteronomous.[95] The idea of the will as universally legislative in terms of objective ends leads to the concept of a "kingdom of ends." This kingdom or realm Kant defines as a "systematic union of rational beings by common objective laws." In language reminiscent of Rousseau Kant argues that a rational being belongs to such a kingdom as a member when he is subject to its laws and that he belongs to it as a sovereign when, "while giving laws, he is not subject to the will of any other." He goes on to show that in such a kingdom of ends, which is only an ideal, everything has either a value or a dignity; whatever has mere value can be replaced by something of equivalent value, but that which is the condition of anything else's having a value—that is, man—has dignity.[96]

Kant sums up his whole argument in a way that shows clearly why his critics have been able to tax him with mere formalism and contentlessness. All of the formulations of the categorical imperative, Kant insists, "are at bottom only so many formulae of the very same law." All maxims that follow the categorical imperative, he says, are characterized by:

1. A *form*, consisting in universality; and in this view the formula of the moral imperative is expressed thus, that the maxims must be so chosen as if they were to serve as universal laws of nature.
2. A *matter*, namely, an end, and here the formula says that the rational being, as it is...an end in itself, must in every maxim serve as the condition limiting all merely relative and arbitrary ends.
3. A *complete characterization* of all maxims by means of that formula, namely, that all maxims ought, by their own legislation, to harmonize with a possible kingdom of ends.[97]

The problem here is obvious: what Kant calls a matter in item 2 is at other times called subjective; and immediately after the passage just quoted he says that while it is better to start from the formula of the categorical imperative (the principle of universality), it is "useful" to consider the other factors as well (that is, the matter of a maxim and the complete characterization of all maxims) in order to bring the moral law "nearer to intuition." Thus, there are problems in Kant if even objective ends-in-themselves are regarded as something introduced into the higher notion of formal universality merely in order to "gain entrance" for morality, intuitively conceived. Kant himself sometimes seems to invite this interpretation. However, since he also insists on the notion of an "independently existing end" that one must "never act against," on the "dignity of man as a rational creature, without any *other* end or advantage to be attained,"[98] it is at least possible that the three elements of a moral maxim—the form, the matter or end, and the "complete characterization"—are all necessary, and no one of them *sufficient* (for example, the form alone). This interpretation, though far from irresistible, is supported by an important passage from Kant's *Tugendlehre*:

> Since there are free actions, there must also be ends to which, as objects, those actions are directed. But among those ends there must be some which are at the same time (i.e., by their very concept) duties. For if there were no such ends, and since no action can be without an end, all ends for practical reason would always be valid only as means to other ends, and a categorical imperative would be impossible. Thus the doctrine of morals would be destroyed.[99]

If this is the case—and it is Kant himself who is saying that morality would be destroyed if there were no objective ends to serve as the object of the categorical imperative—and if what is subjective in a maxim (the end) is not inferior to what is objective (the form) but is only a different and essential aspect of a "completely characterized" maxim, then Kant's moral philosophy is only somewhat problematical but not the piece of arid formalism that Hegel said it was. Even though Kant's proof of the validity of an objective end-in-itself is intersubjective rather than, as he had hoped, strictly objective—since it rests on everyone's having the same view of himself as an ultimate end—the argument is at least persuasive, if not as decisive as Kant may have wished. H. J. Paton, in his splendid *The Categorical Imperative*, has perhaps given Kant's position its most forceful expression. After granting that Kant, in speaking of the idea of an end-in-itself, is "manifestly extending the meaning of the word 'end,'" Paton goes on to say:

> An objective and absolute end could not be a product of our will; for no mere product of our will can have absolute value. An end in itself must therefore be a self-existent end, not something to be produced by us. Since it has absolute value, we know already what it must be—namely, a good will. This good or rational will Kant takes to be present in every rational agent, and . . . hence . . . every rational agent as such, must be said to exist an an end in itself.[100]

This interpretation gains additional force as Kant says in the *Fundamental Principles of the Metaphysic of Morals* that it is the fitness of a person's maxims for universal legislation that "distinguishes him as an end in itself," which gives him dignity as a willing sovereign in a kingdom of ends.[101] This serves to relate the good will, which initially was defined only as an uncaused faculty of willing universally, to the notions of dignity and objective end. The good will has dignity because it is capable of willing the objective end—that is, the dignity of men as independently existing ends. Dignity is then both something the will has and something it respects in its volitions.

It is not only in the *Fundamental Principles* that Kant tries to defend the notion of an end that is not derived from inclination, happiness, or utility. Indeed, one of his most subtle and imaginative defenses of the idea of men as ends-in-themselves is to be found in the *Critique of Judgment*. Part 2 of this work is concerned with, among other things, the possibility of purposiveness in an apparently mechanical world, with showing that while purposiveness cannot be shown actually to exist in a way that satisfies the "determinant" judgment, it can at least be presupposed by human "reflective" judgment in its effort to make the world intelligible to itself. Kant urges that while the purposes of things in the natural world such as plants or animals are imputed by us to those things, which certainly cannot themselves conceive purposes, man is the ultimate purpose of creation on earth because "he is the only being upon it who can form a concept of purposes, and who can by his reason make out of an aggregate of purposively formed things a system of purposes."[102]

This argument, which has an obvious relation to Kant's distinction between acting according to laws and acting according to the conception of laws, or having a will, is also related to the argument in the *Fundamental Principles* about the way in which all men necessarily conceive themselves—that is, as final causes. While this is, strictly speaking, an intersubjective rather than an objective proof, since purposiveness is only subjectively necessary for men, it does have quite a bit of force. The idea of a rational nature as an end-in-itself or of the dignity of a person, a being capable of conceiving worth and purpose, as an end-in-himself is not an arbitrary premise; it is a conception that defines the kind of being who would be capable of understanding what is at issue in Kant's moral philosophy. And if Kant is right in believing that "lower" beings cannot conceive worth or purpose or final ends, let alone conceive of themselves as unconditioned ends, and that God is deduced out of the concept of morality rather than the reverse, then men-as-persons, as partly moral beings, are the only unconditioned thing in nature and must serve as ends-in-themselves if there is to be any such thing. This is why Kant can say, again in the *Critique of Judgment*, that it is not open to us, in the case of man as a moral agent, to ask for what end man exists. "His existence," Kant argues, "inherently involves the highest end." This is true, Kant grants, only if nature is considered as a teleological system in which one mounts from things that are conditioned, or caused, to that which is unconditioned. Everything in a purposive nature is caused except man as *noumenon*, for his will is an uncaused causality and hence "qualifies him to be a final end to which all of nature is teleologically subordinated."[103]

What this means is that for Kant not God but the moral law—which only men can know and follow—is the final cause of creation considered as teleological; man would thus be an end-in-himself because he is the only being capable of conceiving and following the sole unconditioned end that can be known.

What cannot be considered here, fascinating as it is, is whether the "purposiveness" of the *Critique of Judgment* might not serve as a bridge uniting the whole of Kant's thought.[104] Since, that is, Kant argues in *Judgment* that nature can be "estimated," though never known, through "purposes" and "functions" that mechanical causality fails to explain, that persons as free agents both have "purposes" that they strive to realize and view themselves as the "final end" of creation, and that art exhibits a "purposiveness without purpose," which makes it the symbol of morality,[105] it is possible that Kant's special version of teleology might supply the "unity of reason" that brings the various Kantian "realms" into a single realm. And politics, or "public legal justice," would fit into this reading of Kant by being instrumental to the realization of some moral ends—such as no murder—through "legal" incentives. If the *Critique of Judgment* could supply this unity, it would correctly realize what Kant calls Leibniz's "true although not clearly expressed opinion" that the "pre-established harmony" extends "to the agreement between the realm of *nature* and the realm of *grace* (the realm of purposes in relation to the final purpose, i.e. mankind under moral laws)," so that there is "harmony between the consequences of our concept of nature and those of our concept of freedom."[106]

The arguments for objective ends in the *Fundamental Principles* and in the *Critique of Judgment* are certainly the most impressive ones that Kant produces; it is worth pointing out, however, that in other important works he at least alludes to these arguments. In the late work *Anthropology*, for example, he declares that man is "his own last [final] end."[107] And in *Theory and Practice* he reinforces the view that he is trying to exclude only empirical ends (but not all ends) from his moral philosophy when he says that "not every end is moral (that of personal happiness, for example, is not); the end must be an unselfish one."[108] There is also an elaborate argument in the *Critique of Practical Reason* urging that respect for the moral law and for the dignity of men as objective ends is not derived from a feeling of pleasure and could not be, since respect for law and virtue is often painful to our "self-conceit."[109] Perhaps, in the end, Kant's whole position on this matter, problematical as it is, is best summed up in his *Tugendlehre:*

> Man in the system of nature...is a being of little significance and, along with the other animals, considered as products of the earth, has an ordinary value...
>
> But man as a person, i.e. as the subject of a morally practical reason, is exalted above all price. For as such a one (homo noumenon) he is not to be valued merely as a means to the ends of other people, or even to his own ends, but is to be prized as an end in himself.[110]

In his remarkable late work *The Conflict of the Faculties* Kant seemingly translates this very passage into the language of politics.

> In the face of the omnipotence of nature, or rather its supreme first cause which is inaccessible to us, the human being is, in his turn, but a trifle. But for the sovereigns of his own species also to consider and treat him as such, whether by burdening him as an animal, regarding him as a mere tool of their designs, or exposing him in their conflicts with one another in order to have him massacred—this is no trifle, but a subversion of the ultimate purpose of creation itself.[111]

Without suggesting that the problems in Kant's moral philosophy have been solved, it is at least clear that objections of the kind made by Hegel and Mill are really not fair, since they do not even deal with Kant's effort to show how an objective end is possible. In the end, Kant's position ultimately rests on the view that only a good will is capable of both being an objective end and having, or legislating, such an end; and this position is so impressively defended that it is at least reasonable to assume that Kant's moral philosophy is far more adequate than its critics allow. Indeed, if what he says against the derivation of morality from pleasure, happiness, utility, perfection, moderation, the will of God, moral sense, and so on is really correct, as it appears to be, then his moral philosophy is not only adequate but the most adequate of moral philosophies. And if his quasicontractarian politics turns out to be truly instrumental to this most adequate morality, then his success is as nearly complete as that of anyone else in the history of political philosophy.

At this point it is possible to say several things about Kant's moral and political philosophy with some confidence. He is a social contract theorist, though a hypothetical one who limits what a rational and mature people could agree to by his notion of natural law. His conception of will as the capacity for rational self-determination would have been more adequate than the conceptions of Hobbes, Locke, and Rousseau in providing a sound philosophical basis for the notions of consent, promise, and obligation if Kant had wanted to be a traditional contract theorist. The charge that Kant's politics is instrumental to a merely formalistic and contentless morality is unfair, since Kant made notable efforts to link the notion of a good will to the idea of men as ends-in-themselves. While it is not possible to claim that this last element of the Kantian operation would be persuasive to everyone, since it rests on, among other things, hypotheses about teleology, about men as ultimate purposes of nature, about the need for an unconditioned final cause in nature, Kant's moral system certainly seems to be more successful than the systems that he criticizes and to provide what it sets out to provide: an explanation of the conceptual possibility of common moral experience.

What remains is to determine to what extent Kant's political doctrine is congruent with this moral system. In a general way the congruence is obvious: the Kantian republic respects the liberty ("freedom under law") that is essential to moral activity, blocks external impediments to this activity, realizes some of the ends, though not the incentives, of morality, and, if universalized into a world of republics, brings an end to those practices, above all war, that are themselves immoral and therefore make the state the enemy rather than the instrument of morality. But in more particular respects—such as the morality or immorality of disobedience to law and of revolution, or the question of how to guarantee that the state will act according to the Idea of the social contract—problems remain.

Kant's fullest statement of his republicanism and ideal contractarianism is found in the *Rechtslehre*. He begins with an argument that is obviously derived from Rousseau and that in some respects does not fully represent his real view: "The legitimate [or sovereign] authority can be attributed only to the united will of the people. Because all right and justice is supposed to proceed from this authority, it can do absolutely no injustice to anyone." Strictly speaking, this goes too far in the direction of Rousseau; after all, for Kant all right and justice proceed from natural law as applied by the people's united will, not just from popular authority. With this adjustment the statement can be brought into line with the rest of Kant. He goes on to urge that the nature of a citizen in a commonwealth under the united will of the people involves three attributes:

> First, the lawful freedom to obey no law other than one to which he has given his consent; second, the civil equality of having among the people no superior over him except another person whom he has just as much of a moral capacity to bind juridically as the other has to bind him; third, the attribute of civil independence that requires that he owe his existence and support, not to the arbitrary will of another person in the society, but rather to his own rights and powers as a member of the commonwealth.[112]

Again the debt to Rousseau is evident.[113] And again Kant's statement that a citizen need only obey laws to which he has consented must be qualified: sometimes Kant does insist on indirect consent through a representative system, but often he proposes only the notion that a law must be worthy of consent. A slightly less obvious borrowing from Rousseau is also in evidence in Kant's distinction between the sovereign, the ruler, and the courts. Every state, he argues, contains three authorities: the sovereign authority "resides in the person of the legislator" (the united will of the people), while the executive authority resides in the ruler ("in conformity to law"), and the judicial authority resides in the judge. Following Rousseau yet again, Kant calls laws the determinations of the united will of the people, while the determination of the ruler are mere "ordinances and decrees," because they involve "decisions about particular cases and are considered subject to change."[114] Despite this Rousseaueanism, however, Kant does not want to adopt Rousseau's extreme voluntarist notion that "the engagements which bind us to the social body are obligatory only because they are mutual";[115] his theory of natural law and his belief that morality itself requires public legal justice would not admit of such a view.

There is, then, in Kant ordinarily only one form of sovereignty: the united will of the people under the Idea of a social contract. There are, however, different forms of states, and on this point Kant shows a fair amount of flexibility. He is concerned mainly with the advantages and disadvantages of autocracy and of democracy; aristocracy did not interest him. The advantage of autocracy, he suggests, is that it is the simplest of all political forms; for mere political administration this simplicity is good, but insofar as justice and law are concerned, it is the most dangerous because it "strongly invites despotism," which would necessarily involve immorality. On the whole, then, Kant usually comes down against autocracy: "simplification is indeed a reasonable maxim in the machinery of uniting the people through coercive laws, provided that all the people are passive and obey the one person who is above them; but, under such circumstances, none of the subjects are citizens."[116] Democracy, which in its pure, nonrepublican form Kant sometimes calls a despotism,[117] has the disadvantage of great complexity, since it contains three different kinds of relationships: the will of all to unite themselves into a people; the will of all citizens to form a commonwealth; and their will to place at the head of this commonwealth a ruler who is "none other than this united will itself."[118]

Better than either autocracy or democracy, in Kant's view, is true republicanism, or the ideal state. A true republic, he argues, "is and can be nothing else than a representative system of the people if it is to protect the rights of its citizens in the name of the people." Such a system would realize "the spirit of the original contract." Since, however, the contract is only an Idea of reason, a people cannot use the notion of breach of contract as a pretext for disestablishing the old order and creating the ideal state overnight. It is, rather, the obligation of "constituted authority"—apparently the ruler—to "change the government gradually and continually" until a pure republic is finally attained. When such a republic is realized, public legal justice will be "autonomous"—that is, not the property of a feudal aristocracy, a church, or an autocrat. It is worth noting, however, that Kant insists that during the period of transition to a pure republic the old nonrepublican state forms may "continue as long as they are held by ancient, long-standing custom" to be necessary.[119] And this is true even though morality will be better served by a republican than a nonrepublican context.

Kant does not always go this far; indeed, in some works he even defends, or at least allows for, monarchy when it seems unavoidable. Following the lead of Montesquieu, who had argued that large countries require monarchy in order to introduce "dispatch" into ruling and to offset the sheer size of extensive territories,[120] Kant says in *The Conflict of the Faculties* that a people occupying such territories "may feel that monarchy is the only kind of constitution which can enable it to preserve its own existence between powerful neighbors." However, Kant modifies even this quasi-Montesquieuean concession by insisting that as the rest of the world becomes republican, monarchical states will become "progressively more secure from danger." This means, in effect, that monarchies need not be perpetual; since the only excuse for their existence is a fear of external danger, they lose this excuse when the representatives of the people in republics no longer favor war and publicly paid-for adventurism, as against the former capriciousness of kings and ministers. Ultimately, Kant agrees only provisionally with Montesquieu's famous dictum. But until the attainment of universal republicanism—which might well preserve constitutional monarchs as mere executives—autocrats can at least govern in a "republican manner." Kant says: "It is the duty of monarchs to govern in a *republican* (not a democratic) manner, even though they may *rule autocratically*. In other words, they should treat the people in accordance with principles akin in spirit to the laws of freedom which a people of mature rational powers would prescribe for itself."[121]

Kant makes it plain in works such as *Theory and Practice* that it is better to be ruled provisionally by an even somewhat arbitrary autocrat than to be "devoured by ecclesiastics and aristocrats."[122] If he could not agree with Hegel that monarchy is the "constitution of developed reason,"[123] he at least thought it more rational than rule by the vestiges of feudalism. (It is not for nothing that, when Kant wants to give examples of things that a rational people could not agree to, he chooses the perpetual and heritable privileges of the nobility and the churches as the most eligible impossibilities.)[124] Kant thought it at least possible that a monarch might act "by analogy with laws which a people would give itself in conformity with universal principles of right," but he did not believe this of aristocrats and ecclesiastics.[125]

Kant did not confine himself to treating the formal requirements of republicanism. More characteristically he argued that while all legal orders are in some sense instrumental to the possibility of morality, a republican legal order is best calculated to end political immorality, particularly in the form of war. A republican constitution, he says in *Eternal Peace*, is not only "pure in its origin," since it springs from the "pure concept of right"; it also makes possible a perpetual peace in which states will require, internally and externally, fewer immoral acts. In a republic, Kant suggests, where men are citizens and would personally have to undergo all the deprivations of war and violence, they will have "great hesitation in embarking on so dangerous an enterprise." But where men are not citizens, he goes on, "it is the simplest thing in the world to go to war"; for a monarch unrestricted by even the idea of what a rational people could agree to is not a fellow citizen who would have to share the horrors of war with other citizens but "the owner of a state." Of such a ruler he says: "A war will not force him to make the slightest sacrifice so far as his banquets, hunts, pleasure palaces and court festivals are concerned. He can thus decide on war, without any significant reason, as a kind of amusement. . ."[126]

Doubtless Kant exaggerates in these passages the degree to which he actually believed that war is caused simply by the caprice of monarchs and scheming ministers; after all, he indicates in other works that war may even be a "hidden purpose of nature" designed to bring about a new cosmopolitical world order through "sad experience" of violence and devastation.[127] Nonetheless, he does seem to have believed that even if the morality of the public would not necessarily be higher under a republic than in a monarchy, a republic would at least *cause* fewer immoralities simply because rational people would not willingly choose to ruin themselves, for example through war. And if war—always for Kant the chief form of political immorality—can be made less likely, other good consequences will follow: future generations will not be burdened with a huge war debt improperly inflicted on them by predatory ancestors; thus, money saved from war expenditures can be applied to education, and so on.[128]

Kant, then, makes a rather persuasive case for the view that republicanism, or at least a republican manner of governing, will lead to fewer immoralities and the possibility of a better context for morality. However, none of this means that he was willing to justify revolution in order to attain this republicanism more quickly. Indeed, some critics of Kant insist that he went too far in attacking revolution, that his insistence on obedience to law at all costs destroyed his republicanism. At first glance it certainly looks as though Kant's views on revolution, even as a means of hastening republicanism, are not completely coherent. In his late *The Conflict of the Faculties*, which is his most prorevolutionary work, he says that enthusiasm for the French Revolution cannot have been "caused by anything but a moral disposition within the human race," and goes on to urge that "the moral cause which is at work here is composed of two elements. Firstly, there is the *right* of every people to give itself a civil constitution of the kind that it sees fit...And secondly...there is the *aim*, which is also a duty, of submitting to those conditions [of republicanism] by which war, the source of all evils and moral corruption, can be prevented."[129] Yet—and this is perhaps more characteristic—in the *Rechtslehre* Kant calls revolution illegal, a crime deserving of death, and even argues that "it is the people's duty to endure even the most intolerable abuse of supreme authority" because resistance can only be "unlawful."[130]

If the integrity of Kant's political system is to be maintained, this apparent inconsistency must be explained in a convincing manner. The best way to do it is perhaps to say that even in the *Rechtslehre*, which treats revolution as destructive of all legality, Kant grants that the sovereign—that is, the people—can "take his authority from the ruler, depose him, or reform his administration, but cannot punish him." The removal of a particular ruler would not necessarily constitute an assault on the entire legal order. Consequently, Kant allows that it is conceivable that the dethronement of a ruler may be "effected through a voluntary abdication" and even that the people might have some excuse for forcing this "by appealing to the right of necessity," provided the ruler is not punished and provided above all that he is not executed. Executing the former executor of the laws, Kant suggests, is like executing the law itself. If a people simply forces a ruler out of power but lets him live peacefully as a private citizen, Kant is willing to grant that this may be allowable, though he prefers evolution toward republicanism. It is only the killing of a ruler that Kant calls an "inexpiable" crime.[131] His view of revolution, then, while not without its problems, is much more coherent than it is often taken to be, at least sometimes allowing for the removal of a ruler without producing an anarchy that would destroy legality as an instrument to morality.

Even though it is true that Kant makes a persuasive case that republicanism will lead to less future immorality, and that his theory of revolution is not so defective as is sometimes urged, some problems do remain in his theory of public legal justice as something supportive of but not coincident with morality. The most obvious difficulty is that Kant states clearly that what matters in morality is good will, or the maxim of one's action, whereas all that matters in politics and law is that external behavior be consistent with the freedom of everyone under a universal law. In his treatment of crime in the *Rechtslehre*, however, his distinction appears to break down. The reason for punishing a criminal is that he deserves it: his actions, Kant says, must receive "what they are worth." Penalties must be equivalent to crimes, because all other standards (reform, deterrence) are arbitrary; therefore, murderers must be executed so that their "inner viciousness" may be "expiated" and that "blood-guilt" will not be on the hands of a society that out of "sympathetic sentimentality" or an "affectation of humanity" tries to let murderers off easily.[132] The question is, should the idea of what people deserve because of the malevolence of their will be taken into political-legal account? Does this, perhaps, treat politically what can only be a moral matter?[133] Should it not simply be said that murder, from a political-legal point of view, is not consistent with the external freedom of all under a universal law and that murder is punished by negating the negation—the crime—thus affirming the positive rule?

Actually, Kant himself provides for just such a view of punishment in another part of the *Rechtslehre*:

Any resistance which counteracts the hindrance of an effect helps to promote this effect and is consonant with it. Now everything that is contrary to right is a hindrance to freedom based on universal laws, while coercion is a hindrance or resistance to freedom. Consequently, if a certain use to which freedom is put is itself a hindrance to freedom in accordance with universal laws, . . . any coercion which is used against it will be a hindrance to the hindrance of freedom, and will thus be. . . right.[134]

This is obviously a better theory of coercion and punishment than any argument resting on an idea of inner viciousness or what actions are worth, for it keeps punishment, like the law itself, external.

There are problems, then, in Kant's theory of political-legal order as a context for morality, and these problems are seen most clearly when Kant treats, not always with perfect consistency, the notions of revolution and punishment. Usually, however, if one looks at everything he has to say, even on these matters, a consistent view can be drawn out. In the end, Kant's treatment of morality and politics is remarkably coherent and forceful. Politics and legality serve a high purpose in his system: they are the guarantors of those negative conditions that make the dignity of men as ends-in-themselves more nearly possible. They make the exercise of a good will less difficult by removing impediments such as fear of violence that could incline, though not determine, the will to act on maxims that cannot be universalized in a way that is consistent with the rights of man. Politics cannot make men moral, for public legal justice involves only external legislation, not "acting in accordance with duty *from* duty"; nor should it try to make men happy, for Kantian happiness, like Hobbesian felicity, is relative to individuals. But it can create conditions in which liberty, the prime requisite of politics and the precondition of morality, will be guaranteed through the laws of a republic under the Idea of the social contract—an Idea in which Kant raises to their highest pitch the ideals of the contractarian and voluntarist tradition that he inherited and transformed.

⟶⟨ 6 ⟩⟵

Hegel on Consent and Social Contract Theory: Does He "Cancel and Preserve" the Will?

I_T is difficult to think of two philosophers more different than Hegel and Rousseau. Who can imagine Rousseau lecturing regularly and punctually, perhaps on the destructive effects of the arts and sciences, in a university? Still more inconceivable, who can imagine Hegel's *Confessions*? Yet, it is instructive to compare them, for in respect to one restricted but significant problem—that of relating individuals to a social whole by means of their wills in such a way that *will* means only rational and social will and not arbitrariness or caprice or "natural" will—they have a difficulty in common. Their dilemma is much the same insofar as both writers at once value and fear the will as the source of freedom on the one hand and of mere willfulness on the other. (What Rousseau says about the barrenness and destructiveness of the egoistic will in the *Économie politique*[1] surely finds a complex echo in Hegel's *Phenomenology*.) Comparison of the two from other points of view, of course, yields only negative relationships: Hegel was the chief defender of the rationality of the large modern states that Rousseau hated, and his "universal" civil service comes close to the "government by clerks" that Rousseau detested equally.[2] Still, it is worth noting that, however critical of Rousseau Hegel often was, he rarely failed to point out that Rousseau had been right in basing his theory of the state on the idea of will, though he had "reduced" will to "capriciously given express consent" by settling for a mere "general" will, by not insisting on "rational" will.[3] In his criticism of Rousseau Hegel almost certainly failed to appreciate that Rousseau was in fact trying to rationalize will *by* generalizing it, by helping it move away from particularity and capriciousness. In any

case, Hegel's drawing a firm line between *will* and *consent*—
undoing a connection established by St. Augustine and then
reflected in Hobbes, Locke, and Rousseau—makes it impossible to
agree with Plamenatz's judgment that Hegel's political philosophy
is built on consent.[4] One of Hegel's great points is that consent is
capricious and therefore unworthy of the "true" will—the rational
will, or perhaps just reason itself.

At any rate, the content of the will is always critical in Hegel.
Throughout his political writings he attacks unrelentingly the
merely abstract or one-sided view of the will in its numerous
forms: as mere independence or differentiation of the ego from the
outside world, as Stoic indifference to everything but internal
serenity, as willful "heroism of state service" on the part of
medieval "haughty vassals" who act "rightly" only to please
themselves, as the "frenzy of self-conceit" that tries to destroy
everything that is not the much-loved self, as the Kantian rational
will willing empty abstract universals that are the contradiction of
nothing, as the moral "ought-to-be" (again Kantian) that allows
nothing to become actual because morality must be only willed and
not achieved. "Subjectivity," Hegel observed, "is insatiably greedy
to concentrate and drown everything in this single spring of the
pure ego."[5]

In spite of this attack, which is developed at such length and
with so much subtlety in the *Phenomenology*, there is in the
Philosophy of Right and the *Encyclopedia* an equally unrelenting
insistence on the Hegelian state as the actualization of the
"concept" of the will, on the essentiality of "ethical" life in a
concrete historical state in which the will, by itself an abstract
"moment," something even potentially evil because purely particular, is given a content consistent with its own concept: rational
freedom. Indeed, Hegel does not hesitate to define the concept of
the good itself in terms of will: "the good is the Idea as the unity of
the concept of the will with the particular will."[6] (Interestingly, this
is almost the same as Rousseau's definition of virtue in the
Économie Politique.)[7] In ethical life, Hegel urges, the individual will
is "canceled and preserved"—canceled in its particularity, preserved insofar as it is rational—but it is never simply negated.[8]
Its mere subjectivity, which may have any content, is filled with
the objective social ethics of a concrete society at a given point in
history. As we shall see, this leaves Hegel with the difficulty of
showing that history and its agent, the state, are sufficient
embodiments of reason to bear the burden of fitting will with a

proper object. What must be emphasized here is that while Hegel devotes a great deal of his work, particularly most of the *Phenomenology*, to a dissection and repudiation of the destructive and self-destructive forms of mind and will, he never rejects the concept of willing as significant in modern Western civilization. "In the states of antiquity," he notes in the *Philosophy of Right*, "the subjective end coincided with the state's will. In modern times, however, we make claims for private judgment, private willing, and private conscience."[9]

The tone of this statement is indeed a little odd: the phrase "we make claims" is not exactly an assertion of the validity of those claims. It is also true that many of the common forms of explicit social willing are denigrated and even ridiculed by Hegel—social contract theory, above all, as well as the notion that the consent of the governed, or still less public opinion, is what makes the state legitimate. But he says again and again that men must be able to see their true will in the rationality of historically concrete institutions, in which the abstract ought-to-be comes into real existence, and that men feel entitled to find "subjective self-satisfaction" in being parts of a rational institution, in knowing that the concept of the good is only an idea, only a "moment" in the ethical whole, unless it is actualized by the real wills of real men. "The good itself, apart from the subjective will," he says, is only an abstraction without that real existence which it is to acquire for the first time through efforts of that will."[10] Against this "subjective" element Hegel balances a counterweight that keeps the will in its place, saying that "it is to take higher moral ground to find satisfaction in the [objective] action and beyond the gulf between the self-consciousness of a man and the objectivity of his deed."[11] In short, the good itself is abstract, the will alone equally abstract; the former by itself produces only unconscious or "immediate" ethical life, the latter by itself only the belief that whatever one wills is good by definition. It is the union of the two that brings the subjective and the objective together.

A serious problem arises in all this: the *Phenomenology* is devoted to the "unhappy" side of subjective freedom, to a catalogue of the psychological and social disasters that this freedom has brought about.[12] Hegel never makes clear how the Hegelian state, a new self-conscious ethics, is to be possible after the gradual unfolding of a ruinous subjectivism in Western thought; after consciousness has become so estranged from substantial ethical life and so arbitrary that reality is found only within an individual ego and will; after confidence in the infallibility of individual mind has led to catastrophes such as the French Revolution, which Hegel viewed largely as the product of radical subjectivism, of seeing the state as merely "external" and "other."[13] How, in short, the ethical whole of the state in the *Philosophy of Right* is to be possible after the inventory of spiritual disasters of the *Phenomenology*, is not clear in Hegel. Since most of the forms of radical subjectivism that led to "unhappy consciousness" at best and violence and revolution at worst issue out of the Christian tradition that Hegel often calls a great advance in history, it is also not clear whether Christianity and its realm of will and subjectivity was really an advance or the beginning of anarchism and universal moral solipsism; whether Hegel really believed that ancient nonindividualist ethics was something that needed to be superceded or that it flourished in a "paradise of the human spirit."[14] Of course, he may actually have believed both; this would account for a great deal that is equivocal or paradoxical in his work.

Setting some of these difficulties aside for the moment, it is necessary to point out that Hegel always tried to preserve willing as a moral concept, and that many of his most serious problems are caused by this effort. No one has understood Hegel's special brand of voluntarism more clearly than George Kelly, who argues entirely correctly that

> the most striking element, perhaps, of Hegel's political theory, which makes it quite foreign to simplistic forms of organicism, is that he takes the subjective will to be a cornerstone of modern government. Of course he does not stop there: he imposes a higher "Hellenic" or *sittlich* goal of public virtue and public service upon the modern conditions. Yet the origins of this standpoint are not in "nature," but rather in the will, which, being free, produces a system of right as "a realm of freedom made actual, the world of mind brought forth out of itself like a second nature"...In historical terms, the synthesis of will and reason in actualized institutions has far less to do with the anticipation of industrial dilemmas than with the need to mediate revolutionary subjectivism with a legal recovery of the common life and the practice of public virtue.[15]

This attitude distinguishes Hegel sharply from, say, Burke, with whom he is sometimes rather facilely compared. Both, of course, use organic metaphors of growth and decay in their political writings; both speak of the rationality of the historically actual and decry the rationalism of subjectivists and revolutionaries. But Burke makes no effort to synthesize will with these elements.[16] Hegel almost always does and as a result in an infinitely more complicated political philosopher than Burke, though he is careful to balance will with the "objective": "Ethical life is the Idea of freedom in that on the one hand it is the good become alive—the good endowed in self-consciousness with knowing and willing and actualized by self-conscious action—while on the other hand self-consciousness has in the ethical realm its absolute foundation and the end which actualizes its efforts."[17]

It is true, of course, that Hegel strove constantly to identify the real will with the rational will and that he defined freedom, and goodness, and virtue in terms of the reconciliation of "natural" will (impulse, caprice) with the real or rational will. "It is only as having the power of thinking that the will is free," he urges in the *History of Philosophy;* "the unity of thought with itself is freedom, is the free will."[18] It is true that he was able to see the state as something willed, even without any allowance for social contract theory, consent theory, or even approval of elections or opinion, because reason (or freedom-as-reason) connects the real will and the state. More precisely, it provides a content for both: rational freedom, which is seen as substance in the state and as accident in individuals.[19] It is true in general that he treated will as thought striving to actualize itself, since it is "only as thinking intelligence that the will is genuinely a will and free,"[20] since the will is a "moment" of thought, mind as it "steps into actuality."[21] All of this involves a fairly severe circumscription of the numerous meanings that will can have and has had, certainly a circumscription that makes it tolerably easy to relate will to the state via the concept of rational freedom.

Despite all of this, Hegel's is still a theory of will, though will of a rather passive sort, since it ultimately reduces itself to "recognition," to acceptance of the rational that is in actual institutions. Hegel could, however, argue that it is rather crude to look for willing only in explicitly consensual acts, that since "spirit" is actualized in the world through particular minds, everything is willed by somebody and derives at least its subjective value and the whole of its actual existence from being thus willed. "The educated man," Hegel declares, "develops an inner life and wills that he himself shall be in everything he does." Hegel could, then, urge that all social phenomena are precisely willed in a way that social contract theory, with its concentration on the explicitly consensual, never dreamed of. He could argue that mere agreement and consent can endorse and legitimize anything, however insane or evil, that his own view of volition as rational will was both safer and more comprehensive than the contractarian tradition.[22] And none of these claims can be rejected out of hand, because they all have a certain plausibility: after all, one never signs a social contract, but one constantly performs lesser social acts of rational value that depend on being willed.

What Hegel seems to have wanted is what he (once) says the Greeks enjoyed: a "medium between the loss of individuality on the part of man...and Infinite Subjectivity as pure certainty of itself—the position that the Ego is the ground of all that can lay claim to substantial existence."[23] It is essential to point this out, because it shows that Hegel was trying to deal with a problem that was rather like Rousseau's and that his conceptual apparatus, though not his conclusions, links him more closely to the great contract theorists than to a total nonvoluntarist like Burke. In fact, from a very abstract point of view, which is sometimes necessary to clarify obscured relations, Rousseau, Hegel, and Kant are comparable insofar as all three strove to combine the importance of the will with a rational, universal content. This is true even though the general will, the concrete universal, and the categorical imperative are very different indeed; all three philosophers could agree, in different ways, with Hegel's dictum that "everything depends on the unity of universal and particular."[24]

Hegel as a kind of voluntarist was striving to cope in the most serious way possible with a problem that is extremely difficult for anyone who takes up a "moral" position—namely, that my conviction, however valuable it may be from some point of view, will sometimes set itself against what actually exists, calling it immoral or even unreal; and that in the name of morality concrete social institutions of rational value, which "enshrine the convictions of countless individuals," will be assaulted. "Now if I set against these [institutions] the authority of my single conviction-...that at first seems a piece of monstrous self-conceit, but in virtue of the principle that subjective conviction is to be the measuring-rod, it is pronounced not to be self-conceit at all."[25]

Hegel is dealing with a problem that is not only of great speculative difficulty but of great practical moment as well: granting the importance of conviction, conscience, and good will, how can it be said whether or not they are right? Can they even be subjected to a criterion of right without being contradicted? Whatever Hegel's solution to this problem, he has certainly identified the crucial difficulty in "moral" philosophies and in the social consequences to which they lead.[26] This great question is resolved—to the extent that it is ever resolved—quite differently by various philosophers: by assigning to will an objective end defined in terms of natural law or "practical reason," or perhaps even utility. All of these work in some sense—that is, they are coherent—so long as the standard to which will must conform is not antivoluntaristic. Hegel is perhaps the only great voluntarist who insists consistently on a concrete universal as a fit object of volition, and it is this insistence that causes him so much trouble. For standards such as natural law and utility leave room for a certain creative tension between individual minds, the "mind" of the universal standard, and the "mind" of society; whereas in Hegel the identification of objectively ethical purposes with actual states leaves him open to the charge that he is not really preserving will as a moral concept, not even by "canceling and preserving" it.

Hegel, then, resembles some of his predecessors in wanting to retain the will but to give it a content other than itself. His solution to this problem lies in seeing reason and freedom not simply in the mind and will of one person but in the ethical institutions that actually exist in history. "What lies between reason as self-conscious mind and reason as an actual world before our eyes, what separates the former from the latter and prevents it from finding satisfaction in the latter," he wrote in the *Philosophy of Right*, "is the fetter of some abstraction."[27] The Hegelian will must see itself realized in its highest form in these institutions; and this recognition is supposed to combine real volition with the avoidance of mere subjectivism, of conviction as an end in itself. The question then becomes: granting that social institutions are rational, that they embody a "prodigious transfer" of reason into the "outer world," is this a sufficient reason for calling the state not simply rational but "mind on earth" and the "march of God in the world," against which all forms of subjectivism are to be counted for little?[28] Why the objectivity of the state will suddenly become persuasive and effective in an age that Hegel himself characterizes as one of rampant subjectivism, individualism, romanticism, and revolution is none too clear.

This would be less problematical if Hegel were concerned only with the concept of the state; but Hegel wanted to demonstrate the sufficient rationality of the states that actually exist, to see "reason as the rose of the cross of the present." Indeed, he sometimes seems to urge that while men must think only of the concept of the state, they must accept any actual state.[29] What makes Hegel's case even more complicated is that he sometimes grants a distinction between reason itself and the partial rationality of actual ethical institutions. Great difficulty is caused, he says in the *Philosophy of Right*, by the "gradual intrusion of reason, of what is inherently and actually right, into primitive institutions which have something wrong at their roots."[30] But when are institutions sufficiently rational to serve as a "substantive end" for subjectivity—unless history is now totally fulfilled? If it is fulfilled, however, why did the French Revolution, subjectivism's most notable triumph, wind down only at about the time that the *Phenomenology* was being written? His answer on this point is that political revolution is the consequence of the juxtaposition of a "slavish" religion (Catholicism) with a relatively modern political order, and that Germany, as a Protestant power that had long recognized the sphere of "inward freedom," would not undergo revolution because it had the good fortune to have had a Reformation.[31]

This does not seem to be one of Hegel's more persuasive arguments. He presents his readers with an almost insurmountable problem, for the concept that he wants to represent as a positive force in history—subjective freedom being universally actualized—is brilliantly shown to be ruinous and anarchistic in every form except the one (the state) that the very history of that unfolding subjectivism had made possible. Only by representing his own time as one in which subjectivity and objectivity were or could be in perfect harmony could Hegel hope that the modern state would have "prodigious strength and depth because it allows the principle of subjectivity to progress to its culmination in the extreme of self-subsistent personal particularity, and yet at the same time brings it back to the substantive unity and so maintains this unity in the principle of subjectivity itself."[32] Whether he believed that his own time—or indeed any modern time—could support such an ideal is open to some doubt. Indeed, Hegel was not content with the bare idea of the state as something that ought to be but cannot be; as he observes in the *Logic*, "Wholes like the State [or the Church] cease to exist when the unity of their notion and their reality is dissolved."[33]

Hegel is sometimes accused of unreasonably allowing the dialectical unfolding of history-as-mind to end with the Prussian state. This charge is unfair; Hegel never announced that history had ended but merely suggested this in the *Philosophy of Religion*.[34] Yet it does suggest, in however crude a way, that the actualization of freedom ought not to stop until reality is equivalent to its "concept" (hence the radical side of Hegel). The Greek institution of partial freedom (for those who "knew"), for example, contradicted the idea of freedom itself, since it was compatible with slavery for many; thus, a tension was set up between the concept and its actualization. But the concept always strives to attain its intrinsic limits. This expansion, passing from the abstract freedom of the few who know in Greece to the more diffusive but still abstract legal freedom for all in Roman law, finally attained a Christian stage, in which every person is recognized as an ethically perfectible subject capable of knowledge and will. And when the Reformation overcame the gulf between this Christian concept and the unfortunate reality of Catholic worldliness, that concept finally was able to flower in autonomous secular social forms.[35] Part of the objection to Hegel involves the apparent cutting off of this dynamism in his claim that any mature state of his epoch had in it "the moments essential to the existence of the state" coupled with the claim that "the state is. . .the actualization of freedom." Many could agree with Hegel that "it is an absolute end of reason that freedom should be actual" without thinking that this was yet the case or that such freedom should be found simply and only in the state.[36]

Furthermore, Hegel could not recommend that we simply accept the best we can get in the way of rational institutions, as, by analogy, his criticism of Leibniz's optimism in the *History of Philosophy* shows: "If I have some goods brought to me in the market at some town, and say that they are certainly not perfect, but are the best that are to be got, this is quite a good reason why I should content myself with them. But comprehension is a very different thing from this."[37] Something's being tolerable is very different from its being rational. In the end, Hegel's attitude toward the state may not be quite coherent. He says at one point that "we should desire in the state nothing except what is an expression of rationality," which seems to put judgments about such rationality in the minds of persons and particularly of philosophers. But he also urges that since it is easy to find defects in any actual state, and since the state "is no ideal work of art" but "stands on earth and so in the sphere of caprice, chance and error," it is unreasonable to insist on perfection. In a remarkable analogy he adds that "the ugliest of men, or a criminal, or an invalid, or a cripple is still always a living man," the point apparently being that even the most crippled state is still a state.[38] This is put in an even harsher, almost utilitarian way in the *Logic*: the notion of the state, he says, so essentially constitutes the nature of individuals that "they are forced to translate it into reality... or submit to it as it is, or else perish. The worst state, whose reality least corresponds to the notion, is still Idea insofar as it exists."[39]

In the end, he is forced to say that he intends to emphasize only the "affirmative factor" in the state.[40] But this selectivity is not exactly open to one who wishes to emphasize the rationality of what is actual. In any case, since philosophy, as the highest manifestation of "absolute" mind, stands in judgment over the "objective" mind of the state, just as objective mind stands over "subjective" mind in individuals, ultimately philosophy and not history will judge the adequacy of states.[41] However, since Hegel sometimes represents philosophy as retrospective—as "under-standing" what has been rather than "prescribing" what ought to be—[42] and sometimes as absolute, uncontingent knowledge free of historical limitation,[43] it is hard to know whether philosophy will stand above the state or simply make it intelligible. Unless reality fully actualizes a concept—unless a state is not merely more rational than its predecessors but "mind on earth"—then objective mind will always have to yield to absolute mind, or so one might think. Even if "moral" objections can have no weight against "ethics," philosophy will be in another, higher position; and for philosophy reason itself will be more than what is rational. But all of this depends on whether Hegel saw philosophy as absolute or as retrospective; he tries to relate the two—it is not for nothing that the history of philosophy is for him part of philosophy itself—but retrospective understanding seems passive, and Hegel is not passive.

Hegel's efforts to fuse the state, ethics, morality, history, philosophy, and the concept of will into a system based on rational freedom is extraordinarily intricate and problematical. The only way to judge his success is to turn to the details of several of his works. First, though, it is useful to make one further point for the benefit of those who do not think of Hegel as any kind of voluntarist at all. Particularly in the *Phenomenology* it does look as though Hegel may avoid the problems of voluntarism that had troubled Hobbes, Locke, and Rousseau by placing the idea of *consciousness* altogether above this dilemma, by showing that consciousness, and hence the possession of ideas and volitions, is precisely a social product and that minds, though truly particular, are moments of a mind whose content is collective. A great deal of his work inclines in this direction: the long discussion of the nature of language and universal terms in the *Phenomenology* makes no political sense until it becomes clear later in the work that for Hegel a man's thoughts are expressions of ideas collectively arrived at, that consciousness itself is not strictly private, that saying or even thinking anything involves the use of a medium—language—that men collectively create.[44] If the relation of individual to universal could be explained in terms of consciousness, one would find a genuine common element between the individual and the whole: individual minds would be the precondition of the act of thinking, while the content of consciousness would be socially generated. Even in the *Philosophy of Right,* in which for the most part Hegel abandons the idea of consciousness as transcending the subject-object problem and speaks of will, real will, and reconciliation of will, Hegel says at one point that individuals are to the whole as accidents are to substance.[45] And this is congruent with the theory of consciousness in the *Phenomenology.*

Hegel's theory of the state, however, is contained not in the *Phenomenology* but in the *Philosophy of Right,* and in that work the concept of will is uppermost, though in the form of transformed will, as real will equals reason. Had Hegel adhered to a theory of consciousness as something both social and individual and not attempted to incorporate a theory of will into his doctrine, he would not be so problematic. But for various reasons, the Christian-Kantian inheritance among them, he took over the voluntarist tradition and vocabulary and tried to make it consonant with a nearly Platonic view that only knowledge and not volition really matters. One can see at a glance the consequences for a supposedly voluntarist position of this favoring of knowledge and the objective: consent, contract, election, and opinion, so important to social contract theorists, are of little value, but the knowledge of the state's objective requirements possessed by the "universal class" of civil servants is essential.[46] However, since Hegel was far from wholly rejecting the Christian tradition of virtue understood in terms of good acts and good will, he had to convert will into reason, and sometimes into knowledge, in order to uphold both objectivity and subjectivity. This transformation of the concept of will is something to which Hegel devotes a great deal of effort in the early parts of the *Philosophy of Right.* In order to understand, however, what is involved in Hegel's decision to operate with a new concept of consciousness and an older concept of will, one should proceed at once to a consideration of the *Phenomenology*, introduced by a few remarks about the *Philosophy of History*.

Hegel's most familiar and influential though scarcely most important work, the *Philosophy of History*, suggests that the concepts of will, private judgment, and conscience are going to be more important—above all, more highly praised—than they in fact are in the rest of his work. Indeed, reading this work only gives the impression that to Hegel the progressive actualization of freedom in the world is the most important of all considerations and that the main vehicle of this realization was the subjectivity of Christianity after it fell on the receptive "inward-looking tenderness" of the Germanic nations. In the *Philosophy of History* the Greeks, who are treated much more reverently in the *Phenomenology*, appear largely as a people who did not understand the real meaning of freedom, though they are praised in other respects. The Romans are treated as a people who converted freedom into mere legal rights or rights of legal personality. Only the "Germanic" peoples of the Christian era are represented as peoples who, beginning with the idea of the individual as the subject of salvation in religious thought, went on to diffuse this concept of individualism into the spheres of philosophy, literature, and politics.[47] The best account of this diffusion is given by Hegel in the *Philosophy of Right*, though in a tone reminiscent of the *Philosophy of History*: "the right of the subject's particularity, his right to be satisfied, or in other words the right of subjective freedom is the pivot and center of the difference between antiquity and modern times." This right, Hegel declares, appears in an "infinite" form in the Christian religion, and has become the essential principle of a "new form of civilization." Among the "primary shapes" that this right has taken are "love, romanticism, the eternal salvation of the individual," then "moral convictions and conscience," and finally the "other forms." Here, Hegel becomes rather vague, speaking of "what follows as the principle of civil society and as moments in the constitution of the state"; probably he was thinking of the freedom to buy and sell, to contract, and to find "subjective satisfaction" in being part of the actualization of society and state.[48] In any case, his characterization of modern Western civilization as shaped by the principle of subjective particularity is remarkably complete, though even at this point there is an inkling of Hegel's later operations in that salvation, morality, and conscience are mentioned in the same breath with love and romanticism.

In Christianity, Hegel suggests, individual conviction and subjective belief were important for the first time, and religion was no longer simply worship of nature or a mere ritual. What remained was to "introduce the principle into the various relations of the actual world...the application of the principle to political relations." The "molding and interpenetration of the constitution of society" by this principle of subjective freedom was "a process identical with history itself."[49] The Greeks initiated this process but did not sufficiently advance it because they "had not the idea of man and the essential unity of the divine and the human nature according to the Christian view."[50] During the Christian era the Church itself, in Hegel's view, began to corrupt its own principles: authoritarianism infringed on conscience, and concern with mere external show despiritualized religion. "The Church took the place of conscience: it put men in leading strings like children, and told them that man could not be freed from the torments which his sins had merited, by any amendment of his own moral condition, but by outward actions, *opera operata*—actions which were not the promptings of his own good will, but performed by commands of the ministers of the Church..."[51]

Because the Church had begun to insist only on external requirements such as masses and pilgrimages, the Reformation was necessary to restore the true spirit of Christianity: not in the sense of returning to a primitive and unphilosophical community (Hegel condemned those who would reject the philosophy of the Fathers of the Church) but in the sense of eliminating the merely external and sensuous. Since the Reformation time "has had no other work than the formal imbuing of the world with this principle." Furthermore, all human institutions must be given this newly-recovered form: "Law, property, social morality, government, constitutions, etc., must be conformed to general principles in order that they be in accord with the idea of the free will and be rational. Thus only can the spirit of truth manifest itself in subjective will—in the particular shapes which the activity of the will assumes." Spirit, having "gained consciousness" of itself through the Reformation, must now take up the principle of freedom and carry it out "in building up the edifice of secular institutions."[52]

To be sure, there are scattered indications that in the *Philosophy of History* Hegel was mindful of what he built the whole of the *Phenomenology* upon: the destructiveness, both of self and of society, of the various forms of modern subjectivism. When, for example, he suggests that the Sophistic principle "man is the measure of all things" is ambiguous because the term *man* "may denote spirit in its depth and truth, or in the aspect of mere caprice and private interest," he goes on to point out that "this Sophistic principle appears again and again, through different forms, in various periods of history" and makes this more explicit by saying that "in our own times subjective opinion of what is right—mere feeling—is made the ultimate ground of decision."[53] And in the last few pages of the *Philosophy of History* he warns that when the right of subjectivity takes the form of pitting the private will against the rationality of the state (here he is thinking of the French Revolution), will is out of control, has become a mere "frenzy of self-conceit," is no longer one moment of a whole that must include the objective moment of "ethics."[54] Nonetheless, and despite these few passages, the general spirit of the *Philosophy of History* is one of seeing Christian moral theory as a great advance, as something that may in some forms drift toward moral anarchism but that is to be defended in principle.

The *Phenomenology* is a remarkably different as well as a far greater work. Indeed, Judith Shklar exaggerates only enough to make her point when she calls it a "massive assault upon the 'subjectivity' of individualism."[55] Most of this huge book is given over to demonstrating that concentration on the self leads to egoism, to subjectivism, to a denial of the real world—in any case to the deification of arbitrary willfulness and caprice—and ultimately, when subjectivism externalizes itself, to destruction and death. As early as the introduction a rather "Protestant" observation, "To follow one's own conviction is certainly more than to hand oneself over to authority," is demolished by the succeeding explication: "if we stick to a system of opinion and prejudice resting on the authority of others, or upon personal conviction, the one differs from the other merely in the conceit which animates the latter." Hegel strongly condemns the merely private understanding that "always knows how to dissipate every possible thought, and to find instead of all the content, merely the barren Ego."[56] In the *Phenomenology* he seems determined to display the dark, negative, destructive side of subjective particularity, just as in the *Philosophy of History* he displays, on the whole, the positive side.

Hegel's attack on subjectivism and "justification by conviction" in the *Phenomenology* is made all the sharper by his extremely sympathetic treatment of a wholly nonvoluntarist and preindividualistic ethical system—that of the Greeks. True, he grants that the "germ of destruction" always lay within "that very peace and beauty belonging to the gracious harmony and peaceful equilibrium of the ethical spirit." But there is a great deal of nostalgia and regret in Hegel's characterization of ancient ethics. "Virtue in the olden times had its secure and determinate significance, for it found the fulness of its content and its solid basis in the substantial life of the nation"; it had for its purpose not "a virtue merely in idea and in words" but a "concrete good that existed and lay at its hand." And since this purpose was concrete, really existed, it was not "directed against actual reality as a general perversity."[57] The subjective end of indiviuals and the will of the state coincided.

Hegel, as Shklar reminds us, often found it useful to show what he thought the nature of ancient ethics had been by reminding his readers of certain Greek plays, particularly *Antigone* and *Oedipus,* which were ideally suited to a demonstration of the fact that strong individualism and insistence on personal will and conviction (Christian and Kantian notions) were foreign to Greek ethics. It was not exactly the case, however, that such an ethical system was so integrated that there were no elements whatever that could fly apart; on the contrary, Greek ethical communities contained an inherent tension between what Hegel called the "divine law" of the family and its "piety" and the objective "universality" of the city. This tension might break out into open conflict if, as in the case of Antigone, a woman, who for Hegel embodies family piety, defied the state in the service of the family. Both the divine command ordering the burial of her brother and the state's command, issued by its agent Creon, to leave the body unburied were valid for Antigone, but the divine law took precedence. Be it ever so true, Hegel suggests, that "the family...finds in the community its universal substance and subsistence" and that "the community finds in the family the formal element of its own realization," this ideal unity can fly apart so long as minds can choose between different moments of ethical life. It is true that for Hegel individuals in Greek life, as exemplified in Greek tragedy, do not choose *qua* individuals, putting forward their own conviction or intention; the content of choice is determined by the "laws and customs of...class or station." Hence, Antigone chooses as a sister and as a defender of the family, not as a particular self. In antiquity "self-consciousness within the life of a nation descends from the universal only down as far as specific particularity, but not as far as the single individuality." Still, even though fully personal choice and personal will are not involved in a decision like Antigone's, the Greek ethical consciousness "cannot disclaim the crime and its guilt," for "the deed consists in setting in motion what was unmoved, and in bringing out what in the first instance lay shut up as a mere possibility."[58] Guilt is purer, Hegel suggests, if crime is knowingly committed; hence, Antigone's "ethical consciousness" is more complete than that of Oedipus because, though an agent of "divine" law and family piety, she defied the city, whereas Oedipus was ignorant of his situation.[59]

Unlike modern men, however, Antigone does not dwell on the less than fully voluntary character of her choice in an effort to justify herself; in acknowledging her error she indicates that "the severance between ethical purpose and actuality has been done away," that "the agent surrenders his character and the reality of his self, and has utterly collapsed." But this "victory" of the ethical whole, which wants to preserve permanently "a world without blot or stain, a world untainted by any internal dissension," is short-lived, because, according to Hegel, the opposition of ethical powers to one another "have reached their true end only insofar as both sides undergo the same destruction."[60] This destruction might take a merely external form, as when foreign forces attack the city to right the wronged divine laws of the family. But in a deeper sense the destruction is contained within the society itself, in the form of an individualism and self-consciousness that ethical choices help to bring into the light. It is this deeper malaise of subjectivity with which Hegel is really concerned, and with which he knew Plato had been concerned as well: for Hegel the *Republic* represents a monumental effort to refute the rising claims of individualism.[61] In any case, Hegel felt that *Antigone* serves to show in a stroke all of the implications of Greek ethical thought.

However morally undeveloped Antigone may be, Hegel does not throw a very flattering light on her more "advanced" successors. She takes rules for the "unwritten and unerring laws of the gods": the laws simply are. If, however, one insists, as do modern men, on knowing where the laws came from, Hegel says, one makes oneself and one's conviction about the laws what is universal, thus making the laws themselves "conditional and limited." Hegel says, "If they are to get the sanction of my insight, I have already shaken their immovable nature." But true ethical sentiment "consists just in holding fast and unshaken by what is right...it is right because it is the right."[62] Antigone may have no fully developed sense of self, of private will, but she knows what is right. In *Antigone* Hegel sees not the "comic spectacle of a collision between two duties," both representing themselves as absolutes recognized by conscience, but the unavoidable and hence tragic collision of two "laws of nature"—the law of the family and that of the city—through agents—Antigone and Creon—who do not personally choose their fates.[63] Hegel often suggested that Greek ethics was inadequate insofar as it did not sufficiently distinguish between voluntary and involuntary acts, but this did not affect his opinion of the grandeur and the simplicity of that ethos.[64] Sometimes Hegel almost yearns for this wholeness, despite what he calls its inadequacies.

The Greek ethical society, for all its peaceful equilibrium, was destined to collapse because of the necessary way in which mind develops, individually and socially, once the consciousness of subjectivity gets the better of "unconscious" universality. The "harmony" of such an ethical system notwithstanding, it is bound to perish, because it is not "conscious regarding its own nature"; for while the individual in such a social order enjoys a "solid imperturbable confidence," he is unable to conceive of himself as existing in "singleness and independence." The ethical nation lives in a "direct unity with its own substance, and does not contain the principle of pure individualism of self-consciousness"; in it the individual has not yet attained the "unrestricted thought of his free self." After he arrives at an awareness of his singleness and independence, "as indeed he must," his unity with the collectivity is broken; "isolated by himself he is himself now the central essential reality." The actual society comes to be looked on as an abstraction, while the particular ego becomes "the living truth."[65]

Much of the rest of the *Phenomenology* is taken up with illuminating the various forms that the ego as living truth can take. In a remarkably concentrated passage at the beginning of his account of this "slow progression and succession of spiritual shapes," Hegel anticipates all of the private and social forms that consciousness took after the destruction of the Greek ethos.[66] After abandoning the "beautiful simplicity" of the polis, after beginning to come to an "abstract knowledge of its essential nature," spirit, or mind, found itself partly embodied in the "formal universality of right or legality" in the Roman Empire. But since this legalistic world of "crass solid actuality" was unequal to the fullness of spirit, an element of it went inward into the "element of thought," into the "world of belief or faith," the realm of the inner life and of truth—into Christian subjectivity. After a number of stages including the Middle Ages, the Reformation, and the Enlightenment, self-consciousness took the form of "morality," which "apprehends itself as the essential truth," and finally "conscience," in which individual conviction is stated in the form of language— itself universal by definition—ultimately combining subjectivity with the universal requirements of publicity and recognition.[67] Along the way, in his traversal of the spiritual "gallery of pictures," Hegel finds plenty of time to stop for a lengthy critique of Hobbesian psychology together with its political consequences and, later, of Kant's system. By the end Hegel has treated almost every form of subjectivity known up until his time.

Hegel passes rather quickly by the Romans, whose concept of "legal personality" he seems particularly to have disliked and whom he condemned for making the state something purely external and merely a matter of power (the Stoics, he suggested, had some reason to turn inward, to the "pure universality of thought," in such a time of "universal fear and bondage"). He speaks at some length of the kind of ethical life that existed in the Middle Ages, characterizing it as the "heroism of service," a kind of virtue that "sacrifices individual being to the universal and thereby brings this into existence."[68] But this heroic service did not bring about the existence of a real state for two reasons. First, no state has attained its concept until it has a monarch whose will adds a "moment of subjectivity" to the intrinsic rationality of state activity, and this was not yet possible in the Middle Ages. And second, the man who served heroically only seemed to do so; he did not really serve the state, since he was unwilling to serve any real monarch, but was only a "haughty vassal" who served merely to gain the "self-importance" that "honor" brought him.[69] Because of honor and self-importance, the medieval state never became a true state—the "essential reality"—in Hegel's view.

If the medieval state was one of aristocratic particularity rather than genuine universality, of privilege rather than law, the next stage in the unfolding of subjectivity is not seen in a particularly attractive light either. One of the most destructive and contradictory forms of subjectivism is "the law of the heart, and the frenzy of self-conceit," a phenomenon that Hegel deliberately links with the philosophy of Hobbes by a careful choice of terms. When consciousness sets up the law of its heart as the only thing it can recognize as real, Hegel says, it is resisted by others who want to make equal claims for the law of their hearts. If there is any universality in this, he goes on, it is only a "universal resistance and struggle of all against one another," a "state of war of each against all." The cause of this "meaningless insubstantial sport," in Hegel's view, is the "restless individuality which regards opinion or mere individualism as law, the real as unreal, and the unreal as real." It is the individual consciousness trying to be universal that is "raving and perverted," and in such a situation the only possible kind of social order is the one Hegel describes in connection with the worst days of the Roman Empire. In Rome (and implicitly in *Leviathan*), where no true ethical society existed, the "absolute plurality of dispersed atomic personalities" was gathered into a single center that, in contrast to the "pretended absolute but inherently insubstantial reality" of these single personalities, was the "entire content," the "universal power." The power of such a ruler, says Hegel, is "not the spiritual union and concord in which the various persons might get to know their own self-consciousness. Rather they exist as persons separately for themselves, and all continuity with others is excluded from the absolute punctual atomicity of their nature."[70]

Of course, this is not an altogether fair characterization of Hobbesianism: Hegel treats only Hobbesian psychology, and then only to display it as another form of subjectivism. It is perhaps only just to point out that in the *History of Philosophy* Hegel treats Hobbes more moderately and is even willing to allow the affinities between his own political thought and that of Hobbes. The English philosopher, Hegel claims, was significant insofar as he based the idea of the state on "principles which lie within us" rather than on ideals, Scripture, or positive law, and insofar as he maintained that "the natural condition [of men] is not what it should be, and must hence be cast off." In Hobbes, Hegel says, there is "no idle talk about a state of natural goodness"; on the contrary, Hobbes realized that a state of nature is a condition "far more like that of animals—a condition in which there is an unsubdued individual will." Interestingly, in this relatively favorable version of Hobbes, Hegel says not a word about contract theory; on this reading *Leviathan* is not authorized by consent but involves only the "subjection of the natural, particular will of the individual will to the universal will." Hobbes was "really correct" in locating the universal will of the state in the monarch, Hegel urges, but somehow equated this monarchical will with arbitrary will, even with "perfect despotism." This, of course, is as unfair to Hobbes in one way as the characterization of him in the *Phenomenology* is in another; Hobbes could agree with Hegel that the sovereign's will ought to be "expressed and determined in laws."[71] In any event, Hegel's treatment of Hobbes in the *Phenomenology* shows why he thought so little of contract theory, which might involve nothing more than an agreement to limit the most destructive forms of violence. Its content would not be worthy of the concept of the will; freedom would mean mere caprice moderated by the security sufficient to make that caprice somewhat safer.

The law of the heart and the frenzy of self-conceit are already somewhat more advanced than the morality of the haughty vassal, since they at least deal with efforts to universalize will. But the most advanced and subtle form of subjectivism—and, as such, the one closest to the truth, since it strives for universality even though it winds up with the "bare abstraction" of duty as a mere intention—Hegel calls morality, or moral self-consciousness. It is, in his view, a contradictory and muddled position because, in its effort to isolate pure intentions and purposes from the imperfection of the natural world of impulse and inclination, it by definition denies itself the possibility of being actualized in that unfortunately imperfect world and shuts itself up in a solipsism in which only its own conviction can possibly matter. The contradiction, as Hegel explains it, is this: morality has a content—its purpose, its aim—that "has to be thought of as something which unquestionably has to be, and must not remain a problem." But at the same time, since the translation of purpose into reality in an imperfect world would make duty "flawed," morality cannot carry anything out and must think of its intentions "merely as an absolute task or problem." Actually, Hegel suggests, the moral attitude would be negated if any moral task were really completed, because morality "is only consciousness of the absolute purpose *qua* pure purpose, i.e. in opposition to all other purposes"; that is, it is only this purpose combined with a "struggle" against sensibility and impulse. As a result, Hegel says, morality always shifts the completion of anything "away into infinity."[72]

If moral self-consciousness does act, it is not only contradictory but hypocritical—or, as Hegel says more gently, it "dissembles." When it tries to bring its pure purposes into reality it must act in the external world and so through the sensibility of impulses and inclinations; indeed "self-conscious sensibility, which should be done away with, is precisely the mediating element between pure consciousness and reality—in the instrument used by the former for the realization of itself."[73] Morality is not, then, quite candid either with itself or with others: it must use the means it affects to despise. If it acts, it does so through a corrupt medium; if it does not act, then it cannot claim that its intentions are serious. In either case the position is, for Hegel, absurd.

From a purely philosophical point of view this is an effective but somewhat grotesque characterization. Only a foolish "moral" position would ever hold that action is impossible because it cannot be perfect; in fact, it is only by representing intention as a desire to be perfect that Hegel can make his argument plausible. Many moralists, of course, would agree with Hegel that sensibility is only to be controlled, not negated, by a good will; and one of these would be Kant, who in his *Theory and Practice* provides a strong answer to Hegel's charges. No person is expected to renounce the aim of happiness, which is dependent on "inclination" and "sensibility," Kant says, "for like any finite rational being, he simply cannot do so." He need only "abstract from such considerations" of sensible happiness "as soon as the imperative of duty supervenes, and must on no account make them a *condition* of his obeying the law prescribed to him by reason."[74] Hegel, of course, had what he took to be a decisive objection to this: that reason cannot prescribe anything, that if it is to have any practical force at all, it must be as the reason that is in ethical institutions, not as the reason that is simply in minds. Since Hegel's attempted refutation of Kant is absolutely decisive for his system—since he claimed to replace the abstract universal of Kant's categorical imperative with the concrete universal of the state, or "morality" with "ethics"—it is well worth trying to see why Hegel thought that even Kant's version of morality would not work.

In the *Phenomenology* Hegel urges that since there is no "absolute content" in the Kantian system—no ethical content—the only kind of content available is "formal universality," which means merely that a moral position must not be self-contradictory. Only the "bare form of universality" is left in the Kantian system; reason is not the content of moral laws but only their criterion: "instead of laying down laws reason now only tests what is laid down."[75]

These observations are made far plainer in the *Philosophy of Right*, where after praising Kant for giving prominence to "the pure unconditioned self-determination of the will as the root of duty," Hegel goes on to say that to adhere to the moral position without passing on to ethics is to "reduce this gain [of the idea of will] to an empty formalism." He continues, "If the definition of duty is taken to be the absence of contradiction, formal corre- spondence with itself...then no transition is possible to the specification of particular duties." Kant's idea of universalization contains "no principle beyond abstract identity and the 'absence of contradiction.'" But "a contradiction must be a contradiction of something"; if property is shown to be valid independently of mere universality and noncontradiction, or if life is shown to be a good, "then indeed it is a contradiction to commit theft or murder."[76] In Hegel's view, however, Kant never shows that any particular moral content is valid; he only shows that certain kinds of action would be wrong if a certain content were presupposed. In Kant, Hegel insists, men follow duty not for the sake of real content but only for duty's sake; as a result they never know what is in itself good but only that some action would contradict a content that is no content.

It must be granted that Kant invites such criticism, particularly in the *Fundamental Principles of the Metaphysic of Morals*, by not relating the notion of the dignity of persons as ends-in-themselves to the principles of universality and noncontradiction until halfway through that particular work. Nonetheless, that correlation is finally made, though there are difficulties in it, and as a result there is a little ultimate justification for accusing Kant of mere formal- ism.[77] Whatever objections may be brought against Kant, it is not this easy to overturn him. (Obviously, Hegel was not simply unaware of Kant's notion of ends: the brilliant criticism of the *Critique of Judgment* in Hegel's early *Glauben und Wissen* rules this out.)[78] It remains true, of course, that practical reason in Kant is in some ways problematical—no more than a "necessary hypothe- sis"[79]—and that Hegel is able to exhibit a concrete manifestation of reason in the form of an ethical community that will provide concrete duties. But it is doubtful, first, whether the state is a fit object for the "unconditioned self-determination of the will," to use Hegel's own phrase, and second, whether ethical duties will always be right, unless they are defined as necessarily right. So it is hard to see how one is better off with Hegel than with Kant, particularly in view of the fact that Kant never pits morality against the state; indeed he sees the state not as the embodiment of practical reason but as the *conditio sine qua non* of the effective exercise of practical reason in the phenomenal world and as such as something that must always be obeyed.[80]

If it is not impossible to counter Hegel's objection to "morality," and particularly to the Kantian version of it, he has a stronger point when he speaks of the social effects of moral self-consciousness, especially in the *Philosophy of Right*. In the moral position of pure purpose, Hegel fears, concrete social ethics is "reduced to the special theory of life held by the individual and to his private conviction." If good intention and "subjective conviction" become the standard of what is worthy in conduct, then hypocrisy and immorality will disappear, since even the man who is objectively criminal can cite his good intentions as being really important. "My good intention in my action and my conviction of its goodness make it good."[81]

In the additions to the *Philosophy of Right* Hegel makes his argument more explicit by contrasting the modern moral position with the more truly ethical one of older times. "It is a striking modern innovation to inquire continually about the motives of men's actions," Hegel notes, saying that in other times one simply asked whether a man did his concrete duty. But, he goes on—in a remark that is difficult to reconcile with his observations on the superiority of modern morality, unless one recalls that it is meant to synthesize the will with what is "objective"—"the laurels of mere willing are dry leaves that never were green." Conviction, he urges again, is different from right and truth, and "the bad could only be that of which I am not convinced."[82] What Hegel hopes for as the reconciliation of self-conscious, Christianized morality with objectivity he makes clear enough: "The unity of the subjective with the objective and absolute good is ethical life.... Morality is the form of the will in general on its subjective side. Ethical life is more than the subjective form and self-determination of the will; in addition it has as its content the concept of the will, namely freedom."[83] What is objectively right and good—rational actual freedom—by itself "lacks the moment of subjectivity," while morality is only this subjectivity. Both find their union in the state. Hegel could not yet say this in the *Phenomenology*, but the *Philosophy of Right* puts in a clearer perspective his complaint in the earlier work that for moral self-consciousness there is no ethical reality, "no actual existence which is moral."[84] The moral position, for Hegel, takes what is most volatile and solipsistic in the Christian ethos and aims it against the rationality and freedom of a concrete social order.

While Hegel on occasion uses the terms *morality*, or *moral self-consciousness*, and *conscience* almost interchangeably, in the *Phenomenology* he is extremely careful to draw a line between them, for, there being no theory of the state as the reconciliation of objectivity and subjectivity in this work, he wants to make "conscience" the most universal, the most objective, the most social concept in his gallery of forms. He was, doubtless, all the more careful to be clear about this term, in view of the significance attached to it since the Reformation; in a sense Hegel was reclaiming the word from religious sectarians.

Hegel criticizes "moral self-consciousness" because it is completely self-contained; conscience, on the other hand, involves "the common element of distinct self-consciousness," that is, recognition by others. "Doing something," he says, "is merely the translation of its individual content into that objective element where it is universal and is recognized." What is dutiful, what the content of conscience is, is not specified in the concept of conscience; conscience is simply what is "universal for all self-consciousness," which is recognized or acknowledged and thus objectively is. The essence of the act of conscience, Hegel says, is in the "conviction that conscience has about it," but this conviction is not merely private or personal since conscience, by being universalized, by declaring itself and appealing for recognition, can will only what is universal. Hegel tries to clarify this difficult idea in a passage that is central: "When anyone says, therefore, he is acting from conscience, he is saying what is true, for his conscience is the self which knows and wills. But it is essential that he should say so, for this self has to be at the same time universal self." This universality cannot exist in the content of the conscientious act, since for Hegel content is derivative from the actual ethics of a given society at a given time. The universality can lie only in the form of the act of conscience. And this form is the self, which is "actual in language, which pronounces itself to be the truth, and just by so doing acknowledges all other selves, and is recognized by them."[85]

Obviously, a great deal depends on Hegel's view of language, and it is precisely his theory of language that makes his whole doctrine of conscience work. "We see language to be the form in which spirit finds existence. Language is self-consciousness existing for others... [it]... is self separating itself from itself... the self perceives itself at the same time that it is perceived by others: and this perceiving is just existence which has become a self." By concentrating on what is "universal in all selves," by insisting on the embodiment of personal conviction in language, which can only be understood because it uses "universal" terms, any "distinction between the universal consciousness and the individual self is precisely what has been canceled, and the superseding of it *constitutes* conscience."[86]

In the *Philosophy of Right* Hegel makes this point even plainer. The "objective system" of the principles and duties that constitute the content of conscience "is not present until we come to the standpoint of ethical life." He supplements what he says in the *Phenomenology* by declaring that "whether the conscience of a specific individual corresponds with [the] idea of conscience...is ascertainable only from the content of the good it seeks to realize." Since the good is defined in terms of the amount of rational freedom actualized in the state, the state cannot "give recognition to conscience in its private form as subjective knowing, any more than science can grant validity to subjective opinion." It may tolerate rather than recognize less-than-universal forms of conscience, if it is strong enough to afford such toleration; but it need not, and if it is too weak, it should not.[87]

These formulations involve a radical transformation of the idea of conscience: what is only private in conviction is precisely what is "bracketed out." Indeed, Hegel argues that "actual conscience is not this insistence on a knowledge and a will which are opposed to what is universal" and that anyone who acts from a conscience of his own is actually saying that he is "abusing and wronging" others.[88] Doubtless this transformation was important to Hegel's purposes if he wanted to cancel and preserve the Christian and Kantian "realm of subjectivity"—to retain conviction but to require it to universalize itself through language, to appeal for recognition. On Hegel's view of conscience whoever says "Here I stand" must find others to stand there with him: *con-science*, after all, stresses this *with*, this need of "others."

Ironically, the charge of formalism that Hegel makes against Kant could be turned against his own notion of conscience: just as a Kantian conviction may (allegedly) have any content, so may the ethics of any historical society. If the "formalism" of Kant involves accepting the content of everyone's conviction, the formalism of Hegelian conscience involves accepting the content of whatever customs obtain at a given time. Perhaps Ernst Cassirer does not even go too far in saying that it involves the acceptance of whatever power is most effective or successful at any given moment,[89] though this was surely not Hegel's intention, to judge from what he says against the equation of might and right in his contemptuous refutation of von Haller.[90]

Nonetheless, in the absence of a general theory of the state in the *Phenomenology*, and given both his objections to moral subjectivism and his wish to preserve conviction in some form, such a formulation as Hegel's theory of conscience appears to be essential. It is supplanted by the more concrete content of the state in the *Philosophy of Right*. Before turning to that work, however, it is possible to give a slightly more adequate notion of why Hegel could not use the concept of consciousness as the bridge between individuals and the whole in the *Philosophy of Right*, and thus had to speak in terms of will. The reason why Hegel was able to avoid the problems of voluntarism in the *Phenomenology* but got caught up in them in the *Philosophy of Right* is that the latter builds on a concept of institutions as embodying reason, while the former relies mainly on consciousness. While it is true that in the chapter on conscience in the *Phenomenology* the idea of the will is not excluded, it is definitely subordinated to the idea that what links the individual and society is the fact that the former depends on the latter for its very thoughts, its very language. Without language, which makes conceptual thinking possible, individuals would remain at the level of bare perception. The complicated notion of personality would never even appear; the distinction between animal and human life would be diminished. "Conscience is the common element of distinct self-consciousness," but that self-consciousness, as distinguished from perception, is itself socially generated. The theory of language and the theory of conscience as social consciousness put the idea of will in the shade. The reconciliation of self with the whole does not require a will to stop being willful but simply the possibility of understanding the self for what it is: a social product.[91]

What makes this a possibility in the *Phenomenology* is the fact that conscience, the highest stage of social consciousness treated in that work, is not defined in terms of reason, as is the state in the *Philosophy of Right*. It is defined only in terms of formal universality.[92] Of course, in the *Phenomenology* reason is taken to be a very high form of consciousness, but that does not affect the definition of conscience in that work. In the *Philosophy of Right*, however the state, as successor to the abstraction of conscience, must embody reason: and reason, or thinking in general, can avoid the abstractness of being mere ratiocinations or thoughts and actually become reasoning and thinking only when subjective activity is joined with the ideas of reason and thought. (Recall that Hegel criticizes Plato for imagining that there could be rule of thought without everyone thinking, and his claim in the *Logic* that for thought to avoid abstraction substance must be understood as subject,[93] that "mere ideas" have actually to be thought of.) If substance must be subject, as Gadamer especially points out,[94] if thought must give way to thinking, ratiocinations to reasoning, then the concepts of thinking and reasoning, and hence ultimately reason in the state, will in some degree have to become subjective, will require the idea of volition as part of themselves. (Here one recalls what Hegel says about thinking and willing as things that cannot be kept in different pockets.)[95] Consciousness, however, is not consistently defined in this way; will sometimes has a part in it, but it is often defined in terms of linguistic universals common to self and society. When in the *Philosophy of Right* reason becomes what must be actualized—while in the *Phenomenology* there is only a criterion (universality of form, or "conscience") of *whatever* is to be actualized—the idea of will must be made fundamental as part of the concept of reasoning. (This is ironic considering that Hegel treats will in most of its forms as irrational.) Hence, voluntarism, albeit in an odd form—as part of the definition of reason—becomes the precondition of the state-as-reason. The reason that consciousness will not suffice in the *Philosophy of Right* is that consciousness, unlike reason, may have any content from subjectivism and/or egoism to "absolute knowledge." But none of these possibilities forms part of the definition of consciousness. As a consequence, though the idea of consciousness avoids many of the problems of voluntarism, it also avoids the requirement that reason be what is actualized in the state as the necessary concrete content of conscience. Only by representing consciousness as equivalent to reason could Hegel have used it as the foundation of the *Philosophy of Right*. But there were no grounds for doing this, and as a result his theory of the difference between thought and thinking, ratiocination and reasoning, coupled with what there was of a (wavering) respect for Christian subjectivity in his philosophy, led him to construct the *Philosophy of Right* on the basis of a theory of rational will in terms of which the good, freedom, and virtue are then defined. Hegel's own concept of reasoning as the activity of a subject forced him to introduce the very concept of will that he commonly saw as the foundation of a ruinous subjectivism.

It is, incidentally, the fact that the *Philosophy of Right* is built around the notion of rational will that makes it impossible to accept unreservedly Alexandre Kojeve's celebrated reading of Hegel's philosophy as something shaped throughout by the notions of mastery and slavery, by the notion of a dialectical "struggle for recognition" between masters and slaves.[96] The reason, indeed, that this study has given prominence to the *Phenomenology*'s great set-pieces on Antigone and Kant at the expense of the brilliant "Master and Servant" chapter is that Antigone and Kant bear directly on Hegel's notion of will as it finally flowers in the *Philosophy of Right*, while mastery and slavery by contrast are, in Hegel's own words, something long since transcended. In section 57 of the *Philosophy of Right* Hegel insists that

> the position of the free will, with which right and the science of right begin, is already in advance of the false position at which man, as a natural entity and only the concept [of man as mind, as something inherently free] implicit, is for that reason capable of being enslaved. This false, comparatively primitive phenomenon of slavery is one which befalls mind when mind is only at the level of consciousness. The dialectic of the concept and of the purely immediate consciousness of freedom brings about at that point the fight for recognition and the relationship of master and slave.[97]

This passage is difficult to reconcile with Kojeve's insistence that in "having discovered" the struggle for recognition between masters and slaves, "Hegel found himself in possession of the key idea of his whole philosophy."[98] The notions of mastery, slavery, struggle, and recognition are certainly key ideas in one part of the *Phenomenology*; but it is doubtful whether that part shapes all the other parts, and it is simply not true that it shapes the *Philosophy of Right*.[99] It is not surprising that Kojeve's extraordinary *Introduction to the Reading of Hegel* says next to nothing about the *Philosophy of Right*. There is little that it can say; for, as George Kelly has pointed out, the master-slave relationship simply cannot be used as "the synoptic clue to a whole philosophy."[100] Kojeve's reading is especially helpful to those who, like Jean Hyppolite, are working for a Hegel-Marx rapprochement, for the notions of slavery and struggle are clearly important in that connection.[101] But it throws little light on Hegel's final political thoughts, which ground "right and the science of right" in "the position of the free will." It is to that "right," and to that "will," that one finally turns.

The *Phenomenology* ends, so far as forms of society are concerned, with conscience, with expressing oneself universally not in the Kantian sense but in the sense of getting one's conviction universally recognized and of not insisting on conscience as something private and, as Hegel will have it, "capricious." The chapter on conscience however, came near the end of a work in which will in all of its forms is treated quite unfavorably, particularly as compared with the ethics of the Greeks and their "statuesque virtue free from moral ambiguity."[102] By contrast, the *Philosophy of Right* strains to incorporate a transformed theory of will as a moral concept: modern ethical life, "the good become alive," is that good "endowed in self-consciousness with knowing and willing," is "actualized by self-conscious action." This willing and actualizing assume some concrete social, though not political, forms. Whether a man will belong to the agricultural, business, or universal class in civil society, for example, is partly a matter of birth, capacity, and accident; but the "essential and final determining factors are subjective opinion and the individual's arbitrary will, which win in this sphere their right, their merit, and their dignity." On this point Hegel criticizes Plato for allowing the question of vocations to be left to the ruling class.[103]

This willing is put in a proper perspective by several other remarks of Hegel's, most particularly by his suggestion that when confronted with the claims that are made for the individual will "we must remember the fundamental conception that the objective will is rationality implicit or in conception, whether it be recognized or not by individuals."[104] This assertion, reminiscent of Rousseau in its intimation that people may have a real will that they fail to recognize (though not of his claim that they may be "forced to be free"),[105] helps to reinforce Hegel's view that thinking is the highest form of willing and that subjective mind must will the state as a concrete, rational content. The perspective is broadened by his striking—at first sight even startling—assertion that to the "ethical powers which regulate the life of individuals" those individuals are "related as accidents to substance."[106] It was surely no accident that Hegel, possessed of an incomparable knowledge of the history of philosophy, should have chosen to describe the relation of men to the state in the way that Spinoza had described the relation of men to God: as beings not truly individual in themselves but real only to the extent that they participate in the One that alone has reality.[107] Hegel modifies this Spinozistic concept of the relation between substance and accident by allowing that the "substantial order" of the state is attained in the self-consciousness of individuals.[108] This is not surprising in view of his belief that either mere self-consciousness or mere unwilled good are abstractions and that, *pace* Spinoza, "true individuality and subjectivity is not a mere retreat from the universal," provided one sees that the universal is the highest state of being that the individual can will or recognize.[109]

In any case subjective opinion, whatever right and dignity it may win in civil society, wins none—at least none directly—in the guiding of the state. "What the service of the state really requires is that men shall forego the selfish and capricious satisfaction of their subjective ends; by this very sacrifice they acquire the right to find their satisfaction in, but only in, the dutiful discharge of their public functions."[110] To a large extent satisfaction replaces the active forms of willing that are excluded. Indeed, Hegel makes a great deal of use of the term, since it seems to allow a kind of assent that is not an active political consent. In the state the idea of the good provides the will with a satisfying object, and this is essential since "the subjective will has value and dignity only insofar as its insight and intention accord with the good." Hegel drives this point home with a rather harsh observation: "What the subject is, is the series of his actions. If these are a series of worthless productions, then the subjectivity of his willing is just as worthless. But if the series of his deeds is of a substantive nature, then the same is true also of the individual's inner will." This passage is extraordinary in that it juxtaposes with great boldness the inner will and substantiality, which can only mean the state, without allowing any significance whatever to that will if it is objectively wrong. (Sometimes, somewhat paradoxically, Hegel does affirm that even mere belief cannot be touched by politics since, as far as "moral conviction" is concerned, a person "exists for himself alone, and force in that context is meaningless.") This he does too in a theory of the state that claims to take account of will—at least the real will.[111]

Perhaps it is because he employs the idea of will in so attenuated a way that Hegel must use the weakest form of voluntarist language (*find subjective satisfaction* rather than the stronger terms *consent, agree,* or *authorize*) whenever he uses the idea of volition in a political sense. In the absence of will in any active sense in Hegel's theory of the state—not only contract theory but also most elections, participation, opinion, and conscience conventionally defined are denigrated[112]—what is left is will as recognition, above all as acceptance of the rationality of the universal. The recognition of conscience in the *Phenomenology* becomes the recognition of the state in the *Philosophy of Right*. Since the only worthwhile will is the rational will, and since rationality cannot be found in mere Kantian moral universality, it must be looked for in the concrete rationality of the customs and institutions around us: "the state exists immediately in custom, mediately in individual self-consciousness, knowledge and activity."[113] The state, Hegel says in a characteristic passage from the *Encyclopedia*, "provides for the reasonable will—insofar as it is in individuals only implicitly the universal will—coming to a consciousness and understanding of itself and being found."[114] And if, as Aristotle holds, thinking is the highest form of action, then man wills by knowing, by recognizing, by accepting the state as a content.[115] Man is then truly free, since true freedom "consists in the will finding its purpose in a universal content, not in subjective or selfish interests."[116]

Hegel's view of the state as something recognized by the rational will and not merely consented to has been sympathetically restated by Michael Oakeshott in his splendid *On Human Conduct*.

> The claims that the conditions of *das Recht* [right or law] are themselves fully satisfied in the "goodwill" or benevolence of the agent, or in the "sincerity" or conscientiousness of his engagement in self-enactment, or that the "authenticity" of his conduct absolves it from the imputation of fault, are ill formulated. So far from identifying *das Recht*, they merely deny it. They are, however, exaggerated rather than merely false. The "authenticity" of conduct cannot be a sufficient identification of the conditions which constitute *das Recht*, but it stands for a principle of the highest importance; namely, that the only conditions of conduct which do not compromise the inherent integrity of a Subject are those which reach him in his understanding of them, which he is free to subscribe to or not, and which can be subscribed to only in an intelligent act of Will. The necessary characteristic of *das Recht* is not that the Subject must himself have chosen or approved what it requires him to subscribe to, but that it comes to him as a product of reflective intelligence and exhibiting its title to recognition.[117]

When Hegel's political philosophy is taken as a whole, it becomes perfectly clear why he could not allow any of the traditional manifestations of will in politics—contract, consent, agreement, election, opinion, conscience—to have any considerable weight in his state. It is possible to apply to these manifestations a criticism that he made of mere opinion in general: "What is right these [modern] principles locate in subjective aims and opinions, in subjective feeling and particular conviction, and from them follows the ruin of the inner ethical life and a good conscience, of love of right dealing between private persons, no less than the ruin of public order and the law of the land." So strongly did Hegel resent subjectivism by the time he wrote this passage in the preface to the *Philosophy of Right* that, dropping his usual insistence on the moral inadequacy of Platonism, he even likened modern moral ideas to the "maxims which constitute superficiality in this sphere, i.e....the principles of the Sophists which are so clearly outlined for our information in Plato."[118] The tension in the *Philosophy of Right* is very great indeed; there is a struggle to incorporate into a general theory of freedom-as-reason a form of human activity—willing—that in almost every shape he detests.

Not surprisingly, Hegel had a good deal to say about social contract theory, which he was determined to expose as a bad form of voluntarism. Since he believed that contractual relationships enshrine no more than the arbitrary wills of the contractors, and not something universal, he could view social contract theory only with loathing.[119] Not that Hegel was contemptuous of contracts in themselves or of the work and property that they reinforce: work has, for him, a "universal" character that binds society together by making it strive for common ends, and contracts are part of this process. But some things are too important to be seen as contractual, and therefore merely legal—among them marriage and the state. Theorists who conceive political legitimacy in terms of contract have "transferred the character of private property into a sphere of a quite different and higher nature." To conceive of the state as a bargain was as offensive to Hegel as it had been to Burke. He was willing to grant that contract theory contains one moment of truth insofar as it stresses the importance of "will as the principle of the state." But, particularly in the case of Rousseau, only a general will, not a rational and universal will, can arise out of mere agreement, and this vitiates the whole theory. In treating will as mere contract, Hegel claims, Rousseauean theory concentrates too much on "opinion" and "capriciously given express consent," and these are of little value to Hegel.[120]

In the additions to the *Philosophy of Right*, he enlarges on his objections to contract theory. The relation of individuals to society, he urges, can be looked at in only two ways: "either we start from

the substantiality of the ethical order, or else we proceed atomistic-
ally and build on the basis of single individuals." The second point
of view leads to a mere juxtaposition of persons; it excludes mind,
because mind requires the unification of the particular and the
universal. In another passage Hegel emphasizes the naturalness of
the state in language heavily indebted to Aristotle. We are citizens
of the state by birth and by what we require as rational beings, not
by something as arbitrary as agreement: "the rational end of man is
life in the state, and if there is no state there, reason at once
demands that one be founded." In his view it is false to hold that
the state is something optional that may or may not be founded at
the whim of contracting parties; "it is nearer the truth to say that it
is absolutely necessary for every individual to be a citizen."[121]

In Hegel's view the deficiencies of the contractarian position are
not merely theoretical either. In the French Revolution such
abstract conclusions came into power in the form of fanatics who
destroyed everything existent and tried to build a truly rational
state. The result was "the maximum of frightfulness and terror."[122]
The universal freedom of thinking that a new and more rational
order can simply be willed by fiat and good will, he says in the
Phenomenology, can produce only negative action: "it is merely the
rage and fury of destruction." The only achievement of the illusion
of willing new and better things is death, "a death that achieves
nothing, embraces nothing within its grasp."[123]

It is not surprising to find Hegel hostile to the idea that the state
is the consequence of an agreement, however much its actuality
may depend on will in a weaker, or at least very different sense.
However, he is opposed not only to the idea that the origin and/or
legitimacy of the state is traceable to some consensual act but also
to less comprehensive manifestations of political will such as
elections and public opinion. To be sure, Hegel develops at some
length the idea that estates-assemblies ought to exist, at least as a
"mediating" force between "civil society," with its multiplicity of
interests, and the universality of the state. But Hegel says quite
clearly that the estates only add something to the intrinsically
rational determinations of the "universal class" of civil servants,
who "necessarily have a deeper and more comprehensive insight
into the nature of the state's organization and requirements."
Those who insist on "summoning the estates" (here he surely has
France of 1789 in mind) generally make the mistake of thinking
that "the deputies of the people, or even the people themselves,
must know best what is in their best interest" and that their will to

promote it is "undoubtedly the most disinterested." This kind of reasoning, however much it might appeal to a Bentham or a J. S. Mill, does not appeal to Hegel; "to know what one wills, and still more to know what the absolute will, reason, wills, is the fruit of profound apprehension and insight, precisely the things which are not popular." Here, Hegel carries to its extremest point his earlier claim that true will simply is reason. Given this, and given the nonvalue of conviction qua conviction, it is not surprising that he suggests that the real will of a state can never be found in a popular assembly, since "profound apprehension and insight" are "not popular," but only in the determinations formulated by that class that has "the universal as the end of its essential activity."[124]

It is scarcely necessary to point out at much greater length what Hegel's opinion of public opinion is: no more than Plato could he accept the doctrine that opinion must be set above knowledge. If knowledge is the province of the universal class, and at best only "glimmers more or less dimly" in the opinion of the public, then that opinion will not suddenly have a social value that it intrinsically lacks.[125] Though the idea of the universal class does not involve the actual rule of philosophy or philosophers, it does involve the predominance of knowledge; an opinion, however, as Hegel says in the *History of Philosophy*, "is merely mine" ("*die Meinung ist mein*"). While Hegel does not quite claim for knowledge what he claims for philosophy ("philosophy contains no opinions...philosophy is objective science of truth"), knowledge is first in the state, and opinion's main justification is either the possibility of its absorbing knowledge or its absolute harmlessness.[126]

Hegel has little difficulty in relating his view of opinion to what he had said in the *Phenomenology* about the identity of the purely personal with the bad and the universal with the good: "the bad is that which is wholly private and personal in its content; the rational, on the other hand, is the absolutely universal, while it is on peculiarity that opining prides itself."[127] As he goes on to show, just as the only social will worthy of respect is that which wills the state as its rational, substantive end, so too the only respectable opinion is that which accepts the state: "Subjectivity is manifested in its most external form as the undermining of the established life of the state by opinion and ratiocination when they endeavor to assert the authority of their own fortuitous character and so bring about their own destruction. But its true actuality is attained in the opposite of this, i.e. in the subjectivity identical with the substantial will of the state..."[128]

Since he is no absolutist, Hegel does not propose to stifle opinion, except when it is directly dangerous; and danger is entirely relative to historical circumstances.[129] But the security of opinion is the same as the security enjoyed by poor men against thieves: poverty.[130] Freedom of public communication, Hegel says, is controlled in part by law but mainly "by the innocuous character which it acquires as a result principally by the rationality of the constitution," and to a secondary degree by the fact that the publication of the debates of the estates leaves the public with "nothing of much importance to say.[131]

As consent, election, and opinion are very much weakened in Hegel's system, and as at the same time he wants to see the modern principle of subjectivity embodied in the state, there is little alternative to injecting this "sphere of subjectivity" into the monarch. In the additions to the *Philosophy of Right* Hegel makes the greatest effort to contrast the modern principle of subjective volition with what he sees as the inadequacy of ancient morality. He then suddenly refines the new principle down to its tiniest compass: "This 'I will' constitutes the great difference between the ancient world and the modern, and in the great edifice of the state it must therefore have its appropriate objective existence...In a well-organized monarchy, the objective aspect belongs to law alone, and the monarch's part is merely to set the subjective 'I will.'"[132]

Just as ethics requires the union of objective good with subjective actualization of this good, so too the objectively correct law formulated by the universal class needs the actual consent of a real person if the "individual aspect of the state" is to attain actuality. This actual will cuts short the "perpetual oscillation" between mere possibilities and, "by saying 'I will,' makes its decision and so inaugurates all activity and actuality."[133] In a monarch, too, will has an objective existence; that is, it is not just anyone's will but the unification of rational law with the principle of subjectivity.

Hegel makes clear in several works how important it is that this will be a real will, not a fiction or a metaphor. In the *Encyclopedia*, for example, he says that "in the perfect state...subjectivity is not a so-called 'moral person,' or a decree issuing from a majority (forms in which the decreeing will has not an *actual* existence), but an actual individual—the will of a decreeing individual— monarchy. The monarchical constitution is therefore the constitution of developed reason."[134]

It may be thought a little extraordinary that the very subjectivity that Hegel had spent the whole *Phenomenology* in assaulting in individual minds should now be represented in the person of a monarch as the "constitution of developed reason," particularly when, as Hegel says, the monarch need be no extraordinary person at all. "It is wrong... to demand objective qualities in a monarch; he has only to say 'yes' and dot the 'i.'" Neither is it self-evident why will must be the will of one person only in order to have any actual existence. Indeed, Hegel comes close to saying that individual wills are so important that there can be only one. "Not individuality in general, but a single individual, the monarch," is what is necessary.[135] Marx was not at all wide of the mark when he complained in his *Critique of Hegel's Philosophy of Right* that "personality and subjectivity... never exhausts the spheres of its existence in a single one, but in many ones," though Marx was clearly wrong in treating Hegelian monarchy as interchangeable with *l'etat c'est moi*, since Louis XIV did not confine himself to "dotting the 'i.'"[136]

Nor does this theory of monarchical will simply represent the difference between the fragmented medieval polity undermined by the "haughty vassal" and the modern unified state. Hegelian will is not just sovereign command, as in legal positivism; it expresses the principle of subjectivity. But it was precisely this principle of subjectivity that had to find full expression somewhere in a rational state, since for Hegel reason involves willing. In individual men the subjective will had been allowed only as rationality, only as acceptance and recognition of the rational, only as striving toward that end. But if the will can be allowed to expand safely somewhere, the person of the monarch is the ideal place, for he adds only the "moment of subjectivity." As a result Hegel can say, for example, that state councilors may be discharged at the "unrestricted caprice" of the monarch, without saying the withering things that he usually says about caprice.[137] A reader unsympathetic to Hegel might be excused for thinking that he has given to monarchs everything that is dangerous or arbitrary in individuals or, even more, that this is demanded by the very concept of the rational state. This ingenious transmogrification of the idea of will as the principle of the modern state, in which will is raised to its highest pitch—rationality—for ordinary men but is left largely unrestricted in the one who represents the unity of the state, or rather *is* the unity of the state, is truly brilliant, truly original. Whether it meets Hegel's aim of showing that will is canceled and preserved in the modern state is another matter altogether. If one is willing to see the principle of subjectivity defined in one way for monarchs and in a very different way for citizens, the whole system works; if not, then it is not clear why this principle must find its fullness only in monarchy.

In the end, after everything that Hegel has to say about the good and the bad social forms of willing has been considered, it turns out that he is right in his assertion that his political philosophy has canceled and preserved the will.[138] But it has canceled it in every form thought politically important since the time of Hobbes while preserving it only (1) in the subjectivity of monarchy; (2) in the fact that nothing in the world becomes actual unless will translates ideas into existence, which is true but politically not very important; or (3) in the idea that whatever is rational and recognized as rational is willed, which is again true in a certain sense but politically even less important. Hegel shows to brilliant effect the precise weaknesses and dangers of every form of voluntarist theory, and his effort to transform the theory of the will until it becomes congruent, and sometimes even identical, with reason itself is equally brilliant. It is more than that. To draw together incredibly diverse phenomena—thought, religion, the good, the virtuous—in terms of reconciliation of object and subject, of abstract and concrete, and to fit true volition into such an edifice surely shows a capacity for systematic explanation that has not been remotely equaled by anything since Hegel's death. But his own claim to have canceled and preserved the will is, appropriately enough, both true and false.

--⊰{ 7 }⊱--

Conclusion

BY NOW it is clear that the great age of social contract theory—defined by the works of Hobbes, Locke, Rousseau, and Kant, coupled with Hegel's demolition efforts—was both greatly strengthened and greatly weakened by the attempt to explain the meaning of contract and consent in terms of voluntary acts. The strength of the tradition lies in the fact that it supplied a metaphysic of morals to show why men are obligated by virtue of free acts of their own, why human will can be understood as a kind of moral causality that makes intelligible such notions as promise, responsibility, imputability, and the like. Its weakness lies in the incoherencies that arise from the fact that will is sometimes equated with appetite or desire, as in the notion of willfulness, but is sometimes treated as a moral capacity or faculty capable of producing moral effects such as obligations and legitimate governments. It is also clear that if the contemporary renaissance of contractarianism brought about by John Rawls, Michael Walzer, G. R. Grice, and others avoids some of the weaknesses of a contractarianism that relies on a voluntaristic metaphysic of morals, this advantage is sometimes offset by the taking of voluntariness as a morally consequential idea to be a simple and unproblematical given that has no need of explanation. Before passing on to these contemporary efforts it is useful to recall what the reliance on a theory of voluntariness did to the consent and contract theorists of the great age of social contract theory.

By looking back on the development of social contract theory, and more generally on the question of will and political legitimacy, it is possible to see the range of problems that emerged and that remain as well in contemporary contractarianism. In Hobbes, and to a lesser extent Locke, the difficulty is to find a doctrine of consent that is plausible and consistent with a definition of will in terms of physiological psychology alone—that is, in terms of impulse, appetite, desire, and uneasiness. Despite what Hobbes says about consent, and about being obligated to obey because one has voluntarily promised to do so, he formally defines will as the "last appetite in deliberating," or the last impulse before acting.[1] As a result of this definition, Hobbes argues that animals, no less than persons, have wills.[2] The will no longer seems to be a moral cause that can bind a person to duties. *Voluntary* can describe any act from lifting one's arm to promising to obey; both are unlike, for example, the circulation of the blood, over which volition has no control.[3]

One can understand how a moral or political obligation could arise out of a will defined, in Kantian terms, as the capacity to act according to the conception of a law, since this would involve a conscious decision, the understanding and application of a rule.[4] But it is not clear how such an obligation can issue out of a will understood as an appetite. As a result, even though Hobbes urges in *Leviathan* that human wills "make the essence of all covenants," that political legitimacy is based on voluntary acts of consent, he was never able to show how an obligation can be derived from an appetite. As we have seen, his problem becomes clear if his use of *will* in some key passages is substituted for his definition of will: thus, for example, from "the last appetite makes the essence of all covenants" one can derive no notion of political obligation or of legitimate authority, no idea that once a man has freely obligated himself to obey, "it is his duty not to make void that voluntary act of his own."[5] The only reason that Hobbes's system works is that he appears not to use the concept of will as his definition requires. Indeed, Hobbes's famous dictum that there can be "no obligation on any man which ariseth not from some act of his own"[6] is unintelligible unless the act is really his, actually arises out of his own consciously and freely produced maxims (to use Kant's term). If there are no maxims but only causally determined natural impulses and last appetites, then there is no accounting for responsibility, imputability, obligation, and other moral concepts that Hobbes himself uses constantly. And so it seems that Michael Oakeshott was right when he argued in his 1937 review of Leo Strauss's *The Political Philosophy of Hobbes* that "Hobbes...never had a satisfactory or coherent theory of volition" and that "a writer so completely devoid of a satisfactory philosophy of volition lacks something vital to modern political thought."[7]

Locke insists in the *Second Treatise* that "voluntary agreement gives...political power to governors for the benefit of their subjects,"[8] but in the *Essay Concerning Human Understanding* he defines will, at least initially, in terms of uneasiness, or "uneasiness of desire."[9] At first glance Locke would thus appear to be beset by problems fully comparable to Hobbes's: after all, if a Hobbesian volition is an appetite and a Lockean volition is a desire or an uneasiness, it is equally difficult to derive a voluntarist and contractarian theory of right and obligation from either of them. If it is true that the reformulation "the last appetite makes the essence of all covenants" throws Hobbes's problem into high relief, so too Locke's contractarian utterances lose most of their force if "voluntary agreement gives...political power to governors" is translated into "uneasy or desirous agreement gives...political power to governors." Plainly, Locke intended *voluntary* in the *Second Treatise* to mean something more than a restless desire for some absent good, but his account of volition in the first edition (1690) of the *Essay* seems not to allow for that something more. It is true, of course, that in the revised (1694) version of the *Essay* Locke overcame most of these difficulties with his notion of "suspending" the operation of the will while striving to determine that will in terms of intrinsic goods. The revised theory of volition separates out uneasiness as something immediately causal and makes intelligible the free choice of, for instance, an indifferent judge who can execute the law of nature.[10] No one has seen this more clearly than Hans Aarsleff, who points out that "without this power of suspension, all men would invariably, like automatons, be immediately absorbed in the nearest pleasure; there would be no distinction between will and desire—indeed willing would become a meaningless and empty concept—and men would follow satisfactions as varied and contrary as their tastes."[11]

In Rousseau these difficulties appear in a still more acute form. He sometimes treated moral notions as if they simply arise in a developmental process, in the course of socialization, as in his public *Letter to Archbishop Beaumont*.[12] Nevertheless, particularly when speaking of contract and obligation, he often fell back on a moral theory in which the wills of free men are taken to be the causes of duties and of legitimate authorities.[13] Thus, in an argument against obligations based on slavery in the *Social Contract*, Rousseau urges that "to deprive your will of all freedom is to deprive your actions of all morality"; that no notion of right can be derived from mere force because "to yield to force is an act of necessity, not of will."[14] In the *Discourse on Inequality*, in a passage that seems to anticipate Kant, he insists on the importance of free agency, arguing that while physics might explain the "mechanism of the senses," it can never make intelligible "the power of willing or rather of choosing," a power in which "nothing is to be found but acts which are purely spiritual and wholly inexplicable by the laws of mechanism."[15] Despite this voluntarism in his moral and political philosophy, which led to the general claim that "civil association is the most voluntary act in the world,"[16] Rousseau's fear of arbitrary willfulness, of particularism and egoism, led him to suspect the notion of will as much as to praise it. As a result he claimed, in his *Political Economy*, that "the most absolute authority is that which penetrates into a man's inmost being, and concerns itself no less with his will than with his actions."[17] Only consent can create duties, but men do not know what they ought to consent to; hence, great legislators such as Moses or Lycurgus must somehow guide, or "generalize," the wills of men while leaving those wills free.[18] This requirement got Rousseau into serious difficulties. Throughout his work he tries to retain will as a source of morality but to control or sometimes even to obliterate it as a source of self-love and inequality through a process of socialization and education that seems to lessen the autonomy of individuals.

Kant's practical philosophy offers a coherent and consistent concept of volition in which free will is a "necessary hypothesis," a "moral cause" that makes duty, responsibility, and the like intelligible.[19] This hypothetical free will serves as the foundation of a moral order that is meant to be paralleled one day in an external social system (universal republicanism) in which man will be as socially autonomous as he was always morally autonomous. But the relation of Kant's moral philosophy to his politics is problematical, because in Kant's politics some matters are governed by his special versions of natural law (the categorical imperative)[20] and natural rights (men conceived as ends-in-themselves), while some other matters are governed by hypothetical contractarianism, as in Kant's insistence that rational men could never agree to the existence of a class of hereditary nobles who do not merit their rank.[21] And it is sometimes unclear what kind of equilibrium can or should be found between Kant's special versions of contractarianism, natural law, and natural rights—a problem that also arises in considering Locke's complete concept of political right, which is neither purely contractarian nor based solely on natural law and rights.[22] Perhaps one can simply say that Kant hoped that rational citizens would agree out of enlightened self-love to some of the very things, such as "republicanism" and "eternal peace," that are also the ends or purposes of a good will; then the ideal contract would be the legal analogon of the kingdom of ends. In any case, Kant's greatest contribution to social contract and consent theory was the development of a theory of will as the capacity to shape conduct in terms of understood principles, a definition that makes intelligible any theory of right and obligation that depends on voluntariness—whether on Hobbes's "wills" which are the "essence of all covenants" or on Locke's "voluntary agreement" which "gives political power to governors" or on Rousseau's "free will" without which one's actions are deprived "of all morality." A coherent and consistent theory of will as a kind of moral causality, as something distinguishable from appetite and desire and uneasiness and willfulness, was what Kant brought to a contractarian tradition that had been resting on a slightly incoherent metaphysic of morals.

In Hegel one finds a consciousness of the importance of a morality based on will and choice, coupled with a fear of subjectivism and solipsism; in this he resembles Rousseau.[23] However, not only did Hegel not see any parallel between his views and Rousseau's; he actually accused Rousseau—for Hegel the supreme contractarian—of reducing "the union of individuals in the state to a contract and therefore to something based on their arbitrary wills, their opinion, and their capriciously given express consent." In Hegel's view this led to the destruction of "the absolutely divine principle of the state, together with its majesty and absolute authority."[24] This is ironic, given Rousseau's efforts to overcome arbitrariness and caprice. Hegel's fear of subjectivism on the part of egocentric "beautiful souls" led him to make a distinction between private morality and social ethics, a distinction that is made questionable by the fact that while states as "ethical substances" may be rational and may be conservators of freedom, they do not themselves constitute reason or freedom.[25] The desire for concreteness, for transcendence of the never-ending Kantian ought-to-be, appears to lead Hegel to the acceptance of whatever level of ethics has been reached at a given point in history. But Hegel provides a telling criticism of what he calls "justification by conviction," of theories that make will or choice the sole criterion of what ought to be done, a criticism beautifully and acidly summarized in his remark that "the laurels of mere willing are dry leaves that never were green."[26]

Considering the practical philosophies of these five theorists with care necessarily involves thinking about the most important questions in social contract theory: What kind of theory of moral personality could account for willing as moral causality, as a source of legitimacy and of obligation? Is will or choice in itself a complete and adequate standard of political right? How can will be related to a standard such as natural law or rights that will not negate it?

The philosophical foundations of social contract theory, and Hegel's attempted canceling of much of this foundation, have been dwelt on at some length, not so much because those foundations, in the works of Hobbes, Locke, Rousseau, and Kant, are perfect but because these philosophers at least try to settle questions that seem to arise irresistibly whenever contract theory is considered carefully. It is not so clear that these irresistible questions are treated with as much thoroughness by contemporary contract theorists, particularly when will is at issue.

To be sure, the notion of will as moral causality continues to be used in contemporary social contract theory; but it is only used, not supplied with a "transcendental deduction," to borrow one of Kant's phrases.[27] In Michael Walzer's deservedly much-read *Obligations*, for example, the idea of voluntarism figures quite prominently: "To insist that obligations can only derive from willful undertakings is to restate the theory of the social contract...One does not acquire any real obligations...simply by being born or by submitting to socialization within a particular group. These come only when to the fact of membership there is added the fact of willful membership."[28] But the moral significance of voluntariness is not treated independently, perhaps because the social contract tradition that Walzer embraces (with reservations) and extends had already done so much with that concept. For example, he cites with apparent approval Hobbes's famous dictum that there can be "no obligation on any man which ariseth not from some act of his own."[29] Of course, it is not Walzer's aim to supply a metaphysic of morals to explain why voluntary acts obligate; indeed, he says disarmingly, "I am simply going to assume...that obligations derive only from consent. . . and the reader must judge for himself whether descriptions and arguments rooted in that assumption are at all helpful." The considerable value of his work lies in showing how social life as a whole can be made more nearly voluntary when states are mature enough to recognize, without feeling threatened, the legitimacy of their citizens' voluntarily joining "secondary associations with limited claims to primacy," such as an association of conscientious objectors who deny only the state's right to make them fight, not its sovereignty in general.

> The possibility of becoming a conscientious objector establishes the *possibility* of incurring an obligation to fight in the army. But if the groups within which men learn to object are repressed by the state, that possibility disappears, for in one important sense at least the state is no longer a voluntary association. Only if the possible legitimacy of countergroups with limited claims is recognized and admitted can the state be regarded as a group of consenting citizens.[30]

Walzer's innovations in extending the range of contract theory are possible mainly because he can appeal to traditional arguments such as Hobbes's dictum, in effect summoning up the force of a voluntarist argument without actually making it *in extenso*.

A comparable reliance on an implicit voluntarist theory is to be found in John Rawls's *A Theory of Justice*, a work that has done more to revive interest in social contract theory than any other contemporary contractarian argument. Rawls urges that it is important that society come "as close as a society can to being a voluntary scheme," that men be "autonomous" and that "the obligations they recognize [be] self-imposed," but nowhere does he treat the concept of will or the moral significance of voluntariness. Rawls probably lays relatively little emphasis on an explanation of voluntarism because of his desire to use "thin" and widely accepted premises, such as the notion of "rational choice" in an "original position" that is "fair." The idea of will, however, is anything but a widely accepted notion; on the contrary it is a cause of violent philosophical disagreement. In his effort to revive contract theory and to weaken the claims of utilitarianism and "intuitionism," Rawls has a reason for using more generally acceptable and intelligible premises; but the implicit voluntarist element remains in his argument—for example, in his distinction between "natural duties," which involve no voluntary act, and "obligations," which are voluntarily self-imposed.[31] In the latest reformulation of his theory of justice, "Kantian Constructivism in Moral Theory," the notions of will and voluntariness drop out altogether. But that may have been occasioned by the fact that Rawls wished to underline the word *rational* in his rational choice theory, that he wished to draw a sharp distinction between his own theory and "so called 'radical' choice: that is, a choice not based on reasons, a choice that simply fixes, by sheer fiat, as it were, the scheme of reasons that we, as citizens, are to recognize, at least until another such choice is made." Indeed, Rawls insists that "radical choice, commonly associated with Nietzsche and the existentialists, finds no place in justice as fairness."[32] It is conceivable that will and voluntariness do not appear in "Kantian Constructivism" simply because of possible irrationality—or at least nonrationality—in a Nietzschean "will to power" or a Sartrean voluntary "leap towards existence." Rawls's wish to state what his theory is *not* may have led him to understress part of what it is.

In a few works, particularly in Joseph Tussman's *Obligation and the Body Politic*, there is a constant use of the notion of voluntariness unaccompanied by any indication that problems in the notion of will account for much that is problematical, even incoherent, in the social contract tradition. For Tussman true obligations are to be found in a "voluntary group" composed of "a number of individuals...in pursuit of a common purpose"; but for him "the difficulty is not in understanding what a voluntary group is" but rather "in seeing the body politic *as* such...a group."[33] As a result, he devotes his main efforts to refuting various arguments such as Hume's against viewing the body politic as a voluntary group and treats the notion of voluntariness itself as wholly unproblematical.

Something roughly comparable is true of A. J. Simmons's more recent study *Moral Principles and Political Obligations*, which also builds on an unexamined notion of voluntariness. To be sure, Simmons finally concludes that political obligation through consent or "the personal performance of a voluntary act which is the deliberate undertaking of an obligation" cannot be made to work; that consent theorists have so far failed to "show us how government by consent can be made a reality." In the end, Simmons says that while there can be no moral obligation to support a state,—even one's "own"—there may still be good reasons for selective obedience. Before arriving at "philosophical anarchism," however, Simmons does say that "consent theory has provided us with a more intuitively appealing account of political obligation than any other tradition in modern political theory." He shows very successfully exactly why consent is an "appealing" doctrine. A consent theory, he contends, "characteristically advances... four central theses." The first is that "man is naturally free," a claim that "connects in obvious ways to consent theory's contention that our political bonds must be freely assumed" through people's "having voluntarily acted in ways which bind them." The second characteristic thesis is that "man gives up his natural freedom (and is bound by obligations) only by voluntarily giving a 'clear sign' that he desires to do so." The third is that "the method of consent protects the citizen from injury by the state." And the last is that "the state is an instrument for serving the interests of its citizens." Simmons then goes on to say persuasively that "there is a sense in which consent theory might be thought not just appealing, but to be the ideal account of political obligation ... which holds that only the voluntary giving of a clear sign that one finds the state acceptable (and is willing to assume political bonds to it) can ever obligate one to support or comply with the commands of that state's government."[34]

Given all this, it is perhaps surprising that Simmons abandons consent, albeit reluctantly, on the grounds that "consent theory is not... devoid of difficulties." The difficulties, to be sure, are perfectly real; Simmons avoids the further difficulty of asking why voluntary acts obligate morally despite his constant use of the terms *voluntary* and *willing*. Perhaps an examination of will as problematical would only have hastened his flight from consent, however appealing, to his final assertion that "political theory cannot offer a convincing general account of our political bonds."[35] There seems to be a lingering suspicion in Simmons's work that Locke would be right about voluntary agreement's giving political power to governors if only that voluntary agreement could be actualized. For Simmons obligation through consent is not so much wrong as unattainable.

There are some important contemporary contract arguments that do not rely on even an implicit voluntarism. The best example is surely G. R. Grice's remarkably effective *The Grounds of Moral Judgement*. He bases his theory of obligation on the notion of having a "better reason" for doing whatever is in question; thus, "A ought to do X" implies that A has a better reason for doing X than for doing Y or Z and that it is reasonable for him to contract with others to do X.[36] While Grice works out this view with unusual thoroughness and consistency, it is still questionable whether defining obligation exclusively in terms of having reasons, even better reasons, solves the traditional problems of contractarianism. After all, having a reason for doing anything is really a matter of understanding, not of striving to effect something; and if the old distinction between understanding, volition, and action is of any value, simply having a reason does not involve anything but understanding. One has not yet made a reason that he understands the "maxim" of his action. Moreover, if willing is bracketed out in favor of having better reasons, it becomes difficult to distinguish between error and evil and between a mistake and a crime, since the concepts of moral evil and of crime involve some notion of voluntary wrongdoing, not just having a better reason. It is in this kind of connection that one appreciates the force of what Hobbes says about an act of one's own being necessary for obligation, particularly if the Hobbesian dictum is understood in terms of what Kant says about making a reason or principle the maxim of action. In Grice there is a rational obligation rather than a true obligation to keep a contract. Still, Grice's book is a formidable effort to construct a complete contract doctrine—accounting for promises, political obligations, natural law, natural rights— without any reference to voluntarism.[37] In its ambitious scope it resembles the great contractarian systems of the seventeenth and eighteenth centuries.

The advantage over contemporary theorists of the social contract tradition from Hobbes to Kant is not just that it makes a case for the importance of voluntariness but that it first shows openly how problematical are the metaphysics underlying a theory of obligation and legitimacy based on voluntary consent and choice, and then goes on to show how hard it is to balance voluntary acts of one's own against natural law and natural rights in establishing a complete concept of political right. Hobbes, Locke, Rousseau, and Kant are open to attempted demolitions such as Hegel's because they deploy so many kinds of difficult arguments at once, because they try systematically to account for every main concept they use.[38] They go beyond merely employing the ideas of will and voluntariness in practical arguments to considering, not always with equal success, what those ideas might mean.

Despite the importance of a coherent theory of will in social contract theory, contractarianism does not involve an extreme voluntarist position. This can best be seen by comparing contractarianism with existentialism. It is surely the case that both social contract theory and existentialism are instances of voluntarism in practical philosophy, compared with, say, Platonism; but it is not true that existentialism simply takes voluntarism farther than does contractarianism. In Hobbes and particularly in Locke social contract theory defines *what* ought to be done in terms of either natural law or natural rights, settling mainly the question of *who* ought to rule in terms of pure consent theory.[39] Even Rousseau, for all of his saying that the general will is always right, sometimes tacitly defends natural rights, for example in his statement that a contract of slavery is ipso facto void—though he certainly comes closest to defining what ought to be done, as well as who ought to do it, in terms of will and consent.[40]

Unlike contractarianism, existentialism—represented for present purposes by Sartre—speaks of creating values through will, values that were in some sense nonexistent before being willed, before what Sartre calls the "leap toward existence."[41] We define man, Sartre says, through his voluntary commitments, and it is absurd to call a commitment "irresponsible."[42] But, to make a Hegelian objection, commitment is a very abstract term: it may have any concrete content whatsoever. A man may be committed to justice or to equality or to sadism or to genocide. What would seem to be crucial is not the content of the commitment—for that content could be judged only by using the idealist and a priori standards whose validity Sartre denies—but the commitment itself as a choice. Yet, Sartre does not want to say that all commitments are of equal value and deserve equal praise: he condemns fascism, for example, very strongly, though he would have to grant that some people might voluntarily have chosen it and might be committed to it. He cannot condemn fascism as inhuman or antihuman, because this would involve a notion of the essence of humanity that existentialism cannot allow.[43] Sartre is in the very difficult position of wanting to define man in terms of free choices without saying that all choices are of equal worth. Thus, he says that in willing is involved one's "image" of what all men should be, that one must will universally.[44] But it is not clear why one cannot will that only he shall be free or satisfied or well treated and that no other person matters. And if one says that others do matter, it is arguable that one falls back into idealism or into the essence of what it is to be human. A writer like Kant had good grounds for insisting that no one ever make an exception of himself in moral activity, that one always will universally; but how, or whether, Sartre can insist on responsibility is not so clear.[45] In the end it seems that even existentialism is not a pure form of voluntarism, since it ultimately has recourse to responsibility, universality, and other idealist notions; but existentialism at least aims to be the purest form of voluntarism. Contractarianism never has to look into quite so deep an abyss.

Whatever may be the advantages and disadvantages of existentialism, it looks as though it should be possible to construct a scale or continuum of voluntarism on which all practical philosophies that depend in any degree on a concept of will as moral causality can be placed. Thus, it can be said that (1) there is little reliance on will in most of ancient moral and political philosophy, though this is less true of Aristotle than of Plato;[46] (2) will is confined mainly to questions of sin and good acts—that is, to private acts—in the Christian philosophy that succeeded Platonism and Aristotelianism; (3) will is raised to a central, but not exclusive, social and political place in the great age of social contract theory;[47] and (4) will is made supreme, an actual creator of moral value, in existentialism, though even its adherents fall back on idealism when confronted with the problem of commitment to inhuman or antihuman "leaps toward existence." On this fourth step of the continuum one might also place Max Weber, at least insofar as he treats a moral person as an "acting, willing person" who "weighs and chooses from among values involved according to his own conscience and his *personal* view of the world."[48] Historically, this is not just a continuum but an ascending scale in which the proportion of voluntarism and the moral weight of willing are constantly on the increase. And it is arguable that Hegel's complaints about "justification by conviction" on the part of "beautiful souls," which were unfairly aimed at Kant—or more precisely at Kantianism—have more force as this voluntarism displaces and replaces an equilibrium between will, natural law, and natural rights, an equilibrium that Locke and Kant especially tried to find.

In any case, the arguments of Locke and Kant, together with those of Hobbes, Rousseau, and Hegel, have to be given serious attention as we examine the philosophical foundations of consent and social contract theory. To be sure, there is little reason to think that contractarianism will become wholly coherent and intelligible until the concept of will is clarified; on the other hand, such a clarification does not seem to be imminent, despite a stream of "definitive" pronouncements on this point over the last three hundred years. So long as will sometimes, or rather for some people, means desire, inclination, or appetite, there will be some who see consent and choice not as a moral but as a psychological notion, as a mere converging of wishes, fundamentally indistinguishable from J. S. Mill's famous claim that "the sole evidence it is possible to produce that anything is desirable is that people do actually desire it."[49] On the other hand, voluntarists who urge that a distinction between will and appetite or desire is both necessary and possible (Kant always, Rousseau sometimes, Hobbes and Locke fitfully) maintain that obligation and authorization necessarily involve will as moral causality: that to have a reason is not necessarily to have a duty, and that one must distinguish between mere cognition and activity, via the concept of will understood as consciously making a reason or principle the maxim of one's action.

By now it will be evident that the solution favored here is to say that if contractarian theories are to have any serious weight, then a minimalist hypothetical theory of will such as Kant's appears to be indispensable. This is a weak way of putting the case; but to say more—to defend, for example, a pure contractarianism as the sole criterion of political right—would require something more than the commentary on the great social contractarians offered here.[50]

What is to be hoped for, in any event, is a bringing together of the recent innovations in consent and contract theory with the metaphysic of morals that the chief contractarians of the seventeenth and eighteenth centuries tried to supply—not because the answers are all correct but because the scope of the inquiry is. It is not that a new devotion to the metaphysics of morals underlying contractarianism will make contractarian arguments better. Indeed, among contemporary contract theorists Robert Paul Wolff has done the most with the metaphysics of contract and consent and has at the same time (arguably) gone the farthest wrong. In his *Defense of Anarchism,* while borrowing the "cloak" of Kant's "legitimacy," Wolff develops the notion that only a "unanimous direct democracy" in which everyone actually consents to everything is legitimate because only in such a scheme is everyone truly "autonomous"—autonomy not being preserved, in this view, by such elements of Lockean politics as representative government, and majoritarianism. Wolff's political position turns on the idea that autonomy is "the primary obligation of man"; that this autonomy can be politically preserved only in a unanimous direct democracy in which everyone "gives laws to himself"; that, failing the creation of such a democracy, it is necessary to come down in favor of philosophical anarchism. This political theory might, Wolff says, "if I may steal a title from Kant (and thus perhaps wrap myself in the cloak of his legitimacy)," be called *Groundwork on the Metaphysics of the State.*[51]

What is interesting here is that Wolff has turned autonomy into a substantive moral duty, into "the primary obligation of man," whereas Kant's argument (whose authority Wolff would like to "steal") is that unless man is considered, from a hypothetical point of view, as an autonomous being, then none of his substantive moral duties—summarized in the general notion of treating persons as ends—would be conceivable.[52] That is, Kant holds that while the objective reality of autonomy cannot be demonstrated, it must nevertheless be presupposed as the *conditio sine qua non* of conceiving oneself as responsible, good, or just; that a being that could not conceive itself as an autonomous moral cause could never imagine itself responsible or good or just. For Kant, then, autonomy is a necessary point of view, or a necessary hypothesis, in explaining the possibility of the common moral concepts that we actually use; but autonomy is not itself a substantive moral duty. It is rather the hypothetical condition of being able to conceive any duties. Since Kant would not say that we have a duty to be autonomous, he would not support Wolff's politics either; indeed, while Kant prefers republicanism, he supports any legal order that creates a context for self-moralization by removing impediments to that process.[53]

It is a serious enough problem to borrow the cloak of Kant's legitimacy only to drape it around a non-Kantian argument; but even more serious is the problem of relating the common moral duties—such as refraining from murder—to Wolff's primary obligation of autonomy. For example, does one act autonomously by refraining from murder to the extent that refraining from murder becomes an example of autonomous action? Is the obligation, then, one of not murdering, or is it one of not violating one's own autonomy by murdering? That is, if the primary obligation of man is autonomy, the refusal to be ruled, are all obligations ultimately obligations to oneself? Along what lines should we view secondary obligations to others? To say that everyone's autonomy is to be respected would take care of both self-regarding and other-regarding obligations; but this is not what Wolff argues, though Kant of course does.[54] Moreover, if our primary obligation were to respect the autonomy of everyone, the anarchism that Wolff supports when unanimous direct democracy cannot be attained would not irresistibly follow: after all, respect for the autonomy of everyone could be said to necessitate a legal order insofar as respect is an imperative rather than an achieved fact; but if the primary obligation is "autonomy, the *refusal* to be ruled," then anarchism appears to be more nearly inevitable, and perhaps even more natural than unanimous direct democracy itself. Wolff may possibly think that having a primary obligation to be autonomous is equivalent to having an obligation to respect the autonomy of everyone, but this is not true. Thus, he has not only transmogrified Kant, whose authority has been illegitimately borrowed; he has provided too easy and convenient a foundation for his anarchism.

If there is a metaphysic of morals that can shore up social contract theory without falling into Wolff's difficulties—and most of such a metaphysic is arguably to be found in Kant's philosophy—then bringing together recent innovations in contract theory and such a metaphysic could help to insure that the renaissance of contract theory that now appears to be unfolding in the work of Rawls, Walzer, Grice, and many others does not draw up short at the notion of a voluntarism that is at least implicit in most of it, so that inquiry into the foundations of contractarianism does not stop before what we take to be the "extreme limit of moral inquiry" is reached. Robert Paul Wolff at least asks the right kinds of questions, even if his interpretation of Kant occasionally seems questionable; a more orthodox treatment of Kant's theory of will as moral causality, if fused with some of the recent expansions and refinements of consent and contract theory, might lead to an unusually cogent and powerful political philosophy. Indeed, since the social contract tradition is alive and even more vital at this moment than at any other time since the death of Kant, all that is necessary is that contemporary contractarianism avail itself of what Hobbes, Locke, Rousseau, and Kant labored to produce and Kant largely achieved: a coherent metaphysic of morals, a coherent account of the relation of will to political legitimacy.

Notes
Index

Notes

1. How Coherent Is the Social Contract Tradition?

1. The best brief historical account of social contract theory is still Sir David Ritchie's "Contributions to the History of the Social Contract Theory," in *Darwin and Hegel* (London: Swan Sonnenschein, 1893), pp. 196–226.

2. See, inter alia, T. H. Green, *Lectures on the Principles of Political Obligation* (London: Longmans, 1941), pp. 49–50; Ernest Barker, *The Social Contract* (Oxford: Oxford University Press, 1947), pp. v–xii.

3. In Edmund Burke's *Reflections on the Revolution in France* (Indianapolis: Library of Liberal Arts, 1955), p. 110, the idea of a social contract has become purely metaphorical: "Each contract of each particular state is but a clause in the great primieval contract of eternal society, linking the higher with the lower natures, connecting the visible and invisible world."

4. See David Hume's essays "Of the Obligation of Promises" (in *A Treatise of Human Nature*, bk. 3) and "Of the Original Contract," both in *Hume: Theory of Politics*, ed. F. Watkins (Edinburgh: Nelson, 1951), pp. 61–71, 193–214, for a formidable criticism of the voluntarist and contractarian positions.

5. G. W. F. Hegel, *Philosophy of Right*, trans. T. M. Knox (Oxford: Clarendon Press, 1942), additions, pp. 280, 288–289.

6. Ibid., p. 157. When the "abstract conclusions" of consent theory came to power during the French Revolution, Hegel says, "they afforded for the first time in human history the prodigious spectacle of the overthrow of the constitution of a great actual state." This "experiment," he adds, "ended in the maximum of frightfulness and terror."

7. Understanding *phenomenology* in the Hegelian sense.

8. Pelagianism, of course, was officially branded a heresy, but this did not keep it from reappearing in the works of such writers as Erasmus. See

Robert F. Evans, *Pelagius: Inquiries and Reappraisals* (New York: Seabury Press, 1968), pp. 90–121.

9. Cited by Sheldon Wolin in *Politics and Vision* (Boston: Little, Brown, 1960), p. 152; original in *Reformation Writings of Martin Luther*, ed. Bertram Lee Woolf (London: Lutterworth Press, 1952), 1:114, 318.

10. On this point see particularly H. C. Mansfield, Jr., *The Spirit of Liberalism* (Cambridge, Mass.: Harvard University Press, 1978), p. 45.

11. A. W. Adkins, *Merit and Responsibility* (Oxford: Oxford University Press, 1960), pp. 2–4.

12. Michael Oakeshott, *Rationalism in Politics* (London: Methuen, 1962), pp. 249–251. Here, in the compass of three pages, Oakeshott presents a wonderfully lucid account of three kinds of moral-political experience.

13. The notion of political obligation does not appear at all in Plato's *Republic*; it does, of course, appear in the *Crito*, but only with respect to Socrates' particular case. Plato, *Collected Dialogues*, ed. E. Hamilton and H. Cairns (New York: Bollingen Foundation, 1961), pp. 35–39.

14. Adkins, *Merit and Responsibility*, pp. 8, 316–318.

15. Aristotle, *Politics* 3.9.8.1280b, in *The Politics of Aristotle*, trans. Ernest Barker (Oxford: Clarendon Press, 1946), p. 119. Aristotle was arguing against the Sophist Lycophron, whose views on the social contract are known only through Aristotle's brief quotations. For a good short account of contractarianism in Greek thought see W. K. C. Guthrie, *A History of Greek Philosophy* (Cambridge: Cambridge University Press, 1969), 3: ch. 5; see also W. K. C. Guthrie's reply to R. G. Mulgan's "Lycophron and Greek Theories of Social Contract," in *Journal of the History of Ideas*, 40 (January–March 1979), 128.

16. Plato, *Republic* 1.338a, in Plato, *Collected Dialogues*, p. 588.

17. Plato, *Euthyphro*, 9c–11b, in Plato, *Collected Dialogues*, pp. 177–179. With Plato's *Euthyphro* begins the tradition—later upheld by Grotius and Leibniz and attacked by Descartes and Hobbes—that eternal truths are prior to the will of God, that they are not created. Obviously, either defending or attacking this view exposes one to apparently insoluble difficulties.

18. For a good brief treatment of *bona voluntas* in Roman thought see Neal W. Gilbert, "The Concept of the Will in early Latin Philosophy," *Journal of the History of Philosophy*, 1 (October 1963), 17–35.

19. Augustine, *De Libero Arbitrio* 3.1, trans. R. P. Russell as *The Free Choice of the Will*, in *The Fathers of the Church* (Washington, D.C.: Catholic University of America Press, 1968), 59:167.

20. Augustine, *De Civitate Dei* 14.3, cited in Gilbert, "The Concept of the Will," p. 32.

21. Augustine, *De Libero Arbitrio* 2.1.109–110; Augustine, *De Trinitate* 13.6.9, trans. Robert Meagher, in *An Introduction to Augustine* (New York: New York University Press, 1978), p. 203.

22. Augustine, *De Spiritu et Littera* 54, cited in Gilbert, "The Concept of the Will," p. 33.

23. Augustine, *De Libero Arbitrio* 2.19.53, Meagher, *An Introduction to Augustine*, p. 176.

24. Blaise Pascal, *Pensées*, in *Oeuvres de Blaise Pascal*, ed. L. Brunschvicg (Paris: Librairie Hachette, 1904), 2:385. For a full treatment of general and particular will in Pascal see Patrick Riley, "The General Will before Rousseau," *Political Theory*, 6 (November 1978), 486–488; cf. Nannerl O. Keohane, *Philosophy and the State in France* (Princeton: Princeton University Press, 1980), pp. 262–282, for a superb study of Pascal's political and moral thought.

25. See Riley, "The General Will before Rousseau," pp. 501–508. Cf. Alberto Postigliola, "Da Malebranche à Rousseau: le aporie della volontà generale e la rivincita del 'ragionatore violento,'" in *Studi filosofici* (Naples: Istituto Universitario Orientale, 1978), pp. 101–129. (A shortened version was published in French as "De Malebranche à Rousseau: les apories de la volonté générale et la revanche du raisonneur violent," in *Annales Jean-Jacques Rousseau*, 1972–1977, ed. C. Wirz (Geneva: A. Jullien, 1980), pp. 123–138.

26. Thomas Aquinas, *Summa Theologica*, trans. Fathers of the English Dominican Province, 2nd rev. ed. (London: Burns Oates and Washbourne, 1922), pt. 1, quest. 83, art. 3, pp. 152–153.

27. One way of getting around these difficulties is to adopt Leibniz's solution and say that God permits but does not will free human actions; cf. G. W. Leibniz, *Theodicy*, ed. A. Farrer (New Haven: Yale University Press, 1952), pp. 182–183.

28. Ordinarily St. Thomas suggests simply that subjects obey even tyrannical rulers; in the *Summa Theologica*, pt. 2, quest. 104, art. 5, however, he allows that "in matters touching the internal movement of the will man is not bound to obey his fellow man, but God alone. . .a subject is bound to obey his superior within the sphere of his authority [only]." Trans. D. Bigongiari, in *The Political Ideas of St. Thomas Aquinas* (New York: Hafner, 1953), p. 170.

29. William of Ockham, *Quodlibeta* 3, quest. 13, in *Ockham: Philosophical Writings*, trans. and ed. Philotheus Boehner (Edinburgh: Nelson, 1957), p. 145; see also Jürgen Miethke, *Ockhams Weg zur Sozialphilosophie*, (Berlin: Walter de Gruyter, 1969), p. 304.

30. William of Ockham, *Tractatus de Praedestinatione et de Praescientia Dei et de Futuris Contingentibus*, trans. M. M. Adams and N. Kretzmann as *Predestination, God's Foreknowledge, and Future Contingents* (New York: Appleton-Century-Crofts, 1969), p. 23.

31. William of Ockham, *Dialogus*, pt. 2, tract 2, bk. 3, ch. 6, cited by Paul Sigmund, in *Nicholas of Cusa and Medieval Political Thought* (Cambridge, Mass.: Harvard University Press, 1963), pp. 96–97; see also A. S. McGrade, *The Political Thought of William of Ockham* (Cambridge: Cambridge University Press, 1974), pp. 185–189.

32. McGrade, *The Political Thought of William of Ockham*, p. 189: "His [Ockham's] limited conception of governmental functions is a natural

consequence of the view that virtue and vice are centered in an inner region [will] that the external coercion of secular power does not touch."

33. Nicholas Cusanus, *De Concordantia Catholica*, bk. 2, ch. 14, cited by Sigmund, *Nicholas of Cusa*, p. 140; bk. 3, ch. 4, in F. W. Coker, ed., *Readings in Political Philosophy* (New York: Macmillan, 1938), p. 264.

34. Sigmund, *Nicholas of Cusa,* p. 155.

35. Francesco Suarez, *A Treatise on Laws and God the Law-Giver,* in *Excerpts from Three Works,* ed. G. L. Williams (Oxford: Oxford University Pres, 1944), p. 66.

36. Ibid., p. 380.

37. Ibid., pp. 380; 383; 375, 545; 370.

38. John Locke, *Two Treatises of Government,* ed. Peter Laslett (Cambridge: Cambridge University Press, 1967), p. 162: "governments must be left. . .to the old way of being made by contrivance and the consent of men."

39. On the voluntarization of Western practical thought by Christian ideas the best study still is Hegel's; see *Philosophy of Right,* p. 84. (For an interpretation of this passage see Chapter 7.) Among recent studies the best is Hannah Arendt, *The Life of the Mind: Willing* (New York: Harcourt Brace Jovanovich, 1978), pp. 3–7, 84–110. Arendt exaggerates only a little when she says that "the faculty of the Will was unknown to Greek Antiquity and was discovered as a result of experiences about which we hear next to nothing before the first century of the Christian era" (p. 3). She goes on to add, with no exaggeration, that "the problem for later centuries was to reconcile this faculty with the main tenets of Greek philosophy." Unfortunately, those later centuries are rather skimped by Arendt, who leaps from Duns Scotus and "the primacy of the will" (pp. 125–146) to Nietzsche and the "repudiation of the will" (pp. 149–172). This repudiation is questionable, and at least Rousseau and Kant ought to have separated Scotus and Nietzsche. Despite this oddity Arendt's book is the best recent work of its kind.

40. Barker, *The Social Contract,* pp. vii–xi.

41. John Rawls, *A Theory of Justice* (Cambridge, Mass.: Harvard University Press, 1971), pp. 11–18.

42. G. R. Grice, *The Grounds of Moral Judgement* (Cambridge: Cambridge University Press, 1967), pp. 36–74.

43. Jean-Jacques Rousseau, *The Social Contract,* in *Rousseau: Political Writings,* ed. F. Watkins (Edinburgh: Nelson, 1953), pp. 115–119, 8–17.

44. H. D. Thoreau, *On the Duty of Civil Disobedience,* in *Walden* (New York: New American Library, 1960), p. 223: "the only obligation which I have a right to assume, is to do at any time what I think right." And in a bizarre addendum to democratic theory he adds that "any man more right than his neighbors, constitutes a majority of one already" (p. 230).

45. It is true that in book 5 of *De Rerum Natura* Lucretius urges that some early social relations were established on the basis of treaties of friendship; but this does not amount to a contractarian, let alone a

voluntarist, position. On Lucretius see Ernest Barker, *From Alexander to Constantine* (Oxford: Clarendon Press, 1956), pp. 181–184.

46. Thomas Hobbes, *Leviathan*, ed. Michael Oakeshott (Oxford: Basil Blackwell, 1957), p. 377; cf. pp. 207, 309.

47. Thomas Hobbes, *De Cive (The Citizen)*, ed. S. Lamprecht (New York: Appleton-Century-Crofts, 1949), p. 157n.

48. A. E. Taylor, "The Ethical Doctrine of Hobbes," in *Hobbes Studies*, ed. K. C. Brown (Oxford: Basil Blackwell, 1965), pp. 35–55.

49. Rousseau, *The Social Contract*, pp. 38, 117.

50. Immanuel Kant, *The Metaphysical Elements of Justice*, trans. J. Ladd (Indianapolis: Library of Liberal Arts, 1965), sect. 49D, p. 97; sect. 52, pp. 112–113.

51. Hegel, *Philosophy of Right*, p. 280.

52. Aquinas, *Summa Theologica*, pp. 152–153.

53. One of the best late statements of the Scholastic view is in the work of Leibniz: "to will is nothing but the striving which arises from thought, or to strive for something which our thinking recognizes." Revision note for the *Nova Methodus*, in *G. W. Leibniz: Philosophical Papers and Letters*, ed. L. Loemker (Chicago, University of Chicago Press, 1956), 1:556.

54. Bishop Bramhall in his confrontation with Hobbes defended this distinction vigorously. See Thomas Hobbes, *English Works*, ed. W. Molesworth (London, 1841), 5:278–279 inter alia.

55. Hobbes, *Leviathan*, pp. 37–38.

56. Ibid., pp. 137–138.

57. Moritz Schlick, *Problems of Ethics*, trans. David Rynin, (New York: Prentice-Hall, 1939), pp. 143–158. Schlick begins by asserting that the "pseudo-problem...of the freedom of the will" has "long since been settled"; that it is "one of the great scandals of philosophy" that "so much paper and printer's ink is devoted to this matter"; that "I should be truly ashamed to write a chapter on 'freedom.'" If freedom means anything, Schlick asserts, it means "the opposite of compulsion": "a man is *free* if he does not act under compulsion, and he is compelled or unfree when he is hindered from without in the realization of his natural desires." (This is very close to Hobbes's idea of freedom as the absence of external impediment.) But the notion that desires themselves are undetermined is absurd; it is a mere flight from causality. And so in punishment, Schlick declares, the only question is, "Who, in a given case, is to be punished?" He insists that "consideration of remote causes" of wrongdoing "is of no help," partly because the weight of those causes cannot be determined, partly because those remote causes "are generally out of reach." To be sure, for Schlick those remote causes really do determine desires, and freedom—even that expressed in crime—is the mere acting out of those desires, so that freedom is *caused*. But none of this distresses Schlick. How moral ideas are conceivable at all in his view is not clear.

58. See Hobbes, *Leviathan*, p. 307, where he urges that wills "make the essence of all covenants."

59. Ludwig Wittgenstein, *Philosophical Investigations,* trans. G. E. M. Anscombe (Oxford: Basil Blackwell, 1968), vol. 1, part 615, p. 160.

60. John Locke, *An Essay Concerning Human Understanding,* ed. A. C. Fraser (New York: Dover, 1959), pp. 328–329.

61. Immanuel Kant, *Fundamental Principles of the Metaphysic of Morals,* trans. T. K. Abbott (Indianapolis: Library of Liberal Arts, 1949), pp. 11, 63–80.

62. Gilbert Ryle, *The Concept of Mind* (New York: Barnes and Noble, 1949), pp. 62–82. Surely, Ryle makes too much of the fact that the will cannot actually be found or observed in action. It is open to doubt whether he himself does not use the notion of voluntariness in assessing merit and demerit; see, for example, pp. 72–74.

63. On this point there is a fine paragraph in Isaiah Berlin's "Does Political Theory Still Exist?" in *Philosophy, Politics and Society,* 2nd ser., ed. P. Laslett and W. G. Runciman (Oxford: Basil Blackwell, 1967), p. 33: "Rationality rests on the belief that one can think and act for reasons that one can understand, and not merely as the product of occult causal factors which breed 'ideologies,' and cannot, in any case, by altered by their victims. So long as rational curiosity exists—a desire for justification and explanation in terms of motives and reasons, and not only of causes or functional correlations or statistical probabilities—political theory will not wholly perish from the earth."

64. Kant, *Fundamental Principles,* pp. 63–80.

65. T. H. Green, *Prolegomena to Ethics,* 3rd ed., ed. F. H. Bradley (Oxford: Clarendon Press, 1890), pp. 92–93, 106.

66. For the political consequences of Green's theory of will see *Lectures on the Principles of Political Obligation,* pp. 121–141.

67. Rawls, *A Theory of Justice,* pp. 11–13; cf. pp. 251–257, where Rawls relates his own contractarianism to that of Kant, emphasizing, as might be expected, the notion of what a rational being could consent to rather than willing itself.

68. Rawls probably lays relatively little emphasis on voluntarism because of his desire to use "weak" and widely accepted premises such as the notion of rational choice; the idea of will, however, is a cause of violent philosophical disagreement. In addition, Rawls argues for "natural duties," an idea with which voluntarism is not invariably congruent. But he has done more to revive social contract theory than any other contemporary writer. Cf. Rawls's latest reworking of his ideas in "Kantian Constructivism in Moral Theory," *Journal of Philosophy,* 77 (September 1980). Here the terms *will* and *voluntary* have disappeared completely, and it is stressed that Rawlsian "justice as fairness" is not a theory of "radical choice" of the sort "associated with Nietzsche and the existentialists" (p. 568).

69. G. W. F. Hegel, *The Phenomenology of Mind,* trans. J. B. Baillie (New York: Harper, 1967), p. 490.

70. Hobbes, *Leviathan,* pp. 37–38, 31.

71. Kant, *Fundamental Principles*, p. 44.

72. Hobbes, *De Cive*, pp. 65–66.

73. Thomas Hobbes, *Liberty and Necessity*, in *English Works*, 4:265–266; cf. Thomas Hobbes, *English Works*, 5:273–274.

74. For the ablest recent defense of the view that obligation ordinarily turns on consent and covenant in Hobbes see Brian Barry, "Warrender and his Critics," in *Hobbes and Rousseau*, ed. M. Cranston and R. S. Peters (Garden City, N.Y.: Anchor, 1972), pp. 37–65.

75. Hobbes, *Leviathan*, p. 307.

76. Rousseau, *The Social Contract*, pp. 7, 9.

77. Jean-Jacques Rousseau, *Discourse on Inequality*, in *The Social Contract and Discourses*, trans. G. D. H. Cole (New York: Everyman, 1950), p. 208.

78. Jean-Jacques Rousseau, *Political Economy*, in Cole, *The Social Contract and Discourses*, p. 297.

79. Rousseau, *The Social Contract*, pp. 40–45. He states, "The general will is always right, but the judgment which guides it is not always enlightened." As a result, the legislator must help men to "bring their wills into conformity with their reason." The bringing together of the legislator's genius with the people's inalienable right to consent will "effect a union of understanding and will within the social body" (pp. 40–41).

80. This worry is clearly behind Michael Walzer's complaint, in "Philosophy and Democracy," *Political Theory*, 9 (August 1981), 384–385, that "Rousseau's legislator...raises the most serious questions about Rousseau's fundamental argument, that political legitimacy rests on will (consent), and not on reason (rightness)."

81. Hegel, *Philosophy of Right*, pp. 83, 91, 109.

82. See particularly G. W. F. Hegel, *Philosophy of History*, trans. J. Sibree (New York: Dover, 1956), esp. pp. 18, 250.

83. Hegel, *Philosophy of Right*, pp. 197–208.

84. Kant, *Fundamental Principles*, esp. p. 11.

85. Kant, *The Metaphysical Elements of Justice*, pp. 125–127, 19–21.

86. Ibid., p. 111–114; cf. Immanuel Kant, *Eternal Peace*, in *The Philosophy of Kant*, ed. C. J. Friedrich (New York: Modern Library, 1949), pp. 452–453.

87. Friedrich Nietzsche, *The Twilight of the Idols*, in *The Portable Nietzsche*, trans. W. Kaufmann (New York: Viking, 1954), pp. 499–500: "today we no longer have any pity for the concept of 'free will': we know only too well what it really is—the foulest of all theologians' artifices, aimed at making mankind 'responsible' in their sense, that is, *dependent on them.*"

88. Nietzsche, *Twilight of the Idols*, p. 500.

89. Ibid., p. 509. That this mastery and assertion are not political is clearest in the very passage in which Goethe, Heine, and Wagner are praised: "all great ages of culture are ages of political decline: what is great culturally has always been unpolitical, even *anti-political*" (Nietzsche's

italics). He adds that "what matters most...always remains culture." The worst thing of which Nietzsche can be fairly accused is aestheticism.

90. Arthur Schopenhauer, *The World as Will and Representation,* trans. E. F. Payne (Indian Hills, Colo.: Falcon's Wing Press, 1958), 1:410–411. With denial and surrender, Schopenhauer argues, "the never-satisfied and never-dying hope that constitutes the life-dream of the man who wills" is replaced by "that peace that is higher than all reason...Only knowledge remains; the will has vanished."

91. Friedrich Nietzsche, *Beyond Good and Evil,* in *The Portable Nietzsche,* p. 446.

92. Friedrich Nietzsche, *The Will to Power,* trans. W. Kaufmann (New York: Random House, 1967), pp. 369, 366–367.

93. Cf. Sigmund Freud, "Thoughts for the Times on War and Death," in *Civilisation, War and Death,* ed. J. Rickman (London: Routledge and Kegan Paul, 1968), p. 5: "our conscience is not the inflexible judge that ethical teachers are wont to declare it, but in its origin is 'dread of the community' and nothing else." Cf. the equally important observations on the will in *Psychopathology of Everyday Life* and in *Totem and Taboo.* In the former Freud explains will by reducing it to a feeling. "Like all normal feelings, it must be justified by something. But, so far as I can observe, it does not manifest itself in weighty and important decisions on these occasions, one has much more the feeling of a psychic compulsion." In *Basic Writings of Sigmund Freud,* ed. A. A. Brill (New York: Modern Library, 1938), pp. 161–162. In *Totem and Taboo* the most highly developed of all voluntarist ethical theories—Kant's—is made to seem intelligible only if treated psychologically and anthropologically: "The moral and customary prohibitions which we ourselves obey may have some essential relation to this primitive taboo the explanation of which may in the end throw light upon the dark origin of our own 'categorical imperative'" (*Basic Writings,* p. 824).

94. Jean-Paul Sartre, *Existentialism and Humanism,* trans. P. Mairet (London: Methuen, 1948), p. 28.

95. Ibid., pp. 29, 49. It should be noted, however, that for Sartre choice has nothing to do with caprice. Even if there are objective moral rules, Sartre is saying, we must sometimes—in a conflict of duties, all of them worthy—choose between rules; and there is no ultimate rule that tells us which rule is to take precedence. It is not clear, however, whether Sartre's examples prove what he wants to show. For example, he says that we cannot say a priori whether in wartime a young man ought to stay with and protect his family or join the resistance, since both of these are praiseworthy. But what of a young man who abandons both his family and the resistance to read and paint in a quiet corner of Vichy France? In his case there would be a great deal "in common between art and morality," and no a priori rule can condemn him. What Sartre is really praising is making hard choices between equally worthy moral objectives; but his voluntarism, at least as generally stated, goes far beyond this.

96. For the view that contractarianism is all procedure and no substance see Mansfield, *The Spirit of Liberalism,* p. 46: "the principle of consent has shown a remarkable capacity to become preoccupied with itself...in consequence, the people's attention is diverted from the worth of policy to its formulation, from the uses of power to its legitimation by consent."

97. Cf. Hanna Pitkin, "Obligation and Consent," in *Philosophy, Politics and Society,* 4th ser., ed. P. Laslett, W. G. Runciman, and Q. Skinner (Oxford: Basil Blackwell, 1972), pp. 45–85. Pitkin discusses with care and discrimination the question of whether all obligations must be voluntarily assumed, self-imposed.

98. Hegel, *Philosophy of Right,* pp. 8, 32–33, 83, 87–88, 99, 26: "will is thinking reason resolving itself into finitude."

99. For a contemporary voluntarist such as Robert Paul Wolff the autonomy of the will is taken so far that he finds it necessary to say "that the defining mark of the state is authority, the right to rule. The primary obligation of man is autonomy, the refusal to be ruled." See *In Defense of Anarchism* (New York: Harper, 1970), p. 18. Wolff suggests that he wants to wrap this doctrine in the cloak of Kant's legitimacy. But Kant would never have said that there is a duty to be autonomous; he said that autonomy is the condition of having a duty. And this is why Kant does not endorse the philosophical anarchism that Wolff would like to derive from Kantianism.

100. The notion of *bona voluntas,* however, has some weight in Cicero; see Gilbert, "The Concept of the Will," pp. 22–23.

101. J. L. Talmon, *The Origins of Totalitarian Democracy* (London: Secker and Warburg, 1955), pp. 38–40. It is remarkable that interpreters of Rousseau cannot be content with calling him paradoxical or contradictory even when these are precisely the terms required; usually the either-or principle intervenes, and Rousseau is seen as either a liberal or a totalitarian.

102. Hobbes, *Leviathan,* p. 307.

103. Cf. ch. 6 of Hobbes's *Leviathan,* pp. 37–38, where will is defined in purely psychological terms, with the moral use of the term *voluntary* given in the seventh paragraph of ch. 14, p. 86.

104. In Locke's *Essay,* pp. 332–336, it is uneasiness rather than appetite and aversion that moves the will; but apart from this Hobbes and Locke share many difficulties, to the extent that they both affirm and weaken voluntarism.

2. Will and Legitimacy in the Philosophy of Hobbes

1. Thomas Hobbes, *Leviathan,* ed. Michael Oakeshott (Oxford: Basil Blackwell, 1957), pp. 307, 86.

2. Ibid., p. 141.

3. On this point see particularly A. E. Taylor, "The Ethical Doctrine of

Hobbes," in *Hobbes Studies,* ed. K. C. Brown (Oxford: Basil Blackwell, 1965), pp. 44–55.

4. For this view of Hobbes see Leslie Stephen's *Hobbes* (New York: Macmillan, 1904), pp. 208–209: "Hobbes' real theory comes out when we drop the imaginary contract altogether...Men act for their own preservation as stones fall by gravitation." Stephen's view is restated by J. W. Gough in *The Social Contract,* 2nd ed. (Oxford: Clarendon Press, 1957), p. 111: "The sovereign's authority is made to consist of the combined powers...of all his subjects, conferred on him by the terms of the contract, but an obligation to abide by that contract is clearly not the real reason why they obey him. Their ruling motive is desire for protection— for the preservation of their lives." To be sure, Gough does not follow Stephen in calling the social contract imaginary; but why genuine contractual obligation is not consistent with a desire for preservation as a motive is never made clear. Cf. Michael Oakeshott's introduction to his edition of *Leviathan* (Oxford: Basil Blackwell, 1957), pp. lviii–lxi, in which he argues that a logical "duty" to obey the sovereign is one of four kinds of duty in Hobbes. See also Frederick Watkins, *The Political Tradition of the West* (Cambridge, Mass.: Harvard University Press, 1962), pp. 79–80.

5. Thomas Hobbes, *De Cive (The Citizen),* ed. S. P. Lamprecht (New York: Appleton-Century-Crofts, 1949), p. 32n.

6. Hobbes, *Leviathan,* chs. 6, 21, 46; and Thomas Hobbes, *Liberty, Necessity and Chance,* in *Hobbes' English Works,* ed. W. Molesworth (London, 1841), 5:34, 272–273, 293–294, 424.

7. Hobbes, *Leviathan,* p. 32: "these words of good, evil and contemptible are ever used with relation to the person that useth them; there being nothing simply and absolutely so."

8. On this point see the original and independent argument of H. C. Mansfield, Jr., in "Hobbes and the Science of Indirect Government," *American Political Science Review,* 65 (March 1971), 106.

9. Useless thanks to equality. Hobbes, *Leviathan,* chs. 13–15.

10. The question of Hobbes's religious doctrines is judiciously treated by Willis B. Glover in his "God and Thomas Hobbes," in Brown, *Hobbes Studies,* pp. 141–168. Glover properly stresses the oddity rather than the alleged atheism of Hobbes's theology.

11. Hobbes, *De Cive,* pp. 195–196.

12. Hobbes, *Leviathan,* pp. 37–38.

13. Thomas Hobbes, *Liberty and Necessity,* in Molesworth, *Hobbes' English Works,* 4:265–266. Cf. Hobbes, *Liberty, Necessity and Chance,* pp. 273–274.

14. Hobbes, *Liberty, Necessity and Chance,* pp. 47, 388.

15. Thomas Aquinas, *Summa Theologica,* trans. Fathers of the English Dominican Province, 2nd rev. ed. (London: Burns Oates and Washbourne, 1922), pt. 1, quest. 83, art. 3, pp. 152–153: "the proper act of a free-will is choice, for we say that we have a free-will because we can take one thing while refusing another."

16. Aristotle, *Ethics*, ed. and trans. John Warrington (London: Dent, 1963), 5.1135a–1137b, pp. 107–114.

17. Hobbes, *Leviathan*, chs. 6, 21, 46.

18. John Plamenatz, in his *Man and Society* (New York: McGraw-Hill, 1963), 1:127, however, suggests that it is "perhaps not important" to determine just how significant consent is in Hobbes's thought; and Stuart M. Brown, in his "The Taylor Thesis: Some Objections," in Brown, *Hobbes Studies*, pp. 57–71, goes farther than most commentators in treating covenant in Hobbes as an unproblematical given.

19. Hobbes, *Leviathan*, pp. 377, 309, 141.

20. Ibid., p. 307. This phrase is extracted from the middle of a sentence dealing with covenants between God and Abraham and his family.

21. Ibid., p. 132.

22. Hobbes, *Liberty, Necessity and Chance*, p. 180. This passage is given full weight by Brian Barry in his helpful article, "Warrender and his Critics," in *Hobbes and Rousseau*, ed. M. Cranston and R. S. Peters (Garden City, N.Y.: Anchor, 1972), p. 64.

23. The idea of a commonwealth by acquisition causes one problem for Hobbes, however: in contract there must be acceptance by both sides ("without mutual acceptation there is no covenant"). But this makes the sovereign-by-conquest a party to a covenant and thus gives him contractual obligations to those whom he defends. This is ordinarily something that Hobbes wants to avoid. See Hobbes, *Leviathan*, p. 90.

24. Hobbes, *De Cive*, pp. 46, 50; cf. Hobbes, *Leviathan*, pp. 100–101.

25. Hobbes, *Leviathan*, p. 63.

26. Hobbes, *De Cive*, p. 50; cf. Hobbes, *Leviathan*, p. 100. Leo Strauss suggests in *The Political Philosophy of Hobbes* (Chicago: University of Chicago Press, 1963), pp. 57–58, that Hobbes's thoughts on mastery and slavery serve as the "philosophic basis" of the great "Master and Servant" chapter of Hegel's *Phenomenology of Mind*. For an argument against this ingenious suggestion see Patrick Riley, "Introduction to the Reading of Alexandre Kojève," in *Frontiers of Political Theory*, ed. M. Freeman and D. Robertson (Brighton, Sussex: Harvester Press, 1980), pp. 279–281.

27. Hobbes, *Leviathan*, p. 172.

28. Hobbes, *De Cive*, p. 198. In *Leviathan*, p. 19, Hobbes expands this discussion into the nominalist doctrine that only words are universal and are imposed by agreement on a certain range of phenomena by virtue of some common quality or accident. How common qualities are recognizable if there are only universal names but no universal essences is a fascinating question that cannot be gone into here.

29. Hobbes, *Leviathan*, pp. 238–241.

30. Hobbes, *Liberty, Necessity and Chance*, p. 179. It would be difficult to reconcile this passage with Eldon Eisenach's argument in *Two Worlds of Liberalism: Religion and Politics in Hobbes, Locke and Mill* (Chicago: University of Chicago Press, 1981), p. 106, that in Hobbes "men see double: in Part II of *Leviathan* they see their own construct, and in Part III they see a Vicar of

Christ." This line between a construct and a Vicar of Christ cannot be drawn, since Hobbes's whole point in *Liberty, Necessity and Chance* is that if the sovereign is a vicar—an authorized interpreter of Scripture—this is because his subjects "assent" to view him in that light. Thus, the sovereign's vicarate is constructed by popular assent.

31. Hobbes, *Leviathan*, pp. 268, 269–270.

32. Ibid., pp. 234–235; cf. the similar argument in Hobbes, *De Cive*, pp. 177–178.

33. The definition of law in ch. 26 of Hobbes's *Leviathan*, p. 172, seems to require "former obligation," and God's simple power does not seem to involve obligation; but ch. 35 speaks of God as an omnipotent lawgiver.

34. Hobbes, *Leviathan*, p. 179. Cf. Michael Oakeshott, "The Moral Life in the Writings of Thomas Hobbes," in *Rationalism in Politics* (London: Methuen, 1962), p. 282. The chief merit of this wonderful essay, apart from the notability of its style, is its ability to show Hobbes's greatness at every turn, even when it is being critical. It becomes less than wholly persuasive only when Oakeshott asserts that the social contract need not be seen as obligatory and that only civil law gives rise to real obligations in Hobbes. Against this the present reading holds that no laws would be obligatory if the lawmaker were not authorized, and that this authorization comes precisely from an "act of one's own." But Oakeshott's essay is essential to any serious reader of Hobbes.

35. Hobbes, *De Cive*, p. 179.

36. Hobbes, *Leviathan*, p. 234.

37. Benedict de Spinoza, *A Theologico-Political Treatise*, in *Works of Spinoza*, trans. R. H. M. Elwes (New York: Dover, 1951), 1:200.

38. Hobbes, *Leviathan*, pp. 84–85: "The right of nature...is the liberty each man hath, to use his own power, as he will himself, for the preservation of his own nature; that is to say, of his own life." Hobbes's use of the word *own*, not just once but twice, before *nature* and *life* makes it doubly difficult to extract the right to rule out of natural right: political rule is not the aptest means of preserving one's own life. For a powerful attempt to extract the right to rule from natural right alone, to the detriment of contract or transfer, see Sheldon Wolin, *Politics and Vision* (Boston: Little, Brown, 1960), pp. 283–285.

39. Hobbes, *Leviathan*, pp. 144, 91.

40. On this point see particularly ch. 21 of Hobbes's *Leviathan*; but cf. ch. 28.

41. Hobbes, *Leviathan*, p. 104.

42. Cicero, *De Republica* 3.22.33, in Ernest Barker, *From Alexander to Constantine* (Oxford: Clarendon Press, 1956), p. 196: "true law is right reason comformable to nature; it is universally diffused, unchanging and eternal...all nations, at all times, will be bound by the one eternal and immutable law."

43. Hobbes, *Liberty, Necessity and Chance*, p. 180.

44. Hobbes, *Leviathan*, pp. 93–105, esp. p. 104.

45. Here, of course, Hobbes is to be contrasted with Spinoza and Locke, both of whom make consent important not only in founding the state but in its ordinary operation. Spinoza in particular looked on democracy with favor, despite his theory of absolute sovereignty. See Spinoza, *A Theologico-Political Treatise*, pp. 205–207.

46. See Oakeshott, "The Moral Life in the Writings of Thomas Hobbes," pp. 249–250.

47. F. S. McNeilly, in his careful and discriminating *The Anatomy of Leviathan* (New York: Macmillan, 1968), pp. 100–117, shows convincingly that in his later works Hobbes was careful to use the more abstract term *aversion* in preference to his earlier term *fear*. In McNeilly's view Hobbes is only distorted by emphasizing fear, particularly in *Leviathan*.

48. Thomas Hobbes, *The Elements of Law*, ed. F. Tönnies (Cambridge: Cambridge Univesity Press, 1928), pp. 47–48.

49. On this difficult point see T. H. Green, *Prolegomena to Ethics*, 5th ed. (Oxford: Clarendon Press, 1906), pp. 102–104. There appears to be a direct line leading from Hobbes's treatment of reasons and causes to the contemporary theory of rationalization in Freudian theory: in both Hobbes and Freud reasons seem to have an ex post facto character.

50. Hobbes, *Elements of Law*, p. 48.

51. For a brief but penetrating analysis of the concept of will in *Leviathan* see A. I. Melden, *Free Action* (London: Routledge and Kegan Paul, 1961), pp. 5–6.

52. Hobbes, *Leviathan*, p. 38.

53. Cf. note 15. Thomas Aquinas does not say that will is not will when appetite is not entirely governed by the rationality of the cognitive power; he simply says that appetite should accept the counsel of that power.

54. Hobbes, *Leviathan*, p. 445.

55. Ibid., p. 446. Hobbes adds that a man who believes in free will also believes that "if a man do an action of injustice, that is to say, an action contrary to the law, God . . . is the prime cause of the law . . . but no cause at all of the injustice." Since God causes everything, the notion of free will is "vain philosophy" (p. 445).

56. Hobbes, *Liberty, Necessity and Chance*, p. 293: "nothing is determined by itself, nor is there any man in the world that hath any conception answerable to those words."

57. G. W. Leibniz, *Theodicy*, ed. A. Farrer (New Haven: Yale University Press, 1952), part 288, pp. 302–303. For an analysis see Patrick Riley, *The Political Writings of Leibniz* (Cambridge: Cambridge University Press, 1972), pp. 10–17.

58. Hobbes, *Leviathan*, p. 445.

59. Ibid., pp. 137–138.

60. See the interesting paper of J. W. N. Watkins, "Philosophy and Politics in Hobbes," in Brown, *Hobbes Studies*, p. 251. "Hobbes claimed to be an uncompromising materialist," Watkins notes, "but his account of mind is really an epiphenomenalist rather than a strictly materialist one."

61. Hobbes, *Liberty, Necessity and Chance*, pp. 34–35.

62. Hobbes, *Leviathan*, p. 84. Sometimes, however, *liberty* is used in a moral or political sense; see, for example, pp. 85, 141.

63. Hobbes, *Liberty, Necessity and Chance*, pp. 80, 84, 79.

64. Ibid., pp. 155–156.

65. Ibid., p. 52. Hobbes's claim that we blame people because of their voluntary acts that "please us not" justifies Nietzsche's indignant assertion that "the doctrine of will has been invented essentially for the purpose of punishment, that is, because one wanted to impute guilt." See Friedrich Nietzsche, *Twilight of the Idols*, in *The Portable Nietzsche*, trans. W. Kaufman (New York: Viking, 1954), p. 499.

66. Ibid., p. 114.

67. Ibid., pp. 115, 116.

68. John Dunn, "Individuality and Clientage in the Formation of Locke's Social Imagination," in *John Locke: Symposium Wolfenbüttel 1979*, ed. R. Brandt (Berlin: Walter de Gruyter, 1981), p. 56. This article fails to treat Hobbes sympathetically; in compensation the treatment of Locke is brilliant, perhaps the subtlest and finest of Dunn's many writings on Locke. In this essay Dunn seems to have captured Locke's "intention," which is his stated aim.

69. Hobbes, *Liberty, Necessity and Chance*, pp. 278–279.

70. Ibid., p. 293; cf. Hobbes, *Liberty and Necessity*, p. 274, a passage that makes any distinction between different kinds of will impossible. Since, Hobbes says, "of voluntary acts the will is the necessary cause," and "the will is also caused by other things whereof it disposeth not," such as appetites and aversions, "it followeth that voluntary actions have all of them necessary causes, and therefore are necessitated."

71. Ibid., pp. 308–309; but cf. Bramhall's next sentence, which is weak.

72. Ibid., pp. 279, 346–347.

73. Ibid., pp. 358, 401.

74. Hobbes, *Leviathan*, p. 104.

75. Hobbes, *Liberty, Necessity and Chance*, pp. 215–216.

76. Ibid., pp. 294, 55.

77. Ibid., pp. 272–273.

78. Immanuel Kant, *Fundamental Principles of the Metaphysic of Morals*, trans. T. K. Abbott (Indianapolis: Library of Liberal Arts, 1949), pp. 3–23, 63–80.

79. Hobbes, *Liberty, Necessity and Chance*, p. 424.

80. Michael Oakeshott, "Logos and Telos," in *Government and Opposition* (Spring 1974), 237–244, esp. p. 242. Oakeshott adds that "the device Hobbes sets before his readers, that of association in terms of the recognition of the authority of rules of conduct, has no counterpart in a universe composed of bodies characterized solely by inertial motion" (pp. 243–244). One sees how close is the relation between this reading of Hobbes and Oakeshott's own theory of *respublica* as rule recognition in *On Human Conduct* (Oxford: Clarendon Press, 1975), pp. 147–148. "*Respub-*

lica...is a manifold of rules and rule-like prescriptions to be subscribed to in all the enterprises and adventures in which the self-chosen satisfactions of agents may be sought...it is relationship in terms of the recognition of rules...that relation of somewhat 'watery' fidelity called civility."

81. G. W. Leibniz, *Meditation on the Common Concept of Justice*, in Riley, *The Political Writings of Leibniz*, p. 47; Leibniz accuses Hobbes not only of changing the meaning of words but of "speaking a language different from that of other men."

82. Taylor, "The Ethical Doctrine of Hobbes," pp. 44–55.

83. Hobbes, *De Cive*, p. 157.

84. Hobbes, *Leviathan*, p. 83.

85. Hobbes, *Elements of Law*, p. 60.

86. Hobbes, *Leviathan*, p. 109.

87. Hobbes, *Elements of Law*, p. 60.

88. Hobbes, *De Cive*, pp. 36–37.

89. Ibid., pp. 45, 157.

90. Ibid., p. 44.

91. Ibid., p. 65; cf. the comparable argument in Hobbes, *Elements of Law*, pp. 79–80.

92. Hobbes, *Leviathan*, pp. 172, 141, 377.

93. Hobbes, *Elements of Law*, p. 52.

94. Hobbes, *Leviathan*, p. 86.

95. Benedict de Spinoza, *The Improvement of the Understanding*, in *The Philosophy of Spinoza*, ed. J. Ratner (New York: Modern *Library*, 1927), pp. 175, 176, 203–204.

96. Spinoza, *Theologico-Political Treatise*, p. 200.

97. Ibid., p. 204. C. E. Vaughan, in his *Studies in the History of Political Philosophy Before and After Rousseau* (New York: Russell and Russell, 1960), 1:25, destroys this crucial difference between Hobbes and Spinoza by saying that "the first thing [Hobbesian] men had to do was to hand over all their individual rights." "Hand over" is Spinoza's phrase, not Hobbes's. But the rest of Vaughan's chapter is a brilliant and often very funny polemic against Hobbes. For example: "A covenant, purely material in its [appetitive] origin, purpose and sanction, comes in the end to rest mainly, if not solely, for its moral consequences. Hence the [Hobbesian] despot, established in the first instance for pure convenience, is in the final issue maintained merely as a painful duty...It is a kind of inverted rake's progress to which the reader has been witness. The author, who at the beginning was possessed by the very demon of force and fraud, presents himself at the end repentant, clothed, and in his right mind" (pp. 38–39).

98. Hobbes, *Leviathan*, p. 91.

99. Ibid., pp. 92–93.

100. Spinoza, *Theologico-Political Treatise*, pp. 204–205.

101. Hobbes, *Leviathan*, pp. 85–86.

102. Ibid., pp. 129, 203.

103. The word *will* barely appears in Spinoza's *Theologico-Political Treatise*.

104. Hobbes, *Leviathan*, p. 94.

105. Ibid., p. 92.

106. Ibid., p. 89; here Hobbes says that without "right and force" on the part of the state, covenants have no status.

107. It is Michael Oakeshott's view, in his introduction to *Leviathan*, p. lx, that the social contract itself need not, and perhaps cannot, be obligatory. But if this is so, it becomes impossible to say where the sovereign got the authority to make the civil laws that Oakeshott thinks are unquestionably obligatory.

108. G. W. Leibniz, *Judgment of the Works of the Earl of Shaftesbury*, in *The Political Writings of Leibniz*, p. 196.

109. Hobbes, *Leviathan*, p. 85; but note the qualifications.

110. Ibid., pp. 91–92, 89.

111. Ibid., p. 97.

112. Taylor, "The Ethical Doctrine of Hobbes," p. 38. Taylor, of course, was among the first to suggest that Hobbes's theory of obligation can and should be separated from his psychology, that the two can be seen as independent of each other: "If we grant Hobbes' assumptions about the dependence of civil society on the 'covenant,' and the character of the 'covenant' itself, the duty of obeying the civil law, even when I personally think it to be iniquitous, follows as part of a consistent deontology. It is not a logical necessity of the system that we should also accept the egoistic moral psychology. Even if we reject this psychology *in toto*, so long as we grant the premises that civil society rests upon a covenant to obey whatever shall be enacted as the 'law of the land,' and that breach of covenant is always a violation of duty, the conclusions he wishes to draw will follow" (pp. 44–45).

Waiving the question of whether Hobbes's moral psychology is egoistic or simply egocentric, is it possible to "reject this psychology *in toto*" and preserve the dutiful nature of the covenant? It is hard to see how. "Covenanting" is a voluntary act, and a voluntary act is an act of the will; but the will is precisely a part of the moral psychology that Taylor would like to do without. It is one thing to say that Hobbes's theory of will is not adequate to account for the moral importance of voluntary acts; it is quite another to say that that theory is expendable. Hobbes's theory of duties cannot be detached from his theory of will, because wills, as he says, "make the essence of all covenants," and most duties are the result of covenant. At most it can be said that Hobbes intends terms such as *promise, duty, authorization,* and *obligation* to be understood as part of a deontology, then he has not provided a theory of volition equal to this intention; in fact, his theory of volition seems to contradict any deontological ethics. But this does not mean that one can bracket out that theory of volition.

113. On this point Leo Strauss is particularly good in his *The Political Philosophy of Hobbes*, pp. 44–58.

114. Hobbes, *Leviathan*, p. 97.

115. Hobbes, *Elements of Law*, p. 34.

116. Blaise Pascal, *Les provinciales*, ed. L. Cognet (Paris: Garnier Frères, 1965), pp. 96–98.

117. Hobbes, *Leviathan*, p. 7.

118. Hobbes, *Elements of Law*, p. 34.

119. See Lucian, *Philosophies for Sale*, in *Selected Satires of Lucian*, ed. L. Casson (Chicago: Aldine, 1962), pp. 322–323, in which Socrates is made to say, "I'm the best person in the world to leave with handsome young boys. I don't love their bodies—it's the soul I consider beautiful."

120. Hobbes, *Leviathan*, p. 103. Howard Warrender's interpretation, in his *The Political Philosophy of Hobbes* (Oxford: Clarendon Press, 1957), pp. 267–314, does indeed rely heavily on this passage; but he suggests that the concept of will is not of great importance in this connection (pp. 267–272), though he does say later that for Hobbes morality depends on the distinction between voluntary and nonvoluntary acts (pp. 313–314).

121. Kant, *Fundamental Principles*, p. 15: "if the unfortunate one ...preserves his life without loving it—not from inclination or fear, but from duty—then his maxim has a moral worth."

122. Niccolò Machiavelli, *The Prince*, in *The Prince and Discourses*, ed. M. Lerner (New York: Modern Library, 1950), p. 56.

123. Machiavelli often says that the ordinary rules of goodness must be overridden in the interest of the historical greatness of the state; he justifies Romulus' slaying of Remus on this ground (*Discourses*, bk. 1, ch. 9). See Niccolò Machiavelli, *The Discourses*, in *The Prince and Discourses*, pp. 138–139.

124. Hobbes, *Leviathan*, p. 93. The question is not whether Hobbes believed in duties—clearly he did—but whether he succeeded in showing how such duties are possible, given the premises of his psychology.

125. Ibid., p. 86.

126. Immanuel Kant, *Religion within the Limits of Reason Alone*, in *The Philosophy of Kant*, ed. C. J. Friedrich (New York: Modern Library, 1949), p. 367.

127. Kant, *Fundamental Principles*, p. 44.

128. Hobbes, *Leviathan*, p. 179.

129. Kant, *Religion*, p. 367.

130. Immanuel Kant, *Critique of Pure Reason*, trans. Norman Kemp Smith (London: Macmillan, 1929), pp. 472–473: "'Ought' expresses a kind of necessity...which is found nowhere else in the whole of nature...When we have the course of nature alone in view, 'ought' has no meaning whatsoever."

131. William Shakespeare, *Troilus and Cressida*, act 1, sc. 3, in *The Oxford Shakespeare*, ed. W. J. Craig (New York: Oxford University Press, n.d.), p. 775.

132. Hobbes, *Leviathan*, p. 86.

133. This is seen clearly by F. C. Hood in his *The Divine Politics of Thomas Hobbes* (Oxford: Clarendon Press, 1964), pp. 30–31: "Hobbes's psychology of voluntary actions is restricted to a psychology of deliberation...his later suggestions as to the conduct of the just man are not

covered by this psychology which he expounded in the sixth chapter of *Leviathan*." But Hood also says that "the morality with which Hobbes is concerned in *Leviathan* is the morality of the just man" and that "morality always has references to will" (p. 10). But Hood does not explain this moral will, which is not covered by Hobbes's psychology. Even so, he is one of few writers on Hobbes to give proper weight to this difficulty.

134. For a strong argument against reading Hobbes with Kant's aid see Howard Warrender, "A postscript on Hobbes and Kant," in *Hobbes-Forschungen*, ed. R. Koselleck and R. Schnur (Berlin: Duncker und Humblot, 1969), pp. 155–157: "in fact, the greatest stumbling block for the significant application of ethical theory to politics has been the widespread adoption...of Kantian terminology."

3. On Finding an Equilibrium between Consent and Natural Law in Locke's Political Philosophy

1. John Locke, *Two Treatises of Government*, ed. Peter Laslett (Cambridge: Cambridge University Press, 1967), pp. 401, 324.

2. Ibid., pp. 287–294, 375–376, 317–320.

3. Leo Strauss, *Natural Right and History* (Chicago: University of Chicago Press, 1953), pp. 202–232.

4. T. H. Green, *Lectures on the Principles of Political Obligation* (London: Longmans, 1941), p. 72.

5. C. B. MacPherson, "Natural Rights in Hobbes and Locke," in *Democratic Theory: Essays in Retrieval* (Oxford: Oxford University Press, 1973), pp. 224–232: "it is perhaps not too much to say that, as soon as Locke had shown how the original natural law limits on private appropriation were made ineffective by men's consent...to the use of money, he logically destroyed his natural law system."

6. Willmoore Kendall, *John Locke and the Doctrine of Majority Rule* (Urbana, Ill.: University of Illinois Press, 1965), pp. 63–67.

7. John Plamenatz, *Man and Society* (New York: McGraw-Hill, 1963), 1:220–221.

8. A. P. d'Entrèves, *The Medieval Contribution to Political Thought* (New York: Humanities Press, 1959), pp. 125–126.

9. J. W. Gough, *John Locke's Political Philosophy* (Oxford: Clarendon Press, 1950), pp. 38–39.

10. Hans Aarsleff, "The State of Nature and the Nature of Man in Locke," and R. Polin, "John Locke's Conception of Freedom," in *John Locke: Problems and Perspectives*, ed. John Yolton (Cambridge: Cambridge University Press, 1969), pp. 99–136, 1–18. The Aarsleff essay is especially fine.

11. Ernst Cassirer, *The Philosophy of the Enlightenment*, trans. F. Koelln and J. Pettegrove (Boston: Beacon Press, 1955), pp. 249–250.

12. Ernest Barker, *The Social Contract* (Oxford: Oxford University Press, 1947), p. xviii.

13. Jean-Jacques Rousseau, *The Social Contract*, in *Political Writings*, ed. F. Watkins (Edinburgh: Nelson, 1953), p. 31: "the engagements which bind us to the social body are obligatory only because they are mutual."

14. John Locke, *An Essay concerning Human Understanding*, ed. A. C. Fraser (New York: Dover, 1959), pp. 472–473.

15. John Locke, *Essays on the Law of Nature*, ed. and trans. W. von Leyden (Oxford: Clarendon Press, 1958), pp. 160–179.

16. Locke, *Essay*, pp. 475, 481.

17. Locke, *Two Treatises*, p. 293.

18. Thomas Hobbes, *Leviathan*, ed. Michael Oakeshott (Oxford: Basil Blackwell, 1957), p. 174.

19. Locke, *Essay*, p. 474.

20. Ibid., p. 477. These distinctions are to be found not only in late works such as the *Essay* but in earlier ones such as the manuscript entitled "Obligation of Penal Laws," which Lord King printed in his *The Life of John Locke* (London, 1830), 1:114–117. In that manuscript Locke says that "there are virtues and vices antecedent to, and abstract from, society," such as the duty to love God, but that there are others "which suppose society and laws, as obedience to magistrates, or dispossessing a man of his heritage." In both of these cases—that is, of obedience to magistrates and dispossession of heritages—Locke argues that "the rule and obligation is antecedent to human laws" but that the "matter about which that rule is, may be consequent to them." One of the consequent matters may be "power of persons"—that is, of definite, namable ruling persons as distinguished from magistrates in general. Although natural law enjoins obedience to magistrates, as Locke in this manuscript says it does, it says nothing about the power of persons; it does not say who in particular shall be obeyed.

21. Green, *Political Obligation*, p. 72.

22. Locke, *Two Treatises*, pp. 368–369.

23. Ibid., p. 370.

24. Cf. Immanuel Kant, *Eternal Peace*, in *Kant's Political Writings*, ed. H. Reiss (Cambridge: Cambridge University Press, 1970), p. 121n: "government. . . genuinely makes it much easier for the moral capacities of men to develop into an immediate respect for right." This does not mean, however, that legality replaces morality; legality simply supplies a context within which self-moralization is more nearly possible. (See Chapter 5.)

25. Locke, *Two Treatises*, pp. 289, 299.

26. Ibid., pp. 220–221. Cf. Rousseau, *The Social Contract*, p. 6: "I have said nothing of King Adam or of the Emperor Noah, father of the three great monarchs, who, like the children of Saturn. . . divided the universe between them. I hope that my moderation will be appreciated; for as the direct descendant of one of these princes, and perhaps in the senior line, how do I know that, if titles were verified, I would not find myself the legitimate king of the human race?" Rousseau's brilliant enlargement of Locke's sober point shows that Rousseau was as familiar with the *First*

Treatise as with the *Second.* This is confirmed by the fact that in the *First Treatise* Locke speaks of social bonds as chains, as does Rousseau in the famous opening of his *Social Contract.*

27. Locke, *Two Treatises,* pp. 220–221, 162.

28. Ibid., pp. 291, 342.

29. Ibid., pp. 367, 296.

30. Ibid., p. 301.

31. Barker, *The Social Contract,* p. xviii.

32. Locke, *Essays on the Law of Nature,* p. 185.

33. Ibid., p. 187.

34. King, *The Life of John Locke,* 2:116, 109.

35. John Locke, *A Third Letter for Toleration,* in *The Works of John Locke* (London, 1812), 6:212.

36. Locke, *Two Treatises,* pp. 353, 412, 401–402.

37. Rousseau, *The Social Contract,* p. 40.

38. Locke, *Two Treatises,* pp. 348–349, 289–296.

39. David Hume, "Of the Original Contract," in *Theory of Politics,* ed. F. Watkins (Edinburgh: Nelson, 1951), pp. 193–209. Hume, of course, could not have given much weight to Locke's claim that "voluntary agreement gives...political power to governors," since for Hume will is not a morally consequential idea. This is especially clear in the *Treatise of Human Nature* 3.1.1, in Hume, *Theory of Politics,* p. 14: "Let us choose any inanimate object, such as an oak or elm, and let us suppose that by the dropping of its seed it produces a sapling below it which...at last overtops and destroys the parent tree; I ask if in this instance there be wanting any relation which is discoverable in parricide or ingratitude? Is not the one tree the cause of the other's existence, and the latter the cause of the destruction of the former, in the same manner as when a child murders his parent? It is not sufficient to reply that a choice or will is wanting...It is a will or choice that determines a man to kill his parent; and they are the laws of matter and motion that determine a sapling to destroy the oak from which it sprang." Had King Lear lived to read the *Treatise of Human Nature,* he might well have doubted that ingratitude is "sharper than a serpent's tooth."

40. Locke, *Two Treatises,* p. 295.

41. Locke, *Essays on the Law of Nature,* p. 119.

42. Locke, *Essay,* p. 69.

43. John Locke, *A Letter concerning Toleration,* in *The Works of John Locke,* 6:47.

44. Locke, *Two Treatises,* pp. 286, 208.

45. John Locke, *Of the Conduct of the Understanding,* in *The Works of John Locke,* 6:228.

46. Locke, *Essay,* p. 316.

47. Locke, *Of the Conduct of the Understanding,* p. 228.

48. For an account of the revising and recasting of book 2, ch. 21 of the *Essay,* see Aarsleff, "The State of Nature and the Nature of Man in Locke," pp. 111–112. For the passages that were never actually incorporated into

the *Essay,* see King, *The Life of John Locke,* 2:159–161 (a letter to Le Clerc) and 219–222. The letter to Le Clerc (October 9, 1694) is more conveniently found in *The Correspondence of John Locke,* ed. E. S. DeBeer (Oxford: Clarendon Press, 1979), 5:159–160.

49. Locke, *Two Treatises,* p. 381.

50. For a brief treatment of Suarez's voluntarism and contractarianism, see Chapter 1. Some, though not all, of the parallels between Suarez and Locke are brought out by Quentin Skinner in *The Foundations of Modern Political Thought, Volume Two: The Age of the Reformation* (Cambridge: Cambridge University Press, 1978), pp. 161–166. These fine pages have the merit of calling attention to Suarez's neglected political thought.

51. Hobbes, *Leviathan,* pp. 307, 38, 86.

52. Locke, *Essay,* pp. 313–314, 315, 320, 321.

53. Ibid., pp. 325, 326–327.

54. G. W. Leibniz, *Nouveaux essais sur l'entendement humain,* ed. André Robinet and H. Schepers (Berlin: Akademie Verlag, 1962) p. 181.

55. Locke, *Essay,* p. 322.

56. Ibid., pp. 330, 331, 332.

57. Ibid., pp. 333, 334.

58. Locke, *Two Treatises,* p. 401.

59. Ibid., pp. 221, 162.

60. Locke, *Essay,* pp. 472–473.

61. Ibid., p. 345.

62. Ibid., pp. 345, 346, 361.

63. Ibid., p. 349.

64. Ibid., p. 364.

65. Cf. Immanuel Kant, *Fundamental Principles of the Metaphysic of Morals,* trans. T. K. Abbott (Indianapolis: Library of Liberal Arts, 1949), pp. 63–65.

66. Locke, *Two Treatises,* p. 327. This passage in the *Second Treatise,* and all those like it in the revised *Essay,* are left out of account by Eldon Eisenach in *Two Worlds of Liberalism: Religion and Politics in Hobbes, Locke and Mill* (Chicago: University of Chicago Press, 1981), pp. 90–91, 239, where he asserts that "Locke scholars always seek to resurrect elements of autonomous reason in Locke's politics" and therefore fail to define Lockean voluntary action in terms of pain, pleasure, and uneasiness. But almost everything Eisenach says is grounded on the first (1690) edition of the *Essay,* the edition that Locke himself came to see as inadequate. In Eisenach's reading Locke could not have said that the freedom of man and "liberty of acting according to his own will, is *grounded on* his having *reason.*" But of course the fact is that Locke did say it.

67. Locke, *Essay,* pp. 353, 473.

68. John Locke, letter to William Molyneux (August 23, 1693), in *The Correspondence of John Locke,* 4:722.

69. Locke, *Essay,* p. 347n.

70. John Locke, *Second Reply to the Bishop of Worcester,* in *The Works of John Locke,* 4:492. Cf. the comparable passage in Locke's letter to Molyneux

(January 20, 1693), in *The Correspondence of John Locke*, 4:625–626, where Locke says, "I cannot have a clearer perception of anything than that I am free, yet I cannot make freedom in man consistent with omnipotence and omniscience in God," and finally concludes that "if it be possible for God to make a free agent, then man is free, though I see not the way of it." Both the *Second Reply* and the 1693 letter should be contrasted with John Locke, "Remarks upon some of Mr. Norris's Books, Wherein he asserts P[ère] Malebranche's Opinion of our seeing all Things in God," in *The Works of John Locke*, 10:255–256, in which occasionalist theories of free will are criticized: "A man cannot move his arm or his tongue; he has no power; only upon occasion, the man willing it, God moves it. The man wills, he doth something; or else God, upon the occasion of something, which he himself did before, produced this will, and this action in him. This is the hypothesis that clears doubts, and brings us at last to the religion of Hobbes and Spinosa [sic], by resolving all, even the thoughts and will of men, into an irresistible fatal necessity." It is ironic, of course, that Locke should have lumped Malebranche with Hobbes and Spinoza, since it was precisely Malebranche who invented the idea that freedom is the power to suspend desire while one searches for real good—the doctrine that Locke adopted in the revised (1694) *Essay*. Cf. Nicolas Malebranche, *Recherche de la vérité, éclaircissement I*, ed. G. Rodis-Lewis (Paris: Librairie Philosophique Vrin, 1964), 3:31–34. Cf. also Leibniz's remarks on Locke's reading of Malebranche in G. W. Leibniz, *Analyse et commentaire d'un jugement de Locke sur Malebranche* (1707), in *Malebranche et Leibniz*, ed. André Robinet (Paris: Librairie Philosophique Vrin, 1955), pp. 397–401.

71. Strauss, *Natural Right and History*, pp. 202–232.

72. Locke, *Two Treatises*, p. 289.

73. On Locke's theory of divine workmanship see the brilliant study by James Tully, *A Discourse on Property: John Locke and his Adversaries* (Cambridge: Cambridge University Press, 1980), pp. 35–38. The title suggests a limited scope; in fact the book has valuable things to say about every facet of Locke's thought.

74. Locke, *Two Treatises*, p. 289.

75. Ibid., p. 376.

76. Locke, *Essays on the Law of Nature*, p. 111.

77. Locke, *Essay*, pp. 474, 475.

78. John Locke, letter to James Tyrrell (August 4, 1690), in *The Correspondence of John Locke*, 4:112–113.

79. For the relevant Descartes passages see Anthony Kenny, *The God of the Philosophers* (Oxford: Clarendon Press, 1979), pp. 16–26.

80. Locke, *Essay*, p. 76.

81. John Locke, *Of Ethick in General*, in King, *The Life of John Locke*, 2:122–133.

82. John Locke, *The Reasonableness of Christianity*, in *The Works of John Locke*, 7:140, 142.

83. Cf. Descartes's *Answers to the Six Objections*, 6, in Kenny, *The God of the Philosophers*, pp. 16–26, where roughly the same argument is made.

84. Locke, *Reasonableness of Christianity*, p. 144.

85. Ibid., p. 146: "The greatest part cannot know, and therefore must believe."

86. Locke, *Two Treatises*, p. 289.

87. Locke, *Reasonableness of Christianity*, p. 146.

88. Strauss, *Natural Right and History*, pp. 220, 203, 212.

89. John Locke, *First Letter to the Bishop of Worcester*, in *The Works of John Locke*, 4:9.

90. Locke, letter to James Tyrrell, *The Correspondence of John Locke*, 4:112.

91. Locke, *Essay*, p. 365.

92. Ibid., 2:425.

93. Locke, *Second Reply to the Bishop of Worcester*, p. 476.

94. Locke, *Reasonableness of Christianity*, pp. 107, 111–112.

95. John Locke, letter to William Molyneux (March 30, 1696), in *The Correspondence of John Locke*, 5:595.

96. Locke, *Reasonableness of Christianity*, pp. 141–142.

97. Cf. Hugo Grotius, *De Jure Belli ac Pacis* 1.1.10.

98. Green, *Political Obligation*, pp. 72–74.

99. Cf. ch.2.

100. The passages contrasting submission and consent come from Locke's unpublished notes on William Sherlock's *The Case of the Allegiance due to Sovereign Powers*, and are quoted in John Dunn, *Political Obligation in its Historical Context* (Cambridge: Cambridge University Press, 1980), p. 308. Locke's consent theory is treated at greater length in John Dunn, *The Political Thought of John Locke* (Cambridge: Cambridge University Press, 1969), pp. 140–147. It is to Dunn and his school that we owe much of the best recent Locke scholarship. Sherlock's book was also treated by Leibniz; cf. Patrick Riley, "An Unpublished MS of Leibniz on the Allegiance due to Sovereign Powers," in *Journal of the History of Philosophy*, (July 1973) 319–336. Leibniz's French text is reproduced on pp. 333–336.

101. Locke, *Two Treatises*, pp. 310–320, 305–309.

102. Cf. MacPherson, *Democratic Theory*, pp. 224–226; Strauss, *Natural Right and History*, pp. 234–251.

103. Plamenatz, *Man and Society*, 1:228.

104. Locke, *Two Treatises*, pp. 380, 412.

105. Rousseau, *The Social Contract*, p. 9.

106. Locke, *Two Treatises*, p. 380.

107. Ibid., pp. 351, 350.

108. H. D. Thoreau, *On the Duty of Civil Disobedience*, in *Walden* (New York: New American Library, 1960), p. 230. Locke never allows his voluntarism and contractarianism to spill over into a theory of civil disobedience.

109. Locke, *Two Treatises*, pp. 349–350.

110. Well argued by Kendall in *John Locke and the Doctrine of Majority Rule,* pp. 109–111.

111. See esp. Robert Paul Wolff, *In Defense of Anarchism* (New York: Harper, 1970), pp. 22–27.

112. Rousseau, *The Social Contract,* p. 31.

113. Locke, *Two Treatises,* pp. 367,365–366.

114. Cf. the neglected remarks on property and money in the *First Treatise,* which help to perform this self-correction—particularly p. 188: "as justice gives every man a title to the product of his honest industry...so charity gives every man a title to so much out of another's plenty, as will keep him from extreme want." Cf. also Michael Walzer, *Radical Principles* (New York: Basic Books, 1980), p. 248: "The ability to hold or spend vast sums of money is itself a form of power, permitting what might be called preemptive strikes against the political system...So long as money is convertible outside its sphere, it must be widely and more or less equally held so as to minimize its distorting effects upon legitimate distributive processes." If there can be left Hegelianism, why not left Lockeanism, which seems to be what is offered here?

115. Richard I. Aaron, *John Locke* (Oxford: Clarendon Press, 1936), p. 272. Cf. Dunn, *Political Obligation,* pp. 29–52, in which he argues that consent and contract in Locke are usually misunderstod by those (such as Plamenatz) who wrench the *Second Treatise* out of "its seventeenth century context" in order to graft it onto the "contemporary shibboleth" of "government by consent."

4. A Possible Explanation of Rousseau's General Will

1. Cf. Michael Oakeshott, "Dr. Leo Strauss on Hobbes," in *Hobbes on Civil Association* (Oxford: Basil Blackwell, 1975), p. 148: "A writer so completely devoid of a satisfactory philosophy of volition lacks something vital to modern political thought." This was written in 1937; in his later Hobbes studies Oakeshott softens this judgment.

2. To be questioned, however, is the view of Eldon Eisenach, *Two Worlds of Liberalism: Religion and Politics in Hobbes, Locke and Mill* (Chicago: University of Chicago Press, 1981), pp. 90–91, in which he defines Lockean will purely in terms of pleasure and pain and then, having cut all other ground away, asserts that "such a definition [of will] does not raise the problem of reasonable assent." If Lockean will were always and only a vibration between pain and pleasure, no sense could be made of Locke's claim that "the freedom then of men and liberty of acting according to his own will, is grounded on his having reason, which is able to instruct him in that law he is to govern himself by." In Eisenach's reading Locke could not have said what he actually did say. See John Locke, *Two Treatises of Government,* ed. Peter Laslett (Cambridge: Cambridge University Press, 1967), p. 327.

3. G. W. F. Hegel, *The Phenomenology of Mind,* trans. J. Baillie, (New York: Harper, 1967), pp. 789–790.

4. Rousseau understood will not only as a psychological attribute but also as a moral faculty. By treating the concept of will in psychological terms, however, rather than as a species of moral causality, Judith Shklar, in her brilliant *Men and Citizens: A Study of Rousseau's Social Theory* (Cambridge: Cambridge University Press, 1969), pp. 184–192, is able to make the general will both internally consistent and closely related to Rousseau's psychological theories. That is, by treating the individual will as a defense mechanism ("It is a regulative power, the defensive force that protects the self against the empire of opinion") and the general will as a collective defense mechanism used largely as a weapon against inequality, whose effects for Shklar are mainly psychologically destructive, she is able to make the concept of general will persuasive. This reading, however, seems to involve a weakening of those few passages in which Rousseau speaks in a traditional way of volition as a moral faculty whose endorsement is the source of moral legitimacy; he says, for example, "to deprive your will of all freedom is to deprive your actions of all morality" (*Contrat social*, bk. 1, ch.4). This idea is clearly the foundation of Rousseau's attack on paternalism and on the equation of right and force. It is certainly possible to conceive "the general will one has as a citizen" in a psychological sense if this generality is thought of in terms of factors wholly congruent with producing a group psychology: education, public spectacles and games, the authority of the legislator. But the education and authority that are wholly congruent with the shaping of a group psychology are not so obviously congruent with the free will that Rousseau himself insists on.

5. T. H. Green, *Lectures on the Principles of Political Obligation* (London: Longmans, 1941), pp. 82–83. In this passage Green rather indiscriminately conflates Plato, Aristotle, Rousseau, and Kant.

6. John Chapman, "Political Theory: Logical Structure and Enduring Types," *L'idée de philosophie politique* (Paris: Presses Universitaires de France, 1965), pp. 65–69, includes a helpful passage on the rise of voluntarism and contractarianism.

7. Jean-Jacques Rousseau, *Lettres écrites de la montagne*, in *Rousseau: Political Writings*, ed. C. E. Vaughan (Oxford: Basil Blackwell, 1962), 2:206.

8. Ibid., pp. 199–200. To be sure, Rousseau was trying to give his thought a more traditional cast by appealing to Locke's authority.

9. Leibniz accused Hobbes of adhering to this view. "To say *stat pro ratione voluntas*, my will takes the place of reason," Leibniz insists, "is properly the motto of a tyrant." He traces this line of thought back to Thrasymachus in Plato's *Republic* and urges that Hobbes, "who is noted for his paradoxes, wanted to maintain nearly the same things as Thrasymachus." See G. W. Leibniz, *Méditation sur la notion commune de la justice*, in *Rechtsphilosophisches aus Leibnizens ungedrückten Schriften*, ed. G. Mollat (Leipzig, 1885), pp. 56–65, also in *The Political Writings of Leibniz*, trans. and ed. Patrick Riley (Cambridge: Cambridge University Press, 1972), pp. 45–64.

10. In his letter to Isaac-Ami Marcet de Mezières (July 24, 1762),

Rousseau pointed out that he was not alone in admiring those ancient polities: "indeed many people up til now have regarded the republics of Sparta and of Rome as well-constituted." In *Correspondance complète de Jean-Jacques Rousseau,* ed. R. A. Leigh (Geneva: Institut et Musée Voltaire, 1970), 12:97–98.

11. One solution to this problem is to equate the desirable with what is actually desired: "The sole evidence it is possible to produce that any thing is desirable, is that people do actually desire it." J. S. Mill, *Utilitarianism,* in *The Philosophy of J. S. Mill,* ed. Marshall Cohen (New York: Modern Library, 1961), p. 363.

12. See particularly Jean-Jacques Rousseau, *Discourse on the Arts and Sciences,* in *The Social Contract and Discourses,* trans. G. D. H. Cole (New York: Everyman, 1950), pp. 172–174; Rousseau, *Gouvernement de Pologne,* in *Rousseau: Political Writings,* 2:430, 437–438; Rousseau, *Discourse on the Origins of Inequality,* in *The Social Contract and Discourses,* pp. 247–252, 266–269; Rousseau, *Lettre à M. d'Alembert sur les spectacles,* ed. M. Fuchs (Lille: Giard, 1948).

13. See Rousseau, *Gouvernement de Pologne,* pp. 427–437; Rousseau, *Arts and Sciences,* pp. 153–158; Rousseau, *Économie politique,* in *Rousseau: Political Writings,* 1:253–254; Rousseau, *Rome et Sparte,* in *Rousseau: Political Writings,* 1:314–318; Shklar, *Men and Citizens,* pp. 1–32.

14. Jean-Jacques Rousseau, *Le bonheur public,* in *Rousseau: Political Writings,* 1:325–326.

15. Jean-Jacques Rousseau, *Du contrat social,* in *Political Writings,* ed. F. Watkins (Edinburgh: Nelson, 1953), p. 42.

16. Rousseau, *Le bonheur public,* p. 326.

17. Rousseau, *Contrat social,* p. 58.

18. Ibid., p. 42.

19. Rousseau, *Gouvernement de Pologne,* pp. 166–167.

20. Rousseau, *Économie politique,* in *The Social Contract and Discourses,* p. 308. Cf. Rousseau's letter to Lieutenant Colonel Charles Pictet (September 23, 1762): "The state and morals have perished among us: nothing can cause them to be reborn. I believe that some good citizens remain with us, but their generation is dying out and that which follows will not provide any more." In *Correspondance complète,* 13:100.

21. Jean-Jacques Rousseau, *Émile* (excerpt), in *Rousseau: Political Writings,* 2:145.

22. Rousseau, *Gouvernement de Pologne,* pp. 163–165.

23. Jean-Jacques Rousseau, *Lettre à Monseigneur de Beaumont,* in *Oeuvres complètes,* ed. M. Launay (Paris: Éditions du Seuil, 1971), 3:340–348, esp. p. 348: "my feeling, then, is that the human mind, without progress, without instruction, without cultivation, and such as it is when it leaves the hands of nature, is not in a condition to elevate itself to sublime ideas by itself... but that these ideas are presented to us in proportion as our mind is cultivated."

24. Rousseau, *Contrat social,* p. 9. This crucial sentence seems to have

been overlooked by Stephen Ellenburg, who argues in his *Rousseau's Political Philosophy: an Interpretation from Within* (Ithaca: Cornell University Press, 1976), p. 103n, that "as a term Rousseau's *general will* can obscure his non-individualist meaning, for the word *will* suggests the natural ego of a deliberative individual." Despite the unfortunate term *ego*, it is clear that Rousseau insists precisely on deliberative individuals: in the *Contrat social* he argues that "each individual may, as a man, have a particular will contrary to or unlike the general will he has as a citizen." Plainly, an individual can have either kind of will. In any case, Ellenburg's nonindividualist Rousseau runs counter to too much that Rousseau demonstrably said.

25. Ibid., p. 7.

26. Rousseau, *Discourse on Inequality*, p. 208.

27. Jean-Jacques Rousseau, *Première version du contrat social*, in *Oeuvres complètes*, 2:417. The importance of the "First Version" or "Geneva MS" has been especially well brought out by Roger Masters in his introduction to Jean-Jacques Rousseau, *On the Social Contract* (New York: St. Martins, 1978), pp. 15–20.

28. Jean-Jacques Rousseau, *Émile*, trans. B. Foxley (London: Everyman, 1911), p. 243.

29. Jean-Jacques Rousseau, *Lettres morales*, in *Oeuvres complètes de Jean-Jacques Rousseau*, ed. Henri Gouhier (Paris: Pléiade, 1969), 4:1106. The importance of the *Lettres morales* is decisively established in Shklar, *Men and Citizens*, pp. 229–230.

30. Immanuel Kant, *Fundamental Principles of the Metaphysic of Morals*, trans. T. K. Abbott (Indianapolis: Library of Liberal Arts, 1949), p. 11.

31. Rousseau, *Lettres morales*, pp. 1111, 1107, 1108, 1109.

32. Bertrand de Jouvenel, "Essai sur la politique de Rousseau," in *Du contrat social* (Geneva: Éditions du Cheval Aile, 1947), p. 78.

33. Rousseau, *Émile*, trans. Foxley, pp. 243–244.

34. Rousseau, *Contrat social*, pp. 117, 8.

35. Rousseau, *Économie politique*, trans. Cole (translation slightly altered), p. 297.

36. Cf. Michael Oakeshott, introduction to Hobbes's *Leviathan* (Oxford: Basil Blackwell, 1957), pp. xxxv–l.

37. Jean-Jacques Rousseau, *L'état de guerre*, in *Rousseau: Political Writings*, 1:306. Here Rousseau anticipates by about two hundred years the Hobbes criticism of C. B. MacPherson in *The Political Theory of Possessive Individualism* (Oxford: Oxford University Press, 1962). Cf. Rousseau's letter of January 12, 1762, to Malesherbes: "man is naturally good and...it is through these [social] institutions alone that men become bad," in *Correspondance complète*, 10:25.

38. Rousseau, *Contrat social*, p. 20.

39. Cf. Michael Oakeshott, "The Moral Life in the Writings of Thomas Hobbes," in *Rationalism in Politics* (London: Methuen, 1962), p. 261.

40. Rousseau, *L'état de guerre*, p. 307.

41. Rousseau, *Discourse on Inequality*, pp. 250, 251, 252–253.

42. Rousseau, *Première version du contrat social*, pp. 392–393, 404. To be sure, at this point, Rousseau rejects the idea of general will partly because it had been Diderot's term in his *Encyclopédie* article "Droit naturel." In that piece Diderot had argued for a *volonté générale* of the entire *genre humain*, a general will that all men can naturally find when they consult reason "in the silence of the passions" (Malebranche's phrase from *Recherche de la vérité*). Rousseau's general will is much more particular: the general will of Sparta, of Rome, of Geneva. Both Diderot's rationalism and his universalism are rejected in the *Première version*. For a full treatment see Patrick Riley, "The General Will before Rousseau," in *Political Theory*, 6 (November 1978), 485–516, and in the same issue Nannerl Keohane, " 'The Masterpiece of Policy in our Century': Rousseau on The Morality of the Enlightenment," pp. 475–478. Cf. Robert Wokler, "The Influence of Diderot on the Political Theory of Rousseau," in *Studies in Voltaire and the Eighteenth Century*, 132, 1976: 55–111.

43. Rousseau, *Contrat social*, pp. 24n, 15.

44. Oakeshott, *Rationalism in Politics*, pp. 249–251.

45. David Hume, "Of the Original Contract," in *Hume: Theory of Politics*, ed. F. Watkins (Edinburgh: Nelson, 1951), pp. 163–165.

46. Rousseau, *Gouvernement de Pologne*, pp. 163–165.

47. Rousseau, *Économie politique*, pp. 293–311.

48. Jean-Jacques Rousseau, *Discours sur la vertu du héros*, in *Oeuvres complètes*, 2:118–120.

49. Rousseau, *Économie politique*, pp. 307–309.

50. Though the term *general will* is especially, and rightly, identified with Rousseau—and to a lesser extent with Diderot and Montesquieu—the idea of *volonté générale* was well established in the seventeenth century, though not primarily as a political idea. In fact, the notion of general will was a theological one that referred to the kind of will that God supposedly exercised in deciding who would be granted grace sufficient for salvation and who would be consigned to hell. The question at issue was: If God wills that all men be saved—as St. Paul asserts in a letter to Timothy—does he have a general will that produces universal salvation? And if he does not, why does he will particularly that some men not be saved? Finally, would it be right to save some but not all?

The first work of consequence to treat these questions through an appeal to general will was apparently Antoine Arnauld's *Première apologie pour M. Jansenius* (1644), though Arnauld argued, following Augustine's *De Correptione et Gratia*, that God's original general will to save all men before the Fall turned into a postlapsarian particular will to save only the elect through pity. That is also roughly Pascal's view in the magnificent *Écrits sur la grace*; but Pascal's main achievement was to convert *volonté générale* from a purely theological question into a social one by claiming that men, and not just God, should "incline" toward what is general, that *particularisme* is the source of all evils, above all self-love. In the 1680's

Malebranche both revived and transformed the language of general and particular will, saying that it is because God's operation is general and simple through uniform laws that he cannot particularly save each and every man. Here, general will keeps some men from being saved.

That Rousseau was familiar with all this, and with the controversy over Malebranchism in the writings of Bayle, Fénelon, Leibniz, and Fontenelle, is clear from remarks in the *Confessions* and from the theological *Briefwechsel* between St. Preux and Julie de Wolmar in book 6 of *La nouvelle Héloise.* For a full account of the history of the general will see Patrick Riley, "The General Will before Rousseau," pp. 485–516; cf. Émile Bréhier, "Les lectures Malebranchistes de Jean-Jacques Rousseau," in *Études de philosophie modernes* (Paris: Presses Universitaires de France, 1965), pp. 84–99. Cf. also Alberto Postigliola, "De Malebranche à Rousseau: les apories de la volonté générale et la revanche du raisonneur violent," in *Annales Jean-Jacques Rousseau, 1972–1977,* ed. C. Wirz (Geneva: A. Jullien, 1980), pp. 123–138.

51. Rousseau, *Contrat social,* pp. 37–38.

52. Cf. C. E. Vaughan's introduction to his edition of *Rousseau: Political Writings,* pp. 38–61. Vaughan views Rousseau's contractarianism as a vestigial Lockeanism, which he later abandonned to embrace a Montesquieuean historical method.

53. Rousseau, *Contrat social,* p. 44; cf. Jean-Jacques Rousseau, *Des lois,* in *Rousseau: Political Writings,* 1:331.

54. Rousseau, *Contrat social,* pp. 40–41, 44.

55. Rousseau, *Première version du contrat social,* p. 410.

56. Rousseau, *Contrat social,* p. 44. Cf. Rousseau's letter to V. B. Tscharner (April 29, 1762), in which he says something comparable about wisdom and truth: "you want to begin by teaching men the truth in order to make them wise; but, on the contrary, it would be necessary first to make them wise in order to make them love the truth," in *Correspondance complète,* 10:225.

57. R. Grimsley, in his *The Philosophy of Rousseau* (Oxford: Oxford University Press, 1973), p. 103, treats the general will as "a firm determination to seek the common good," without, however, dealing with the problems and paradoxes in Rousseau's theory of will.

58. Since, for Rousseau, the presocial man is a "stupid and limited animal," becoming a moral and intelligent being only in society, there is a sense in which man's highest nature is social. See Jean-Jacques Rousseau, *Lettre à M. Philopolis,* in *Rousseau: Political Writings,* 1:223.

59. Rousseau, *Contrat social,* p. 25.

60. Ibid.,pp. 42, 113.

61. Ibid., pp. 26, 29–30, 38–40, 32; 25.

62. Ibid., pp. 58, 29.

63. Rousseau, *Économie politique,* pp. 307–308, 309.

64. Rousseau, *Gouvernement de Pologne,* pp. 427–441.

65. Rousseau, *Contrat social,* pp. 40–41.

66. Rousseau, *Économie politique*, pp. 293, 298.

67. Rousseau, *Gouvernement de Pologne*, pp. 427–441; Rousseau, *Rome et Sparte*, pp. 314–320. In ancient polities, Rousseau urges, one saw "a spectacle so touching, and so rare in our century, true citizens loving their brothers and their fellow men, and occupying themselves sincerely with the happiness of the country and of the human race." Letter to V. B. Tscharner (April 29, 1762), in *Correspondance complète*, 10:225.

68. Hegel recognized this still more clearly, as his treatment of Sophocles' *Antigone* shows; see Hegel, *Phenomenology*, pp. 466–499.

69. Jean-Jacques Rousseau, *Histoire des moeurs*, in *Rousseau: Political Writings*, 1:337.

70. Rousseau, *Économie politique*, pp. 302–310.

71. Rousseau, *Contrat social*, pp. 18–19.

72. Ibid, p. 40. It is a passage like this one that leads Richard Fralin to say, in his *Rousseau and Representation* (New York: Columbia University Press, 1978), that in the *Contrat social* "will cannot be represented, no one can will for the people," but that, thanks to the need for the legislator's "understanding," the "people's role in formulating their will" is "much less" than some of Rousseau's "ringing declarations" might suggest. Fralin stops well short of Lester Crocker's claim, in *Rousseau's Social Contract: an Interpretive Essay* (Cleveland: Case Western Reserve University Press, 1968), pp. 14–15, that the phrase *general will* reveals that "what Rousseau has in mind is what we should call the conditioning of men to reflexive behavior." If that was Rousseau's project, then he surely did badly in insisting on general will: for the term *will* reminds us of Rousseau's own claim that "civil association is the most voluntary act in the world."

73. Michael Walzer, "Philosophy and Democracy," in *Political Theory*, 9 (August 1981), 384–385. Walzer's contribution to the revival of contract theory is perhaps second only to Rawls's.

74. Rousseau, *Contrat social*, pp. 53–54.

75. Ibid., pp. 57, 17–18.

76. Ibid., p. 57.

77. Rousseau, *Émile*, trans. Foxley, p. 435.

78. Shklar, *Men and Citizens*, p. 184.

79. Rousseau, *Émile*, trans. Foxley, pp. 141–149, 48.

80. Jean-Jacques Rousseau, *Les rêveries du promeneur solitaire*, in *Oeuvres complètes de Jean-Jacques Rousseau*, ed. M. Raymond (Paris: Pléiade, 1959), 1:1059.

81. Jean Starobinski, *Jean-Jacques Rousseau, la transparence et l'obstacle*, 2nd ed. (Paris: Gallimard, 1971), p. 286.

82. Rousseau, *Contrat social*, pp. 152–155.

83. Jean-Jacques Rousseau, *Lettre à Voltaire*, in *Rousseau: Political Writings*, 2:163.

84. Rousseau, *Contrat social*, pp. 15, 18, 33, 31.

85. Ibid., pp. 117–118.

86. Ibid., p. 20.

87. Ernst Cassirer, in his *Rousseau, Kant and Goethe*, trans. J. Gutmann, P. Kristeller, and J. H. Randall, Jr. (New York: Harper, 1963), pp. 30–43, provides, as always, a balanced view of the relation between Rousseau and Kant.

88. Rousseau, *Première version du contrat social*, in *Rousseau: Political Writings*, 1:462.

89. Jean-Jacques Rousseau, *Jugement sur la polysynodie*, in *Rousseau: Political Writings*, 1:421.

90. On this aspect of Rousseau the most valuable commentary by far is that of Judith Shklar in *Men and Citizens*, pp. 184–197.

91. Particularly in the *Discourse on Inequality* and in the *Première version du contrat social*. See *Rousseau: Political Writings*, 1:451–454.

92. Rousseau, *Contrat social*, p. 9.

93. Jean-Jacques Rousseau, *Lettre à Laurent Aymon de Franquières* (January 1769), in *Correspondance complète*, 37:22–23.

94. Rousseau, *Économie politique*, p. 297.

95. Rousseau, *Émile*, trans. Foxley, p. 444.

96. Rousseau, *Contrat social*, p. 41.

97. Rousseau, *Émile*, trans. Foxley, p. 84; cf. p. 290.

98. John Charvet, *The Social Problem in the Philosophy of Rousseau* (Cambridge: Cambridge University Press, 1974), p. 58.

99. Rousseau, *Lettre à Monseigneur de Beaumont*, p. 341.

5. On Kant as the Most Adequate of the Social Contract Theorists

1. Cited by Ernst Cassirer in his *Rousseau, Kant and Goethe*, trans. J. Gutmann, P. Kristeller, and J. H. Randall, Jr. (New York: Harper, 1963), p. 35.

2. Immanuel Kant, *The Conflict of the Faculties*, excerpted in *Kant's Political Writings*, ed. H. Reiss (Cambridge: Cambridge University Press, 1970), p. 186. For a full translation of Kant's entire work see Immanuel Kant, *The Conflict of the Faculties*, trans. M. J. Gregor (New York: Abaris Books, 1979).

3. Immanuel Kant, *On the Common Saying: 'This May be True in Theory, but it does not Apply in Practice'*, in *Kant's Political Writings*, p. 79.

4. Cited by John Ladd in his introduction to Immanuel Kant, *The Metaphysical Elements of Justice (Rechtslehre)*, trans. John Ladd (Indianapolis: Library of Liberal Arts, 1965), p. xxx.

5. Ibid., p. 97.

6. See Jean-Jacques Rousseau, *The Social Contract*, in *Rousseau: Political Writings*, ed. F. Watkins (Edinburgh: Nelson, 1953), pp. 38–39: "the law considers subjects collectively and actions abstractly; it is never concerned with an individual man or with a particular action." Cf. Nicolas Malebranche, *Traité de la nature et de la grace*, ed. G. Dreyfus (Paris: Librairie

Vrin, 1965), p. 166: for God "to establish general laws, and to choose the simplest ones which are at the same time the most fruitful, is a way of acting worthy of him whose wisdom has no limits," but "to act by particular wills shows a limited intelligence." On the Rousseau-Malebranche rapport see Patrick Riley, "The General Will before Rousseau," in *Political Theory,* 6 (November 1978), 485–516.

7. See David Hume, "Of the Original Contract," in *Theory of Politics,* ed. F. Watkins (Edinburgh: Nelson, 1951), pp. 198–199: "Almost all the governments which exist...have been founded originally either upon usurpation or conquest, or both, without any pretence of a fair consent or voluntary subjection of the people."

8. Kant, *Metaphysical Elements of Justice,* pp. 84–89, 79–80, 111–113.

9. John Locke, *Two Treatises of Government,* ed. Peter Laslett (Cambridge: Cambridge University Press, 1967), pp. 426–438. Despite this Kant and Locke are in some ways quite comparable; for example, both try to balance consent against natural law in a way that Rousseau, for one, does not.

10. Jean-Jacques Rousseau, *L'état de guerre,* in *Rousseau: Political Writings,* ed. C. E. Vaughan (Oxford: Basil Blackwell, 1962), 1:305–306.

11. Kant, *Conflict of the Faculties,* p. 187.

12. Kant did not have to worry about the kind of problem that Rousseau discusses in a letter to Mirabeau: "the great problem of politics"—giving men a general will, making them law abiding—"I compare to the squaring of the circle in geometry." Jean-Jacques Rousseau, letter to M. de Mirabeau (1767), in *Rousseau: lettres philosophiques,* ed. Henri Gouhier (Paris: Librairie Vrin, 1974), p. 167.

13. Immanuel Kant, *Philosophical Correspondence,* trans. and ed. A. Zweig (Chicago: University of Chicago Press, 1967), p. 132.

14. Immanuel Kant, *Fundamental Principles of the Metaphysic of Morals,* trans. T. K. Abbott (Indianapolis: Library of Liberal Arts, 1949), p. 11.

15. This formulation deliberately conflates a number of Kantian premises that are carefully distinguished in H. J. Paton, *The Categorical Imperative* (London: Hutchinson, 1947), pp. 128–222.

16. Immanuel Kant, *Eternal Peace,* in *The Philosophy of Kant,* ed. C. J. Friedrich (New York: Modern Library, 1949), p. 469. For an extended analysis of this work see C. J. Friedrich, *Inevitable Peace* (Cambridge, Mass.: Harvard University Press, 1948), pp. 157–209, 459.

17. Kant, *Metaphysical Elements of Justice,* p. 19.

18. Immanuel Kant, *Critique of Practical Reason,* trans. T. K. Abbott (London: Longmans, 1923), p. 171.

19. Ibid., pp. 186–187; cf. Immanuel Kant, *The Metaphysical Principles of Virtue (Tugendlehre),* trans. J. Ellington (Indianapolis: Library of Liberal Arts, 1964), p. 46.

20. Kant, *Metaphysical Elements of Justice,* pp. 20–21.

21. Kant, *Practical Reason,* p. 164.

22. Immanuel Kant, *Religion within the Limits of Reason Alone,* in *The Philosophy of Kant,* pp. 383–384.

23. Cited by Sheldon Wolin in *Politics and Vision* (Boston: Little, Brown, 1960), p. 389.

24. Kant, *Religion within the Limits*, pp. 404–406. On this point see G. Vlachos's useful study, *La pensée politique de Kant* (Paris: Presses Universitaries de France, 1962), pp. 310–311, which makes extensive use of Kant's posthumously published notes.

25. Kant, *Metaphysical Elements of Justice*, p. 13.

26. Immanuel Kant, *Eternal Peace*, in Reiss, *Kant's Political Writings*, p. 121n. Cf. the remark made by G. A. Kelly in the superb chapter on Kant in his *Idealism, Politics and History: Sources of Hegelian Thought* (Cambridge: Cambridge University Press, 1969), pp. 116–117: "in effect, it should be impossible for citizenship or public law-abidingness to make men moral...a false juncture would be made between the realms of autonomous and heteronomous causation." A possible way out is to say that public legal justice is instrumental only to negative freedom—for example, freedom from fear—so that persons can be positively free by determining themselves to act *from* the moral law.

27. Kant, *Metaphysical Elements of Justice*, p. 100.

28. Immanuel Kant, *Critique of Pure Reason*, trans. N. K. Smith (London: Macmillan, 1933), p. 644.

29. Kant, *Fundamental Principles*, p. 26.

30. Kant holds in the *Tugendlehre* that only a moral "gymnast" would insist that nothing is morally indifferent. See Kant, *Metaphysical Principles of Virtue*, pp. 154–155.

31. Kant, *Pure Reason*, p. 312.

32. Kant, *Metaphysical Elements of Justice*, p. 26.

33. Kant, *Fundamental Principles*, pp. 45–46.

34. Lewis White Beck, *A Commentary to Kant's Critique of Practical Reason* (Chicago: University of Chicago Press, 1960), pp. 199–200. See also the same argument in Lewis White Beck, "Was haben wir von Kant gelernt?" in *Kant-Studien* (1981), no. 1, p. 5, written for the two hundredth anniversary of the *Critique of Pure Reason*.

35. The best example of such a teleological reading is Jeffrie Murphy, *Kant: The Philosophy of Right* (London: Macmillan, 1970), pp. 68–108. A carefully argued counterargument, which diminishes *telos* as much as possible in Kant, is John Atwell's "Objective Ends in Kant's Ethics," in *Archiv für Geschichte der Philosophie*, 56 (1974), pp. 156–171. If objective ends shape Kantian politics—for example, by forbidding murder even if only legal motives can be counted on—then the distinction between ends and incentives might well overcome the difficulty suggested by William Galston in his thoughtful *Kant and the Problem of History* (Chicago: University of Chicago Press, 1975), pp. 200–201. Galston argues that "the sphere of justice or of civil society is said [by Kant] to be that of 'external freedom'...However, as Kant emphasizes in the *Foundations*, the crucial measure of action is intention, for any external motion can be produced by nonmoral causes. It thus becomes very difficult to see how any unequivocal moral meaning can be attached to pure externality." But if public

legal justice realizes some moral ends through legal incentives, then some moral meaning can indeed be attached to external justice; justice would simply fail to be an unqualified good. If by *unequivocal* Galston means that legal justice realizes only a qualified good—a good end—then of course he is right. The distinction between ends and incentives may be the only way to make intelligible Kant's view that morality and legality must be both close together and far apart. Cf. the excellent statement of the relation between morality and legality in Mary J. Gregor, *Laws of Freedom* (Oxford: Basil Blackwell, 1963), p. 31: "The necessity of viewing particular juridical laws as derivations from the categorical imperative...is perhaps more obvious. Law is independent of ethics in the sense that it has no need of ethical obligation in determining its duties. But it cannot be independent of the supreme moral principle; for if its laws were not derived from the categorical imperative, then the constraint exercised in juridical legislation would not be legal obligation but mere arbitrary violence."

36. Kant, *Eternal Peace*, in Reiss, *Kant's Political Writings*, p. 100. If an Ideal contract yields, from self-love, a merely "legal" order that parallels moral requirements—if universalized self-love gets people to abandon something they ought to abandon, such as war—then Harvey Mansfield, Jr., cannot be right when he claims, in *The Spirit of Liberalism* (Cambridge, Mass.: Harvard University Press, 1978), pp. 47–48, that Kant "kept the principle of consent because his formula made it the duty of all, rather than the privilege of a few gentlemen, to be moral." Given Kant's radical distinction between moral and legal incentives, it is questionable whether he viewed political consent as something directly moral or only as something legal that might realize a moral end.

37. Kant, *Metaphysical Elements of Justice*, pp. 109–114.

38. Kant, *Eternal Peace*, in Friedrich, *The Philosophy of Kant*, pp. 434–436.

39. Kant, *Conflict of the Faculties*, pp. 187–188.

40. G. W. F. Hegel, *Philosophy of Right*, trans. T. M. Knox (Oxford: Clarendon Press, 1942), pp. 89–90.

41. G. W. F. Hegel, *The Phenomenology of Mind*, trans. J. Baillie (New York: Harper, 1967), pp. 599–605.

42. On this point see Lewis White Beck, "Les deux concepts Kantiens du vouloir dans leur contexte politique," in *La philosophie politique de Kant* (Paris: Presses Universitaires de France, 1962), pp. 119–137.

43. Kant, *Fundamental Principles*, p. 11.

44. Jean-Jacques Rousseau, *Discourse on the Origins of Inequality*, in *The Social Contract and Discourses*, trans. G. D. H. Cole (New York: Everyman, 1950), pp. 208, 194.

45. Kant, *Fundamental Principles*, p. 30.

46. Jean-Jacques Rousseau, *Lettres morales*, in *Oeuvres complètes de Jean-Jacques Rousseau*, ed. Henri Gouhier (Paris: Pléiade, 1969), 4:1106–1111.

47. Kant, *Pure Reason*, pp. 472–473. For Kant human psychology ("pathology") is part of nature—the same nature that cannot yield an

"ought." Given Kant's radical distinction between morality and pathology, it is a mistake to reconstruct Kantian morality and then politics as a reflection or epiphenomenon of pathology. But this is exactly what Susan Shell does in her highly original book *The Rights of Reason: A Study of Kant's Philosophy and Politics* (Toronto: University of Toronto Press, 1980), pp. 109–122. Beginning with a characterization of Kant that turns him into a Kirkegaard *avant la lettre,* Shell insists that for Kant "man first expresses his sense of right in anger and resentment against the resistance which his will naturally encounters...man's primal indignation represents his unhappy and almost unsupportable awareness of his condition. Morality fortifies and rechannels this indignation while dissipating its initial cause. Morality turns anger inwards against the self, then outwards against other selves...right, properly understood, is rational indignation, anger objectified." She goes on to add that "by universalizing anger, right transforms a physically destructive self-forgetting into a morally constructive one. The rational alternative to self-destruction is the adoption as one's end of a universal legislation which serves all." In this view of Kant—which Shell grounds mainly in her reading of the *Anthropology*—the moral law, as well as right, is a constructive reconstruction of destructive impulses. Surely, this view of morality as the rationalization of the irrational, whatever might be said for it in itself, runs wholly counter to Kant's insistence that the moral law is already a "fact of reason." More strikingly, it runs counter to what Kant says about separating morality and pathology in the *Critique of Judgment:* "the fear that, if we divest...our representations of the moral law and of our native capacity for morality...of everything that can commend it to the senses, it will thereupon be atteneded only with a cold and lifeless approbation and not with any moving force or emotion, is wholly unwarranted." Kant goes on to say that "the moral law...is a sufficient and *original* source of determination within us; so it does not for a moment permit us to cast about for a ground of determination external to itself. If enthusiasm is comparable to delirium, fanaticism may be compared to mania." The additional disparaging things that Kant says about "unbridled" imagination and "brooding" passion make it clear that the moral law, in its pure state, is above and beyond "delusion" and "rational raving." It is absolutely inadmissible, then, to view the categorical imperative as an epiphenomenon of pathology in Kant; the moral law is not simply anger given a constructive turn.

48. David Hume, *Treatise of Human Nature,* pp. 19, 20. In Hume, as in Rousseau, generality is moral, particularity merely self-regarding. But this is not well grounded in Hume: it remains an assertion.

49. Immanuel Kant, *Critique of Practical Reason,* in Friedrich, *The Philosophy of Kant,* p. 231.

50. Kant, *Practical Reason,* p. 182.

51. Kant, *Fundamental Principles,* pp. 34–36.

52. Kant, *Theory and Practice,* p. 64.

53. Cf. Thomas Hobbes, *Leviathan,* ed. Michael Oakeshott (Oxford: Basil Blackwell, 1957), pp. 37–38; John Locke, *An Essay concerning Human Understanding,* ed. A. C. Fraser (New York: Dover, 1959), pp. 308–344. To be sure, Locke later argues that uneasiness can be suspended; see pp. 344–374.

54. Kant, *Fundamental Principles,* pp. 44, 63.

55. Kant, *Practical Reason,* p. 222.

56. Kant, *Fundamental Principles,* p. 63.

57. Ibid., pp. 63–80. For a full exposition of the doctrine that rational beings, though determined as phenomena, must take themselves to be noumenally free see Kant, *Pure Reason,* pp. 464–473.

58. Ibid. Cf. Alexandre Kojève, *Kant* (Paris: Editions Gallimard, 1973), pp. 30–31: "Kant formulates his 'supreme' question as follows: what ought one to do, if the will is free...[?]" This, of course, is disputable: Kant does not say that it is "as if" men were free but are really not; rather, he says that men must necessarily take themselves to be free if they are to understand themselves as responsible moral agents. A Kantian necessary hypothesis is not a mere "as if," Kojève and Hans Vaihinger to the contrary notwithstanding. See Vaihinger's *The Philosophy of As-If,* trans. C. K. Ogden (London: Kegan Paul, Trench, Trubner and Co., 1935), pp. 271–287.

59. Friedrich Nietzsche, *The Twilight of the Idols,* in *The Portable Nietzsche,* trans. W. Kaufmann (New York: Viking, 1954), p. 484.

60. Kant, *Practical Reason,* in Friedrich, *The Philosophy of Kant,* p. 238.

61. Kant, *Fundamental Principles,* pp. 5–8, 72, 73.

62. Ibid., pp. 64–65.

63. Ibid., pp. 68, 69.

64. Ibid., pp. 70–71.

65. Ibid., pp. 75, 76.

66. Kant, *Practical Reason,* in Friedrich, *The Philosophy of Kant,* p. 241.

67. Kant, *Metaphysical Elements of Justice,* p. 22.

68. Immanuel Kant, *Critique of Judgment,* in Friedrich, *The Philosophy of Kant,* pp. 363–364.

69. Hobbes, *Leviathan,* p. 307, cf. p. 377.

70. Ibid., p. 86.

71. On this point see A. E. Taylor, "The Ethical Doctrine of Hobbes," in *Hobbes Studies,* ed. K. Brown (Oxford: Basil Blackwell, 1965), pp. 35–55, in which Taylor compares Hobbes with Kant in an unconventional but partly persuasive way.

72. Kant, *Religion within the Limits,* p. 367.

73. Hobbes, *Leviathan,* p. 141.

74. Kant, *Religion within the Limits,* p. 367.

75. Kant, *Practical Reason,* p. 151.

76. For a good recent defense of Hobbes as a voluntarist who believed in genuine duties see Brian Barry, "Warrender and his Critics," in *Hobbes and Rousseau,* ed. M. Cranston and R. Peters (New York: Anchor, 1972), pp. 37–65.

77. Kant, *Religion within the Limits*, pp. 392–394.
78. Kant, *Fundamental Principles*, pp. 11–12.
79. G. W. Leibniz, *Theodicy*, ed. A. Farrer (New Haven: Yale University Press, 1952), pp. 57, 302–303.
80. Kant, *Fundamental Principles*, p. 26.
81. Kant, *Religion within the Limits*, p. 389.
82. Kant, *Metaphysical Elements of Justice*, pp. 12–14.
83. Ibid., p. 12. Hannah Arendt, however, in *The Life of the Mind: Willing* (New York: Harcourt Brace Jovanovich, 1978), p. 149, almost certainly takes Kant's equation of *Wille* with practical reason itself too literally: that leaves *Willkür*, viewed as uncaused causality, wholly out of account. After all, Kant criticizes the Stoics for making reason immediately causal, without the mediation of will—without taking reason as one's motive. Her further argument that Kant did not believe in "freedom of choice" is apparently grounded in her conviction that for Kant " 'absolute spontaneity' exists only in thinking"; but that, of course, flatly contradicts Kant's crystal-clear claim in *Pure Reason* (A 533/B 561) that without true spontaneity morality itself is impossible: "By freedom . . . I understand the power of beginning a state spontaneously . . . The denial of transcendental freedom must, therefore, involve the elimination of all practical freedom."
84. Kant, *Practical Reason*, p. 204.
85. Kant, *Fundamental Principles*, pp. 44–57.
86. Hegel, *Philosophy of Right*, pp. 89–90.
87. J. S. Mill, *Utilitarianism*, in *The Philosophy of J. S. Mill*, ed. Marshall Cohen (New York: Modern Library, 1961), pp. 326–327.
88. Kant, *Practical Reason*, p. 165.
89. Kant, *Fundamental Principles*, p. 53. One can only sympathize with Sir David Ross's complaint, in *Kant's Ethical Theory* (Oxford: Clarendon Press, 1954), p. 57, that Kant "cannot be said" to make it "at all clear" just how the various formulae imply each other. Among efforts to defend Kant on this point two of the most striking are H. J. Paton's and A. D. Lindsay's. In *The Categorical Imperative*, p. 178, Paton argues that the original formulation of the categorical imperative "bids me act only on maxims which can be universal laws for all men. Since these laws are laws of freedom, this means that in determining my actions I have to take into account the rational wills of other men: I ought to act only in such a way that as rational beings they can act on the same law as I. Hence their rational wills limit my actions and must not be arbitrarily overridden by me . . . I ought not to use them merely as means to the satisfaction of my desires." This is artful, but of course Paton begins by *injecting* man into the original formulation by insisting on legislating universally "for all men." This allows him to move with apparent ease from formal universality to the kingdom of ends, since universal laws are *for* men and the citizens of the kingdom of ends *are* men. This is not to say, of course, that Paton is wrong in his general claim that a full "view of Kant's ethics will show him as the philosopher, not of rigorism, but of humanity" (p. 98). Indeed, he is profoundly right.

A. D. Lindsay, in *Kant* (London: Ernest Benn, 1934), p. 175, says that "the first formula of the categorical imperative," which insists on willing one's maxim as a universal law, "has been reached by seeing that the principle of the will itself is the only thing which has absolute worth, or, in Kant's words, that 'rational nature is an end in itself'"; and so all the formulae are the same. This is as questionable as Paton's procedure: if Paton injects the words *all men* into formal universality, surely Lindsay injects *absolute worth* into the will that wills universal laws. It is not that easy, however, to connect or equate the rational will, which is capable of universal willing, with the good will, which is the only unqualified good. Lindsay's reading works only if will is always good will; but if that were so, Kant's complaints about "radical evil" in *Religion within the Limits* would be quite unintelligible.

90. John Rawls, *A Theory of Justice* (Cambridge, Mass.: Harvard University Press, 1971), p. 251. This remarkable book has brought Kant's political thought back into prominence. That is not to say that Rawls's own thought is purely Kantian; cf. John Rawls, "Kantian Constructivism in Moral Theory," in *Journal of Philosophy*, 77 (Sepetember 1980), 516–517, for Rawls's own view of his debt to Kant.

91. For a good, brief commentary on the notion of objective ends in Kant's moral philosophy see Onora Nell, *Acting on Principle: An Essay on Kantian Ethics* (New York: Columbia University Press, 1975), pp. 106–112.

92. Kant, *Fundamental Principles*, p. 45.

93. Ibid., p. 46. That Kant would not ordinarily have countenanced this kind of argument is clear from a passage in *Practical Reason*, p. 98: "Universal assent does not prove the objective validity of a judgment . . . on the contrary, it is the objective validity which alone constitutes the basis of a necessary universal consent."

94. Ibid., p. 48.

95. Ibid., pp. 45–50.

96. Ibid., p. 50.

97. Ibid., p. 53.

98. Ibid., pp. 53–55. Obviously, the phrase "any other end"—that is, any other end besides "man as a rational creature"—means that there is one objective end; and that objective end is plainly man, the "rational nature" that is an "end in itself."

99. Kant, *Metaphysical Principles of Virtue*, pp. 42–43.

100. Paton, *The Categorical Imperative*, pp. 168–169.

101. Kant, *Fundamental Principles*, p. 55.

102. Kant, *Critique Judgment*, in Friedrich, *The Philosophy of Kant*, pp. 348–349. Cf. the wonderful lines in Wilhelm Windelband's *A History of Philosophy*, trans. J. H. Tufts (New York: Harper, 1958), 2:561: "The problem of the *Critique of Judgment* takes this formulation: Is it a priori possible to judge Nature to be adapted to an end? Evidently this is the highest synthesis of the critical philosophy; the application of the category of the practical reason to the object of the theoretical." For a good general

study of Kant's teleology see George Schrader, "The Status of Teleological Judgment in the Critical Philosophy," in *Kant-Studien*, 45 (1953–1954), pp. 204–235.

103. Ibid., p. 354.

104. Such a reading of Kant—or at least the beginning of one—is to be found in Yirmiahu Yovel's *Kant and the Philosophy of History* (Princeton: Princeton University Press, 1980), the main objective of which is to integrate Kant's historical writings into the critical corpus through reconstructed teleology. For Yovel the historical writings' claims about nature's purposes for mankind can be given a nondogmatic sense only within the confines of *Judgment*'s notion of "reflective" purposiveness. Yovel does very well (pp. 156–198) with Kant's idea of culture—including law, eternal peace, art, science—as the ultimate end of nature in *Judgment*, section 83. If there is a defect in Yovel's study it is that of refusing to connect man as the rational nature that is an end in itself of the *Fundamental Principles* with the man as the final end of creation in *Judgment*. Yovel gives *telos* its full weight everywhere except where it matters most of all: in moral philosophy (see Yovel, pp. 12–13). Yovel's very valuable study could have been better still had he recalled Richard Kroner's words in *Kant's Weltanschauung*, trans. J. E. Smith (Chicago: University of Chicago Press, 1956), pp. 111–112n: "The *Critique of Judgment*... in spite of the new vistas it opens...uniting the opposites of nature and mind, of necessity and freedom...limits the horizon just where it was limited before. The final result is the primacy of ethical thought...it is not the organism but the moral will and moral freedom which must be regarded as the absolute purpose."

105. Immanuel Kant, *Critique of Judgment*, trans. J. C. Meredith (Oxford: Clarendon Press, 1952), pp. 221–225: "taste makes, as it were, the transition from the charm of sense to habitual moral interest possible without too violent a leap, for it represents the imagination, even in its freedom, as amenable to a final determination for understanding." For an extremely careful commentary on the limits of beauty as the symbol of morality see Paul Guyer, *Kant and the Claims of Taste* (Cambridge, Mass.: Harvard University Press, 1979), pp. 351–394. See also Donald W. Crawford, *Kant's Aesthetic Theory* (Madison, Wisc.: University of Wisconsin Press, 1974).

106. Immanuel Kant, "On a Discovery According to which any New Critique of Pure Reason has been Made Superfluous by an Earlier One," in Henry E. Allison, *The Kant-Eberhard Controversy* (Baltimore: Johns Hopkins University Press, 1973), p. 160. Cf. Kant, *Pure Reason*, p. 642: "This systematic unity of ends in this world of intelligences—a world which is, indeed, as mere nature, a sensible world only, but which, as a system of freedom, can be entitled an intelligible, that is, a moral world (*regnum gratiae*)—leads inevitably also to the purposive unity of all things, which constitute this great whole." The *Critique of Judgment* can be viewed as a working up of this passage.

107. Immanuel Kant, *Anthropologie in Pragmatischer Hindsicht,* 3rd ed. (Königsberg, 1820), Vorrede, p. iii: "Der Mensch...sein eigener letzter Zweck ist."

108. Kant, *Theory and Practice,* p. 65n.

109. Kant, *Practical Reason,* p. 170.

110. Kant, *Metaphysical Principles of Virtue,* pp. 96–97.

111. Kant, *Conflict of the Faculties,* p. 185.

112. Kant, *Metaphysical Elements of Justice,* pp. 78, 79.

113. Rousseau, *The Social Contract,* pp. 14–15.

114. Kant, *Metaphysical Elements of Justice,* p. 78.

115. Rousseau, *The Social Contract,* p. 31.

116. Kant, *Metaphysical Elements of Justice,* p. 110.

117. Kant, *Eternal Peace,* in Friedrich, *The Philosophy of Kant,* pp. 438–439.

118. Kant, *Metaphysical Elements of Justice,* p. 110.

119. Ibid., p. 112.

120. Charles Secondat, Baron de Montesquieu, *The Spirit of the Laws,* trans. T. Nugent (New York: Hafner, 1949), p. 54. In a monarchy, Montesquieu argues, the ruler is able "to act with greater expedition" than in republics.

121. Kant, *Conflict of the Faculties,* pp. 182–183n, 187.

122. Kant, *Theory and Practice,* p. 83n.

123. G. W. F. Hegel, *Encyclopedia,* trans. W. Wallace (Oxford: Clarendon Press, 1894), p. 269.

124. Kant, *Metaphysical Elements of Justice,* pp. 97–98.

125. Kant, *Conflict of the Faculties,* p. 184.

126. Kant, *Eternal Peace,* in Reiss, *Kant's Political Writings,* p. 100.

127. Immanuel Kant, *Idea for a Universal History,* in Reiss, *Kant's Political Writings,* pp. 44–53. For a sympathetic appreciation of this essay see Eric Weil, "Kant et le problème de la politique," in *La philosophie politique de Kant* (Paris: Presses Universitaires de France, 1962), pp. 1–32.

128. Kant, *Eternal Peace,* in Reiss, *Kant's Political Writings,* pp. 93–95.

129. Kant, *Conflict of the Faculties,* pp. 182–183.

130. Kant, *Metaphysical Elements of Justice,* p. 87.

131. Ibid., pp. 82, 87–88n.

132. Ibid., pp. 99–106.

133. Whether one can be certain about what people deserve even morally is not so clear in Kant. After all, he says in *Pure Reason,* p. 475n, "the real morality of actions, their merit or guilt, even that of our own conduct, thus remains entirely hidden from us...how much of this character is ascribable to the pure effects of freedom, how much to mere nature...can never be determined; and upon it therefore no perfectly just judgments can be passed." Kant ought to have recalled his own words in constructing his justification of legal punishment.

134. Kant, *Metaphysical Elements of Justice,* in Reiss, *Kant's Political Writings,* p. 134.

6. *Hegel on Consent and Social Contract Theory*

1. Jean-Jacques Rousseau, *Économie politique,* in *Rousseau: Political Writings,* ed. C. E. Vaughan (Oxford: Basil Blackwell, 1962), 1:244–245. Both Rousseau and Hegel were virtually obliged to treat the will as a moral faculty, as the source of obligations and promises, because the notion of voluntariness as an essential component of ethical action, first introduced by Christian doctrine, reached a political zenith in social contract theory as developed by Hobbes, Locke, Rousseau, and Kant. Recall the central place of the general will in Rousseau as well as Hobbes's claim in ch. 40 of *Leviathan* that wills "make the essence of all covenants." On this intricate point see Sir David Ritchie, "Contributions to the History of the Social Contract Theory," in *Darwin and Hegel* (London: Swan Sonnenschein, 1893), pp. 196–226.

2. See ch. 5 of Jean-Jacques Rousseau, *The Government of Poland,* in *Political Writings,* ed. F. Watkins (Edinburgh: Nelson, 1953), pp. 181–182: "practically all small states...prosper merely by reason of the fact that they are small." The "subordinate oppressors" necessary to administer a large state, in Rousseau's view, would be little different from Hegel's "universal class."

3. G. W. F. Hegel, *Philosophy of Right,* trans. T. M. Knox (Oxford: Clarendon Press, 1942), pp. 156–157.

4. John Plamenatz, *Consent, Freedom and Political Obligation* (Oxford: Oxford University Press, 1938), p. 61.

5. G. W. F. Hegel, *The Phenomenology of Mind,* trans. J. Baillie (New York: Harper, 1967), pp. 242–246; 526–537; 391–400; 440–453, and Hegel, *Philosophy of Right,* p. 90; *Phenomenology,* pp. 615–627; Hegel, *Philosophy of Right,* additions, p. 232.

6. Hegel, *Philosophy of Right,* pp. 87–88, 86.

7. Rousseau, *Économie politique,* p. 248: "Virtue is only the conformity of the particular will to the general [will]."

8. On the notion of "canceling and preserving" in Hegel see particularly G. A. Kelly, *Idealism, Politics and History* (Cambridge: Cambridge University Press, 1969), p. 311.

9. Hegel, *Philosophy of Right,* additions, p. 280.

10. Ibid., p. 253. Because this is so, Hegel suggests in the *Encyclopedia,* Plato was wrong in imagining that thought could rule in the person of philosophers only and not in the minds of all men. See G. W. F. Hegel, *Encyclopedia,* trans. W. Wallace (Oxford: Clarendon Press, 1894, pp. 288–289.

11. Hegel, *Philosophy of Right,* additions, p. 251; cf. pp. 259 and 280, as well as the *Phenomenology,* p. 349.

12. Hegel, *Phenomenology,* esp. pp. 251–267.

13. Hegel, *Philosophy of Right,* pp. 157 and 165–174. According to Hegel fanatical religions claiming exclusive spiritual validity for themselves are partly responsible for making men think of the state as nothing better than a "mechanical scaffolding."

14. G. W. F. Hegel, "On Classical Studies," in *Early Theological Writings*, trans. T. M. Knox and R. Kroner (Chicago: University of Chicago Press, 1948), p. 325.

15. G. A. Kelly, *Hegel's Retreat from Eleusis* (Princeton: Princeton University Press, 1978), pp. 113–114. This passage comes from a chapter called "The Neutral State," which is assuredly the most intelligent and helpful sympathetic reading of the *Philosophy of Right* available in English.

16. When Burke says that "society is indeed a contract" (book 7, part 2 of *Reflections on the Revolution in France*), he does so in a way that makes clear that he is no voluntarist: "each contract of each particular state is but a clause in the great primieval contract of eternal society, linking the higher with the lower natures, connecting the visible and invisible world." Contract, for Burke, is nothing more than a metaphor. See Edmund Burke, *Reflections on the Revolution in France* (Indianapolis: Library of Liberal Arts, 1955), p. 110.

17. Hegel, *Philosophy of Right*, p. 105.

18. G. W. F. Hegel, *Lectures on the History of Philosophy*, trans. E. S. Haldane and F. H. Simson (London, 1896), 3:402.

19. Hegel, *Philosophy of Right*, p. 105.

20. Ibid., p. 30.

21. Hegel, *Encyclopedia*, pp. 230–231.

22. Hegel, *Philosophy of Right*, pp. 76–79; additions, p. 248; p. 157.

23. G. W. F. Hegel, *Philosophy of History*, trans. J. Sibree (New York: Dover, 1956), p. 238.

24. Hegel, *Philosophy of Right*, additions, p. 280.

25. Ibid., p. 100.

26. On this point see particularly Immanuel Kant's *The Metaphysical Elements of Justice*, trans. J. Ladd (New York: Library of Liberal Arts, 1965), introduction, section 3, "Of the Subdivision of a Metaphysic of Morals," pp. 18–21.

27. Hegel, *Philosophy of Right*, preface, p. 12.

28. Ibid., p. 167: "The genuine truth is the prodigious transfer of the inner into the outer, the building of reason into the real world, and this has been the task of the world during the whole course of its history." See also pp. 155–157 and additions, pp. 279–285.

29. Ibid., p. 12. See also p. 279: "In considering the idea of the state, we must not have our eyes on particular states." Nonetheless, he holds that any of the "mature states" of his epoch sufficiently embodies this idea.

30. Ibid., p. 138. Hegel, however, does not fail to add that "le plus grand ennemi du Bien, c'est le Meilleur."

31. Hegel, *Philosophy of History*, esp. pp. 452–453.

32. Hegel, *Philosophy of Right*, p. 161.

33. G. W. F. Hegel, *Science of Logic*, trans. W. H. Johnston and L. G. Struthers (London: Allen and Unwin, 1929), 2:397.

34. G. W. F. Hegel, *The Philosophy of Religion*, trans. E. B. Speirs and J. B. Sanderson (London, 1895), 1:246–248. The latest version of Hegel as

a "Prussian" in politics is to be found in J. N. Findlay, *Hegel: A Re-Examination* (London: Allen and Unwin, 1958), p. 327. In this passage Findlay says that Hegel's state, though not "vile," is nonetheless redolent of "the enclosed atmosphere of the small, stuffy waiting-rooms of Prussian officials," and that the *Philosophy of Right* is "small-minded and provincial." The really astonishing claim is Findlay's assertion that Hegel "was not really gifted with deep political and social understanding."

35. Hegel, *Philosophy of History*.

36. Hegel, *Philosophy of Right*, additions, p. 279.

37. Hegel, *History of Philosophy*, 3:341.

38. Hegel, *Philosophy of Right*, additions, p. 285; p. 279.

39. Hegel, *Logic*, p. 398.

40. Hegel, *Philosophy of Right*, additions, p. 279.

41. Hegel, *Encyclopedia*, p. 291: "The notion of the mind has its reality in the mind...The subjective and the objective mind [individual and state] are to be looked on as the road on which this aspect of reality or existence rises to maturity." In sections 572ff. of this work Hegel shows that it is philosophy that is "absolute mind."

42. This is particularly true of the preface to Hegel's *Philosophy of Right*, pp. 10–13: "This book...is to be nothing other than the endeavor to apprehend and portray the state as something inherently rational. As a work of philosophy, it must be poles apart from an attempt to construct a state as it ought to be...To comprehend what is, this is the task of philosophy, because what is, is reason."

43. Hegel, *Logic*, introduction; cf. the chapter on "Absolute Knowledge" in the *Phenomenology* and the one on "Philosophy" in the *Encyclopedia*.

44. Hegel, *Phenomenology*, pp. 644–664, esp. pp. 650–664; see also pp. 162–164.

45. Hegel, *Philosophy of Right*, p. 105.

46. Ibid., pp. 195–208. This is implicit in Hegel's comparison of the triviality of private opinion and judgment with the rationality of the decisions of the "universal class"; see also pp. 197–198.

47. Hegel, *Philosophy of History*, pp. 18, 351–360, 238–240, 279–282; cf. Hegel, *Phenomenology*, pp. 501–506.

48. Hegel, *Philosophy of Right*, p. 84; cf. Hegel, *Philosophy of Religion*, 1:253.

49. Hegel, *Philosophy of History*, p. 18.

50. Ibid., p. 250; cf. Hegel, *History of Philosophy*, 3:4.

51. Ibid., p. 379.

52. Ibid., pp. 416, 417, 422.

53. Ibid., p. 269; cf. Hegel, *Encyclopedia*, p. 161, in which the maxim "Know thyself" is submitted to similar criticism.

54. Ibid., pp. 440–448.

55. J. N. Shklar, "Hegel's Phenomenology: An Elegy for Hellas," in *Hegel's Political Philosophy*, ed. Z. Pelczynski (Cambridge: Cambridge

University Press, 1971), p. 74. Cf. J. N. Shklar, *Freedom and Independence: A Study of the Political Ideas of Hegel's Phenomenology of Mind* (Cambridge: Cambridge University Press, 1976). This splendid book is indispensable to any serious student of the *Phenomenology;* what follows here obviously owes a great deal to this remarkable commentary.

56. Hegel, *Phenomenology,* pp. 136, 138–139.

57. Ibid., pp. 498, 409–410.

58. Ibid., pp. 478, 489, 490.

59. Hegel, *Philosophy of Right,* additions, p. 250.

60. Hegel, *Phenomenology,* pp. 491, 481, 492.

61. Hegel, *Philosophy of Right,* p. 124. Plato, according to Hegel, "could only cope with the principle of self-subsistent particularity, which in his day had forced itself into Greek ethical life, by setting up in opposition to it his purely substantial state."

62. Hegel, *Phenomenology,* pp. 452, 453.

63. Ibid., p. 485. It should be pointed out that while Hegel used Greek art to illustrate truths about Greek ethical life, he paid back this debt by showing how that very ethos gave rise to essential features of Greek art itself. The chorus in Greek tragedy, in particular, as the embodiment of general social judgment passed on individual characters he brilliantly shows to be not only possible but necessary in a culture that is not subjective, whereas in modern tragedy, in which ruin is the consequence of highly personal characteristics rather than a conflict between such established ethical powers as family and city, a chorus would be out of place. What he says about the differences between *Antigone* and *Hamlet* in this connection is incomparably insightful. See G. W. F. Hegel, *Philosophy of Fine Art,* trans. F. P. B. Osmaston (London: G. Bell and Sons, 1920), 4:312–336.

64. Hegel, *Philosophy of Right,* additions, p. 250.

65. Hegel, *Phenomenology,* pp. 378, 379, 710.

66. Ibid., p. 807.

67. Ibid., pp. 460–461. For the relation of this to Hegel's general theory of becoming as the unity of Being and Nothing see Hegel, *Logic,* p. 64.

68. Hegel, *Phenomenology,* pp. 245, 527.

69. Ibid., p. 528. On this point see the incomparable passages in Shklar, *Freedom and Independence,* pp. 155–158.

70. Ibid., pp. 399, 397, 504, 505.

71. Hegel, *History of Philosophy,* 3:316, 317–318, 319.

72. Hegel, *Phenomenology,* pp. 615–627, 635.

73. Ibid., p. 633. Cf. Jonathan Robinson, *Duty and Hypocrisy in Hegel's Phenomenology of Mind* (Toronto: University of Toronto Press, 1977), pp. 44–67.

74. Immanuel Kant, "On the Common Saying: 'This May be True in Theory, but it does not Apply in Practice,'" in *Kant's Political Writings,* ed. H. Reiss (Cambridge: Cambridge University Press, 1970), p. 64.

75. Hegel, *Phenomenology*, p. 445.

76. Hegel, *Philosophy of Right*, p. 90.

77. If Hegel had wanted to consider the strongest possible version of Kant, he would have asked how the ideas of universality and noncontradiction are related to a good will as the only unqualifiedly good thing on earth, and to the notion of persons as "ends in themselves." Cf. John Rawls, *A Theory of Justice* (Cambridge, Mass.: Harvard University Press, 1971), pp. 251–260, for a good defense of Kant.

78. G. W. F. Hegel, *Glauben und Wissen*, trans. W. Cerf and H. S. Harris as *Faith and Knowledge* (Albany: State University of New York Press, 1977), pp. 84–96. Again, by p. 143 Hegel is characterizing Kantian morality in terms of "so-called duties of a formalistic kind that determine nothing."

79. See particularly Immanuel Kant, *Fundamental Principles of the Metaphysic of Morals*, trans. T. K. Abbott (Indianapolis: Library of Liberal Arts, 1949), pp. 63–64.

80. Or almost always. Kant once or twice allows the idea of necessity to have a force he says it ought never to have. See Kant, *The Metaphysical Elements of Justice*, pp. 87–88n.

81. Hegel, *Philosophy of Right*, p. 99.

82. Ibid., additions, pp. 251, 252, 258.

83. Ibid., p. 259; cf. Hegel, *Philosophy of Religion*, pp. 48–50.

84. Hegel, *Phenomenology*, p. 626.

85. Ibid., pp. 650, 663.

86. Ibid., pp. 660, 662.

87. Hegel, *Philosophy of Right*, pp. 91, 168; cf. Hegel, *Encyclopedia*, p. 235: "the discussion of the true intrinsic worth of the impulses, inclinations and passions is thus essentially the theory of legal, moral and social duties."

88. Hegel, *Phenomenology*, p. 670.

89. Ernst Cassirer, *The Myth of the State* (New Haven: Yale University Press, 1946), p. 272: "Hegel could reconcile himself to almost everything—supposing it had proved its right by power." What is remarkable in *The Myth of the State* is the restraint with which Cassirer, though a Kantian, treats Hegel. But even Cassirer, for all his fairness, cannot abide Hegel's claim that "men are as foolish as to forget... in their enthusiasm for liberty of conscience and political freedom, the truth which lies in power" (p. 267); this Cassirer regards as "the clearest and most ruthless program of fascism that has ever been propounded by any political or philosophic writer." But cf. Ernst Cassirer, "Hegel's Theory of the State," in *Symbol, Myth and Culture*, ed. Donald P. Verene (New Haven: Yale University Press, 1979), p. 117: "Hegel's... term 'power'...never means a mere physical but a spiritual force."

90. Speaking of von Haller's notion that "the mightier rules, must rule, and will always rule," Hegel complains that "it is not the might of justice and ethics, but only the irrational power of brute force" which von Haller has in mind. Hegel, *Philosophy of Right*, pp. 157–160.

91. Hegel, *Phenomenology*, pp. 650, 661, 644–663. For a fine account of the importance of language in Hegel's social theory see Hans-Georg Gadamer, *Hegels Dialektik: fünf hermeneutische Studien* (Tübingen: J. C. B. Mohr, 1971), pp. 63–69.

92. Ibid., p. 663.

93. Hegel, *Encyclopedia*, pp. 286–290; Hegel, *Logic*, 1:introduction, p. 60.

94. See especially Hans-Georg Gadamer, "Goethe und die Philosophie," in *Kleine Schriften* (Tübingen: J. C. B. Mohr, 1967), 2:92–93.

95. Hegel, *Philosophy of Right*, additions, p. 226: "The distinction between thought and will is only that between the theorectical attitude and the practical. These, however, are surely not two faculties; the will is rather a special way of thinking, thinking translating itself into existence...we cannot have a will without intelligence." In the main body of the text (pp. 32–33) Hegel urges that the "will's activity consists in annulling the contradiction between subjectivity and objectivity and giving its aims an objective instead of a subjective character," such as willing ethics rather than morality. He attacks Rousseau for allegedly believing that "what is fundamental...is...the will of a single person in his own private self-will, not the absolute or rational will"—a grotesque charge in view of Rousseau's efforts to overcome particularism and egoism.

96. For a discriminating treatment of the strengths and weaknesses of Kojeve's reading of Hegel see Kelly, *Hegel's Retreat from Eleusis*, pp. 29–54. Cf. Patrick Riley, "Introduction to the Reading of Alexandre Kojève," in *Frontiers of Political Theory*, ed. M. Freeman and D. Robertson (New York: St. Martins, 1980), pp. 233–284.

97. Hegel, *Philosophy of Right*, p. 48.

98. Alexandre Kojève, "Hegel, Marx et le Christianisme," in *Critique* (Paris: August-September, 1946), p. 352. In *Introduction à la lecture de Hegel*, ed. R. Queneau (Paris: Gallimard, 1947), pp. 11–58, Kojève is less sweeping, and confines the concepts of struggle and mastery mainly to the *Phenomenology*, with only passing references to the *Philosophy of Right* (p. 437).

99. It is no accident that the only part of Hegel's *Philosophy of Right* that Kojève can use to advantage is the celebrated passage in the preface about philosophy as something "cut and dried": "it is only when actuality is mature that the ideal first appears over against the real and that the ideal apprehends this same real world in is substance and builds it up for itself into the shape of an intellectual realm" (p. 13). Since this might be thought to prefigure Marx's *The German Ideology*, Kojève cites it; see Kojève, *Introduction*, p. 437.

100. G. A. Kelly, *Idealism, Politics and History*, p. 338.

101. Jean Hyppolite, "Marxisme et philosophie," in *Études sur Marx et Hegel* (Paris: Marcel Rivière, 1955), p. 133: "the struggle for life and death...is the root of history for Hegel, while the exploitation of man by

man is only a consequence of it, this consequence serving on the other hand as Marx's point of departure." Cf. Jean Hyppolite, *Genèse et structure de la phenomenologie de l'esprit de Hegel* (Paris: Aubier, 1946), 1:163–171, where the master-slave relationship is integrated much more carefully into a better-balanced reading of the *Phenomenology.*

102. Hegel, "On Classical Studies," p. 326.

103. Hegel, *Philosophy of Right,* pp. 105, 132, 133.

104. Ibid., p. 157.

105. Jean-Jacques Rousseau, *The Social Contract,* in *Political Writings,* book 1, ch. 7, p. 19.

106. Hegel, *Philosophy of Right,* p. 105.

107. See, inter alia, Benedict de Spinoza, *Ethics,* in *The Philosophy of Spinoza,* ed. J. Ratner (New York: Modern Library, 1927), pp. 165–166. At one point in the *History of Philosophy* (3:257) Hegel says that "to be a follower of Spinoza is the essential commencement of all philosophy."

108. Hegel, *Philosophy of Right,* p. 105.

109. Hegel, *History of Philosophy,* 3:261.

110. Hegel, *Philosophy of Right,* p. 191. This is probably because Hegel never presents the will in an ordinary form but always tries to reduce it to reason (hence seeing acceptance of the state as willing) or to desire (hence allowing "caprice" in the economic sphere of civil society to be something meritorious). As M. B. Foster observes in his excellent study *The Political Philosophies of Plato and Hegel* (Oxford: Clarendon Press, 1935), pp. 131–140, the ethical will that relates to the state is "imperfectly differentiated from reason," while the will that "wins its right" in the sphere of free economic activity is "imperfectly differentiated from desire."

111. Ibid., pp. 87, 83; additions, p. 246.

112. Ibid., p. 205.

113. Ibid., p. 155.

114. Hegel, *Encyclopedia,* p. 263.

115. Aristotle, *Ethics,* 1177a-b, trans. John Warrington (London: Everyman, 1963), pp. 227–230.

116. Hegel, *Encyclopedia,* p. 231.

117. Michael Oakeshott, *On Human Conduct* (Oxford: Clarendon Press, 1975), p. 260. In one eloquent paragraph Oakeshott achieves what Kojève does not achieve in hundreds of pages by showing that recognition in Hegel is not a mere epiphenomenon of a "fight to the death for pure prestige."

118. Hegel, *Philosophy of Right,* preface, p. 8.

119. Ibid., pp. 57–64. That Hegel was hostile to contractarian views of society from his earliest writings is clear in the *System der Sittlichkeit* (1802–1803), trans. H. S. Harris and T. M. Knox as *System of Ethical Life* (Albany: State University of New York Press, 1979), pp. 122–123: "The determinate provisions [of a contract]...are treated as the singular aspect of the individuals or of the things about which the contract is made. And for this reason true reality cannot fall within this level."

120. Ibid., pp. 126–129, 59, 156, 157.
121. Ibid., additions, p. 261; p. 242.
122. Ibid., p. 157.
123. Hegel, *Phenomenology,* pp. 604–605.
124. Hegel, *Philosophy of Right,* pp. 195–198.
125. Ibid., p. 205.
126. Cited in W. Kaufmann, *Hegel: a Re-interpretation* (New York: Doubleday, 1966), p. 281. Kaufmann translates from Hoffmeister's critical edition of the *History of Philosophy.*
127. Hegel, *Philosophy of Right,* p. 204. Cf. Hegel, *Logic,* preface to the 2nd edition, p. 43: "the peculiar essence" of anything "consists in the concept of the thing, in the universal immanent in it; as every human individual, though infinitely unique, is so only because it belongs to the class of men." Whoever thinks of Hegel as a romantic should examine this passage with particular care.
128. Hegel, *Philosophy of Right,* p. 208.
129. Ibid., pp. 205–208.
130. This striking turn of phrase has been adapted from Martin Diamond's "The Federalist's View of Federalism," in *Essays in Federalism* (Claremont, Calif., 1961), p. 44.
131. Hegel, *Philosophy of Right,* p. 206.
132. Ibid., additions, pp. 288–289.
133. Ibid., p. 181. Frequently, of course, Hegel is thinking of the sovereign as the will of the state in external affairs, since for him states are the "actors" in world history. But monarchy also serves to represent the principle of subjectivity.
134. Hegel, *Encyclopedia,* p. 269.
135. Hegel, *Philosophy of Right,* additions, pp. 289, 181.
136. Karl Marx, *Critique of Hegel's Philosophy of Right,* ed. J. O'Malley (Cambridge: Cambridge University Press, 1970), pp. 27, 26. The same thought is put in a non-Marxian form by Charles Taylor, in *Hegel* (Cambridge: Cambridge University Press, 1975, p. 440: "this is one of those cases where the detail of Hegel's argument leaves one with a sense of the arbitrary...it is not clear why the realization of the modern idea requires that this be an hereditary monarch."
137. Ibid., p. 187.
138. The most that can be said is that Hegel is a certain kind of voluntarist; but it is a mistake to say, with Plamenatz, that his political philosophy is built on consent (*Consent, Freedom and Political Obligation,* p. 61). One of Hegel's great points is to make consent capricious and therefore unworthy of the true will—that is, the rational will, or perhaps just reason itself.

7. Conclusion

1. Thomas Hobbes, *Leviathan,* ed. Michael Oakeshott (Oxford: Basil Blackwell, 1957), pp. 37–38.

2. Ibid., p. 38; cf. Thomas Hobbes, *Liberty, Necessity and Chance,* in *Hobbes' English Works,* ed. W. Molesworth (London, 1841), 5:80–81, for Hobbes's account of volition in animals.

3. Hobbes, *Leviathan,* p. 31.

4. Immanuel Kant, *Fundamental Principles of the Metaphysic of Morals,* trans. T. K. Abbott (Indianapolis: Library of Liberal Arts, 1949), p. 44.

5. Hobbes, *Leviathan,* pp. 307, 309, 377, 86.

6. Ibid., p. 179. Oakeshott, in his treatment of Hobbes, rightly takes this to be "Hobbes's deepest conviction about moral duties"; see Michael Oakeshott, "The Moral Life in the Writings of Thomas Hobbes," in *Rationalism in Politics* (London: Methuen, 1962), p. 282.

7. Michael Oakeshott, "Dr. Leo Strauss on Hobbes," in *Hobbes on Civil Association* (Oxford: Basil Blackwell, 1975), pp. 147–148.

8. John Locke, *Two Treatises of Government,* ed. Peter Laslett (Cambridge: Cambridge University Press, 1967), p. 401.

9. John Locke, *An Essay Concerning Human Understanding,* ed. A. C. Fraser (New York: Dover, 1959), p. 334.

10. On this point see the brief but excellent remarks of Raymond Polin, "John Locke's Conception of Freedom," in *John Locke: Problems and Perspectives,* ed. John Yolton (Cambridge: Cambridge University Press, 1969), pp. 1–5.

11. Hans Aarsleff, "The State of Nature and the Nature of Man in Locke," in Yolton, *John Locke: Problems and Perspectives,* pp. 110–121. This is the most careful and subtle understanding of the changes that Locke made in the 1694 edition of the *Essay.*

12. Jean-Jacques Rousseau, *Lettre à Monseigneur de Beaumont,* in *Oeuvres complètes,* ed. M. Launay (Paris: Éditions du Seuil, 1971), 3:341.

13. Jean-Jacques Rousseau, *The Social Contract,* in *Political Writings,* ed. F. Watkins (Edinburgh: Nelson, 1953), p. 59: "every free action is the effect of two concurrent causes: a moral cause, or the will which determines the act; and a physical cause, or the power which executes it."

14. Ibid., pp. 9, 7.

15. Jean-Jacques Rousseau, *Discourse on the Origins of Inequality,* in *The Social Contract and Discourses,* trans. G. D. H. Cole (New York: Everyman, 1950), p. 208.

16. Rousseau, *The Social Contract,* in Watkins, *Political Writings,* p. 117.

17. Jean-Jacques Rousseau, *Political Economy,* in Cole, *The Social Contract and Discourses,* p. 297.

18. Rousseau, *The Social Contract,* in Watkins, *Political Writings,* pp. 40–45.

19. Kant, *Fundamental Principles of the Metaphysics of Morals,* pp. 11–30, esp. p. 30.

20. Immanuel Kant, *The Metaphysical Elements of Justice,* trans. John Ladd, (Indianapolis: Library of Liberal Arts, 1965), p. 26: "among external laws [i.e., in a state], those to which an obligation can be recognized *a priori* by reason without external legislation are *natural laws,* whereas those that would neither obligate nor be laws without actual external

legislation are called *positive laws.*" This would serve to distinguish between a duty not to murder and a duty not to violate a traffic regulation.

21. Ibid., p. 97: "a hereditary nobility is a class of persons who acquire their rank before they have merited it...Inasmuch as it can be assumed that no man would throw away his freedom, it is impossible that the general Will of the people would consent to such a groundless prerogative."

22. Of Locke one can fairly say that his politics requires that government be set up by "the consent and contrivance of men," but that that government ought to shape its policies in congruence with the law of nature. No element can be dispensed with: the law of nature does not appoint persons who can indifferently execute it, and so those persons must be appointed by consent and voluntary agreement. Nonetheless, the law of nature is there, waiting, so to speak, to be executed by an impartial "judge." On this point see Chapter 3.

23. On this point see Judith Shklar, *Freedom and Independence: The Political Ideas of Hegel's Phenomenology of Mind* (Cambridge: Cambridge University Press, 1976), pp. 58–69.

24. G. W. F. Hegel, *Philosophy of Right,* trans. T. M. Knox, (Oxford: Clarendon Press, 1942) p. 157. Cf. p. 59, where Hegel condemns contract theory for allowing "the intrusion of this contractual relation...into the relation between the individual and the state," an intrusion that, Hegel says, "has been productive of the greatest confusion in both constitutional law and public life."

25. Ibid., pp. 103–105. Cf. T. H. Green, *Lectures on the Principles of Political Obligation,* (London: Longmans, 1941) p. 8: "Hegel's account of freedom as realized in the state does not seem to correspond to the facts of society...; though undoubtedly there is a work of moral liberation, which society...is constantly carrying on for the individual."

26. Hegel, *Philosophy of Right,* pp. 96–99; additions, p. 252. At the same time, however, Hegel insists that "the good itself, apart from the subjective will, is only an abstraction without the real existence which it is to acquire for the first time through the efforts of that will" (p. 253).

27. Kant, *Fundamental Principles of the Metaphysics of Morals,* pp. 3–8.

28. Michael Walzer, *Obligations: Essays on Disobedience, War and Citizenship* (Cambridge, Mass.: Harvard University Press, 1970), pp. 7–9.

29. Hobbes, *Leviathan,* p. 141; cited by Walzer in *Obligations,* p. x.

30. Walzer, *Obligations,* pp. x, 18–19.

31. John Rawls, *A Theory of Justice* (Cambridge, Mass.: Harvard University Press, 1971), pp. 11–18, 114–117.

32. John Rawls, "Kantian Constructivism in Moral Theory," *Journal of Philosophy,* 77 (September 1980), 568.

33. Joseph Tussman, *Obligation and the Body Politic* (New York: Cambridge University Press, 1960), p. 7.

34. A. John Simmons, *Moral Principles and Political Obligations* (Princeton: Princeton University Press, 1979), pp. 57, 100, 194–195, 61–70.

35. Ibid., pp. 70, 192.

36. G. R. Grice, *The Grounds of Moral Judgment* (Cambridge: Cambridge University Press, 1967), esp. pp. 25–28.

37. Ibid., p. 147: "I think we are in a position to make a take-over bid for the term 'Natural Rights' and the corresponding terms 'Natural Justice' and 'Natural Law.'"

38. With differing degrees of success, to be sure; if what is suggested in this book is correct, then Kant provides the most adequate metaphysic of morals on which to build contractarianism, while Rousseau and Locke do less well and Hobbes least well. Perhaps this was what Rawls had in mind when he urged that "for all of its greatness, Hobbes' *Leviathan* raises special problems" (*Theory of Justice*, p. 11n).

39. On this point see particularly section 81 of Locke's *First Treatise*, where he argues that natural law does not appoint persons but that governors must be given political power by voluntary agreement. Locke, *Two Treatises of Government*, pp. 220–221.

40. Rousseau, *The Social Contract*, in Watkins, *Political Writings*, pp. 8–10. For Rousseau the general will is right if it legislates only general laws that are universally applied; if these procedural safeguards are followed, there is no need to reserve natural rights.

41. Jean-Paul Sartre, *Existentialism and Humanism*, trans. P. Mairet (London: Methuen, 1948), esp. p. 28.

42. Ibid., p. 48: "In every respect I bear the responsibility of the choice which, in committing myself, also commits the whole of humanity. Even if my choice is determined by no *a priori* value whatever, it has nothing to do with caprice."

43. Ibid., pp. 27–28: "What do we mean by saying that existence precedes essence? We mean that man first of all exists, encounters himself, surges up in the world—and defines himself afterwards." For the condemnation of fascism, which is certainly a kind of "surging up in the world," see pp. 35–36.

44. Ibid., pp. 46–48.

45. Ibid., p. 29: "when we say that man is responsible for himself, we do not mean that he is responsible only for his own individuality, but that he is responsible for all men."

46. Cf. Hannah Arendt, *The Life of the Mind: Willing* (New York: Harcourt Brace Jovanovich, 1978), pp. 3–7.

47. Simmons, *Moral Principles and Political Obligations*, pp. 62–65.

48. Max Weber, "'Objectivity' in Social Science," in *The Methodology of the Social Sciences*, trans. E. Shils and H. Finch (New York: Free Press, 1959), p. 53. Cf. Leo Strauss's effective criticism of this piece in *Natural Right and History* (Chicago: University of Chicago Press, 1953), pp. 35–80.

49. J. S. Mill, *Utilitarianism*, in *The Philosophy of J. S. Mill*, ed. M. Cohen (New York: Modern Library, 1961), p. 363. T. D. Weldon, who turns out to be a not-too-subtle utilitarian-libertarian despite his attack on philosophy, makes use of this principle of Mill's in *The Vocabulary of Politics* (London: Penguin, 1953), pp. 176–177.

50. It is not the aim of this book to defend a pure contractarianism as an

adequate political and moral philosophy, but to try to show what kind of voluntarist metaphysic of morals underlies contractarianism, either explicitly or implicitly.

51. Robert Paul Wolff, *In Defense of Anarchism* (New York: Harper, 1970), pp. 21–67, 18–19, 69–82, ix.

52. Kant, *Fundamental Principles of the Metaphysic of Morals*, pp. 57–58, 79–80.

53. Kant, *The Metaphysical Elements of Justice*, pp. 75–80.

54. Wolff, *In Defense of Anarchism*, pp. 12–19; Kant, *Fundamental Principles of the Metaphysic of Morals*, pp. 45–46. For a full account of what Wolff does with and to Kant, cf. Patrick Riley, "On the 'Kantian' Foundations of Robert Paul Wolff's Anarchism," in *NOMOS XIX: Anarchism*, ed. J. R. Pennock and J. Chapman (New York: New York University Press, 1978).

Index

236n39; compared with Kant, 66, 81, 121; compared with Leibniz, 76; compared with Pascal, 89; compared with Rousseau, 92–93, 95, 121; controversy with Bishop of Worcester, 83, 89; correspondence with Molyneux on freedom, 75; criticism of Filmer, 67; dispute with Tyrrell over natural law, 85, 88; distinction between types of law, 63–69, 74–75, 235n20; Green's interpretation of, 65–66, 91; MacPherson's interpretation of, 62, 234; on aliens, 67–69; on citizenship, 64–65; on consent, 1, 8, 61–63, 69, 71–72, 91–92, 202, 220n38; on freedom as power to "suspend" desire, 79–81, 202, 238n70; on liberty, 11; on majority rule, 62, 94–95; on natural law, 8, 61–62, 65–66, 69, 83–91; on natural rights, 61–62; on property, 61–62, 84, 92, 96–97; on representative government, 93–94; on reward and punishment as legal sanctions, 65, 81–82, 83, 85, 87, 90; on revolution, 69; on "voluntary agreement" as basis of political power, 9, 61, 70–71, 74, 78, 91, 202; on will as "uneasiness of desire," 22, 76–79, 202; Plamenatz' interpretation of, 93; Strauss' interpretation of, 87–89

Lucian, 56
Lucretius, 220n45
Luther, Martin, 2–3
Lycurgus, 107, 111, 118

Machiavelli, Niccolò, 57, 233n123
McGrade, A. S., 219n32
McNeilly, F. S., 229n47
Malebranche, Nicolas, 109, 238n70, 245n50, 247n6
Malesherbes, Chrétien-Guillaume de, 243n37
Mansfield, Harvey C., Jr., 218n10, 225n96, 226n8, 250n36
Marx, Karl, 190, 198, 262n101, 264n136
Masters, Roger, 243n27
Melden, A. I., 229n51

Miethke, Jürgen, 219n29
Mill, John Stuart, 147, 212, 242n11, 253n87, 267n49
Molyneux, William, 75, 82, 237n68, 239n95
Montesquieu, Charles Secondat, Baron de, 109, 158, 244n50, 256n120
Moses, 102, 107, 111
Murphy, Jeffrie G., 249n35

Natural law, 6–8, 32, 56–57, 61–74, 78, 82–89, 96–97, 121, 131–132, 138, 203
Natural rights, 31–32, 56–57, 61–62, 92, 97, 203
Nietzsche, Friedrich, 19, 139, 207, 220n39, 222n68, 223n87, 230n65, 252n59
Numa, 102, 118

Obligation (and duty), as based on categorical imperative (in Kant), 15, 130–131, 148–152, 157, 265n20; as based on consent (generally) 1–4, 12, 142, 200–201, 204–205, (in Hobbes) 9, 15–16, 21–22, 23–27, 30–34, 43–45, 48–49, 53–54, 58–60, 201–202, 232n112, (in Locke) 64–69, 70–71, 83, 91, 97, 202, (in Rousseau) 16–17, 64, 99, 102, 104–105, 107–109, 111–112, 117, 122, 202–203, (in Rawls) 13–14, (in Walzer) 205–206; as based on necessity (in Hume), 72–73, 217n4; as "discharge of public functions" (in Hegel), 192–193; as "yoke" (in Rousseau's *Rêveries du promeneur solitaire*), 118–119; autonomy as "primary obligation of man" (in Wolff), 212–214; conflict of duties (in Sartre), 224n95; contractual obligation criticized by Leibniz, 54; difference between moral and political obligation (in Locke) 64–69, 74–75, 93, 97, 235n20, (in Kant) 18, 128–131, 162, 265n20; duty to establish republicanism and eternal peace (in Kant), 160; Hegel's view of duty in *Antigone*, 178–179; Hegel's view of Kantian duty as empty formalism, 183–185;